# BUILDING AN ESL COLLECTION FOR YOUNG ADULTS

# Building
# an *ESL* Collection
# for *Young Adults*

## A Bibliography of
## Recommended Fiction and Nonfiction
## for Schools and Public Libraries

Laura Hibbets McCaffery

**Greenwood Press**
Westport, Connecticut • London

**Library of Congress Cataloging–in–Publication Data**

McCaffery, Laura Hibbets.
　　Building an ESL collection for young adults : a bibliography of
recommended fiction and nonfiction for schools and public libraries
/ Laura Hibbets McCaffery.
　　　　p.　cm.
　　Includes bibliographical references and index.
　　ISBN 0–313–29937–4 (alk. paper)
　　1. English language—Textbooks for foreign speakers—Bibliography.
2. Young adult literature, American—Bibliography.　3. Young adult
literature, English—Bibliography.　4. Young adult fiction—
Bibliography.　5. Young adult libraries—Book lists.　6. School
libraries—Book lists.　7. Public libraries—Book lists.　I. Title.
Z5818.E5M39　1998
[PE1128.A2]
016.4282'4—dc21　　　　98–5271

British Library Cataloguing in Publication Data is available.

Library of Congress Catalog Card Number: 98–5271
ISBN: 0–313–29937–4

First published in 1998

Greenwood Press, 88 Post Road West, Westport, CT 06881
An imprint of Greenwood Publishing Group, Inc.

Printed in the United States of America

The paper used in this book complies with the
Permanent Paper Standard issued by the National
Information Standards Organization (Z39.48–1984).

10 9 8 7 6 5 4 3 2 1

Dedicated to the memory of my father and mother, Glasgow L. Hibbets and Fern Meek Hibbets Rogers. Their belief in the power of education was a constant in my life.

# Contents

# Acknowledgments

I thank the staff of the Allen County Public Library, Fort Wayne, Indiana, particularly the Readers' Services Department, for their support and encouragement. I especially thank the fellow members of the Publishers Liaison Committee of the Adult Lifelong Learning Section of the Public Library Association who have shared their vast expertise with me. I am grateful to all of the other literacy providers and teachers, as well as publishers' representatives, who shared ideas and materials. Heartfelt thanks are due to my family for never complaining about the masses of materials that accumulated and the time I spent at the computer. Last, but not least, I thank the editorial staff who worked with me in publishing this book.

# Introduction

ESL, or English as a second language, is now a factor in education across this country. In the past, ESL was often historically considered a problem of adult education because the people seeking language training were usually adult immigrants. Much of the activity took place in large urban areas and seemingly had little relevance to teachers in middle and high schools. Today the need for ESL materials and supplemental materials has reached an all-time high. *Library Hotline* in August 1995 reported that the ESL product market had reached over $4.5 billion in sales; moreover, it predicted that in the year 2000, at least 45 percent of the school children in California would be Hispanic. This demographic change clearly has ramifications for the border states, but it should make all states aware of the impact that changing demographics will have on the rest of society. No longer can we expect to find the immigrant populations primarily in an urban setting and concentrated in just a few geographic areas. Small towns in rural America as well as smaller cities have growing foreign-born populations.

Although it may seem to some librarians, media specialists, teachers, and tutors that this need for ESL materials has mushroomed only recently, historically it has always been with us. World War II and its aftermath is an excellent starting place to recognize the modern need for ESL materials. World events of the past fifty years have combined to create a large influx of immigrants and refugees into the United States.

The events in my home community of Fort Wayne, Indiana, mirror this half-century of events throughout the nation. The city had a somewhat culturally diverse population base to begin with. Many ancestors of the population had immigrated from Germany. There were small enclaves of Greeks, Macedonians, Chinese, and Japanese. There were Irish and Native Americans, as well as African Americans. Most of these people, however, spoke English. With World War II as the starting point, Fort Wayne welcomed war brides, refugees, and displaced persons. Eastern Europeans and people from the Philippines were new arrivals. Then came Japanese and Korean immigrants, as well as Ethiopian, Cuban, Mexican, and finally boat people from Vietnam and elsewhere in Southeast Asia. As they were settling in, Russians, Bosnians, and people from other Eastern European countries and cultures arrived.

Clearly the language barrier had to be dealt with. Social welfare agencies offered classes in English as a second language, as did the adult education division of the school system. One local elementary school was designated as an ESL school. The local library began collecting materials written in languages other than English in both translations and original publications. Children's materials were made available in languages other than English, and the popular paperback collection began carrying books in foreign languages.

Educators have discovered that ESL is no longer just an adult concept. Material is needed for the entire family. Material for young adult learners and adult learners must be easy to read but with a content level commensurate with their ability to understand.

Schools not only have special classes for ESL students, but also have ESL students mainstreamed in regular classes. Regular and supplemental reading and learning suggestions are needed, and these materials need to be accessible to teachers, media specialists, librarians, and tutors to help provide the needed skills.

One of the most frequent requests that I have received from literacy providers over the past few years is for a bibliography of ESL materials. Local area school teachers—at the middle, secondary, and college levels—have asked for some basic ESL materials for classroom use. Local vocational and technical schools have expressed a definite need for usable bibliographies. I have been asked for bibliographies for both adults and young adults. This book responds to that request.

ESL and literacy in general have been a part of my professional life throughout my career. My career began as a language arts teacher. My first teaching position when I was graduated from Indiana University in the early 1950s took me to the highly industrialized Calumet region of northwestern Indiana, where the steel mills and oil refineries provided employment to immigrants. Many still spoke their native language and had few English skills. In fact, a grade school there used Polish language only.

Several of the junior high students I worked with were refugees or displaced people and could read and write English in varying degrees. Unfortunately, even the best students in the group lacked a background in our cultural literacy, as well as understanding of the colloquialisms and idiosyncrasies of American English. This started my quest for ESL materials at the appropriate interest level and the level of understanding that would bring these students up to speed.

No materials were labeled as ESL then. I haunted the local branch library looking for books, bibliographies, or anything else that would help me. Some of the books I used then might well be included in this bibliography today in new editions or in new format. Books specifically for teenagers were just beginning to be popular, so adult material and children's materials were basically what I had to use. As I recall, I had to use a lot of junior high and upper elementary school material.

My library career took me across the state, where I continued my work with young people. Young adult librarians needed to be cognizant of high-interest, low-level books that would work for adults as well as young adults. In fact, young adult librarians were expected to know which books housed in adult areas were suitable for young adult use. Knowledge of materials suitable for ESL soon was included in the expectations.

Meanwhile, the demand for adult literacy materials was increasing. Many of the immigrants who arrived in Fort Wayne found their own ways to learn. Foreign students at the local colleges expected the library to provide Test of English as a Foreign Language materials but not much else. Most of the foreign language materials were technical in nature and used by engineers in local industries or they were classical materials written in the original language. The Cubans who fled during the Castro Revolution were some of the first who were organized in their approach to learning. In fact, the center they organized still provides ESL for learners in many languages. Classes were provided through local organizations and materials were requested from the library. Young adult materials were used, and Spanish-language materials were purchased.

In the early 1980s, I moved into a position in the newly created Readers Services Department at Allen County and was a member of the committee that created our Adult Basic Reading Collection—a special collection in the library that would supplement the materials needed by the tutors of the Fort Wayne Literacy Council and also be of use to walk-in library patrons. We also created bibliographies. At first we dealt mainly with adult nonreaders. Our needs survey, however, as well as our experience, told us that we needed to expand our scope. At this time, I became supervisor of the collection and wrote the collection development policy for literacy and ESL materials still in use. At the same time I was also appointed to the Board of the Literacy Council, then the official group providing literacy tutoring in Fort Wayne, Indiana. This group joined the coalition in northeast Indiana that was part of the national drive spearheaded by PBS and ABC to fight illiteracy. Our program expanded throughout the county and became the Three Rivers Literacy Alliance. At this time, I was also a member of the Indiana Deaf/Literacy Coalition and worked with other state agencies to improve literacy. When I stepped back from the board after serving ten years, our scope included younger people, families, and ESL students. In fact, ESL demands had more than doubled over the years.

My service on the Publishers Liaison Committee in the Adult Lifelong

Learning Section of the Public Library Association for several years has provided insight into the national need for organized access to ESL materials. This committee reads over a hundred books each year provided by publishers of literacy materials and other publishers that think some specific materials might serve literacy needs. When the committee publishes its Top Title list each year, books that are especially useful for ESL are noted. As contact person for this bibliography for several years, I was often asked for more ESL recommendations, from all levels and all types of educators and throughout North America. ESL and literacy collection development was the topic of one of my American Library Association program presentations and has been a professional priority for me for several years.

The criteria for a book to be included in this bibliography are specific. There are basically eight areas I look at to evaluate a book: format, reading level, content, illustrations, accuracy, indexing, glossary, and bibliography. Once a book meets these criteria, it must also be appropriate for the ESL student— that is, representative of the culture or the topic it describes and also effective in explaining this culture and topic.

The format and layout of the book have to be attractive and suitable for the intended user. (The size of the type and the white space provided are important.) The content must be appropriate for the intended reader and not too childish in content. This means that the book should normally range up to 8 on the Fry Reading Scale. If the rating is higher, the reason for its inclusion is stated—usually the content, topic, and high interest level or the fact that it is a book that the reader would be willing to stretch to read. The content of a book should provide the information advertised in the title or introduction in a useful and concise manner and be presented in a way that is topic or use specific. The content material must be evaluated by the same criteria as the book as a whole. It also should be timely, if not timeless, interesting, and user-friendly. The material must be well illustrated, if illustrations are helpful or necessary to the text. Placement of the illustration in relation to the text is important. For ESL, the pictures should be near the text they describe, and the pictures should be concisely and plainly labeled. Color and black and white are not determiners; the appropriate use of illustrations is. Illustrations should be up-to-date and age appropriate. Childish illustrations can ruin an otherwise readable book; badly done ones make a book hard to use. The material in the book must be as current as possible, if that is a factor, and accurate. The reading level must be appropriate for the intended audience. This means that a teacher and librarian must be able to provide a range of reading materials on the same subject in varying reading levels. Other things that are important are glossaries, indexing, and bibliographies. Glossaries should pick out the main words needed to understand the material in the book and explain them in a concise and explicit manner. I prefer a book that is profusely indexed to one with only the table of contents. I also like cross-references, to reinforce the understanding of ideas. Bibliographies that suggest further and related reading at the same reading level or a step beyond are a positive factor in choosing books.

This bibliography provides materials that can be used mainly as supplemental reading in classes ranging from middle school through high school. Most of the materials are equally suitable for adults. Mainstreamed ESL students can use this material to understand and make use of regular textbooks better. Special ESL classes can use the material as part of the regular instruction. The books highlighting the many multicultural activities in this nation will help instructors prepare ESL students to make a seamless transition from learner to empowered citizen. Most materials are for the intermediate or the upper beginning level of reading in English, but some very easy materials are included. Most of this material is entirely suitable for all learners from grade 5 through adult. Some is specifically geared to youth and is so noted.

This bibliography covers a wide range of subjects to reflect the entire school curriculum, as well as segments of adult and young adult life. Many ethnic groups and diverse cultures are represented, and the materials have been primarily published since 1992. Some classics as well as old standbys and favorites have been included. Modified and abridged classics, as well as abridged and edited best sellers, are included. In many cases, the modern materials have been edited and prepared by the original authors to be appropriate for this particular use. Older books suggested are usually available through the local public library.

Each citation includes the author(s) or editor(s). The title is included in its entirety. The publisher, place of publication, date of publication, edition, and series name are also included. Prices are included for both hardcover and paper when available. If audio cassettes are mentioned, their price is also included. A description of the physical appearance and properties of the book is given, along with a brief summation of the material covered in the book. Each citation contains suggestions for curriculum use.

Interest level and reading level are included for each book. As many subjects as needed will be assigned for each book. The subjects used are Library of Congress. The materials are cross-referenced for subject, title, author, and ethnicity. Both fiction and nonfiction are included and labeled.

Separate indexes are provided for books by author, by title, by subject, and by ethnic group. All indexes are alphabetically arranged. The title index presents the titles of individual stories in collections. It includes multiple authors for individual titles and gives page numbers for each item corresponding to a subject entry. The ethnic group index includes titles of books that correspond to specific ethnic groups in the United States as well as titles of books that are cross cultural in their scope. Books in this index represent the cultures in other countries throughout the world, including information on the peoples, food, holidays, and customs.

Books were chosen for this bibliography from literacy publishers that publish ESL materials and market them as such. Materials were chosen from their adult literacy publications when they fit the criteria I have mentioned. There are other literacy publishers that publish materials that make fine ESL material but are not marketed as such. I winnowed these books out using the criteria already noted. There are also mainstream publishers that publish materials that they believe are appropriate for use by literacy and ESL users, and these are included. Some of the material here I found through reviews in professional journals and others from browsing publishers' catalogs in subject areas. Many are books that have been used for years and have withstood the test of time. Even the ones I found through serendipity met my criteria.

Librarians, media teachers, tutors, and ESL teachers need to be aware of publishers and distributors that routinely have materials suitable for their needs. Such a list is included, showing the type of publisher each is and why each is included. Almost all publishers have at least one book that is appropriate for ESL. The trick is to find it. This bibliography will help do that.

Publishers' catalogs, professional journals, government agency publications, literacy organizations, and professional organizations are all sources of ESL materials. The Internet is an excellent source too, as well as a teaching tool. The individual teacher or librarian has myriad tools nearby to use, including newspapers, magazines, and computers. Professional judgment and personal experience can be the best source of all.

The scope of this ESL bibliography and any ESL collection should be a microcosm of the actual library or media center collection. ESL users have the same needs and requirements as basic students or patrons.

# 1

# Adventure, Mystery, and Suspense

Many of these books are fiction and will provide extra-credit reading materials as well as material for pleasure reading. Mystery and adventure stories are excellent for telling a true story in a manner that is new and easy to read and comprehend. These materials are useful across the curriculum because they deal with history, exploration, biography, discovery, and personal courage. These books provide both fun and leisure reading. The scope of the stories includes the entire world as well as the realm of the imagination.

## NONFICTION

Antonopulos, Barbara. *The Abominable Snowman*. Austin, TX: Steck-Vaughn, 1992. Unsolved Mystery Series Hardcover. $24.26 (ISBN 0–8172–1053–9); paper $11.42 (ISBN 0–8114–6849–6). Fry Reading Level 4+. Interest Level Grade 5–Adult.

Briefly discusses the possibility and the evidence that a large apelike, man-like creature known as the Yeti lives in the Himalayan Mountains. Discusses its footprints, the search by the explorer Sir Edmund Hillary, the villages where it was supposed to have been sighted, a purported scalp, and its American cousin, Bigfoot. Discusses the mythology involved. Black and white and color photographs. For units in popular culture, geography, and legends and for recreational reading. *Subject*: Yeti.

Ballard, Robert D., with Rick Archbold. *Exploring the Bismarck*. New York: Scholastic/ Madison Press, 1990. Hardcover $15.95 (ISBN 0–590–44268–6). Fry Reading Level 4+. Interest Level Grade 5–Adult.

Well-written and illustrated work about the always popular story of the German ship the *Bismarck*, which was sunk in May 1941 during the first stage of World War II after it had wreaked so much havoc on the British navy. Good for intermediate-stage readers and has a broad appeal. History and scientific methods of exploration are discussed. Glossary, excellent picture explanation of the *Bismarck*. Ballad was the explorer who found the *Bismarck* forty-eight years later, in May 1989. For units in world history, geography, oceanography, warfare, and social studies. *Subjects*: Bismarck (Ship); World War, 1939–1945—Naval History; Ships—*Bismarck*.

Barber, Nicola. *The Search for Gold*. Austin, TX: Raintree/Steck-Vaughn, 1998. Treasure Hunters Series. Hardcover $24.97 (ISBN 0–8172–4837–4). Fry Reading Level 4+. Interest Level Grade 5–Adult.

Fun and easy-to-read look at the search for gold across the epochs of time and across the world. Looks at the activities of the explorers and the pirates who went in search of golden treasure. Tells about the unsolved mysteries related to their efforts. Good color photographs. Oversized format. Can be read in sections. Index, glossary. Simple maps. For history, popular culture, and geography units. *Subject*: Buried Treasure.

Barber, Nicola. *The Search for Lost Cities*. Austin, TX: Raintree/Steck-Vaughn, 1998. Treasure Hunters Series. Hardcover $24.97 (ISBN 0–8172–4840–4). Fry Reading Level 4+. Interest Level Grade 5–Adult.

Easy-to-read accounts of the lost cities on five continents. Profiles ghost towns as well and covers unsolved mysteries pertaining to these places. Can be read piecemeal for archaeology in small doses. Includes Knossos, Troy, Machu Picchu, and Angkor, as well as other places. Arrangement makes the material very readable. Photographs and color illustrations. Simple maps, glossary, index, bibliography. Oversized. For units in history, archaeology, geography, social studies, and popular culture. *Subjects*: Extinct Cities; Cities and Towns—Ancient; Civilizations—Ancient.

Barber, Nicola, and Anita Ganeri. *The Search for Sunken Treasure*. Austin, TX: Raintree/Steck-Vaughn, 1998. Treasure Hunters Series. Hardcover $24.97 (ISBN 0–8172–4838–2). Fry Reading Level 4+. Interest Level Grade 5–Adult.

A good book for readers who like adventure and treasure hunting and even underseas exploration. Students will recognize some of the material from television shows. Covers the wreck of the *Mary Rose* and the *Titanic*, as well as other wrecks in the Atlantic, Pacific, Indian Ocean, and other places. Mix of illustrations and photographs in color. Covers current as well as past endeavors and includes some unsolved mysteries on this subject. Discusses the salvaging of the ships. Glossary, index, further reading. Oversized. For units in geography, history, and underseas exploration and for recreational reading. *Subject*: Buried Treasure.

Berke, Sally. *Loch Ness Monster*. Austin, TX: Steck-Vaughn, 1992. Unsolved Mystery Series. Hardcover $24.26 (ISBN 0–8172–1054–7); paper $11.42 (ISBN 0–8114–6858–5). Fry Reading Level 4+. Interest Level Grade 5–Adult.

Covers the legends and the evidence concerning the reasons for and the origins of one of the best known of the mysterious monsters. Discusses the evidence that Nessie really exists. Talks about its looks and features and various hunts for it. Speculates on what it really might be. Illustration and black and white and color photographs. For units in popular culture, myths, legends, and folklore, classes in geography and zoology; and recreational reading. *Subject*: Loch Ness Monster.

Billings, Henry, and Melissa Stone Billings. *Great Adventures*. Austin, TX: Steck-Vaughn, 1991. Great . . . Series. Hardcover $14.94 (ISBN 0–8114–4668–3). Fry Reading Level 3+. Interest Level Grade 4–Adult.

Workbook-style book contains stories about Marco Polo, Captain William Bligh and the *H.M.S. Bounty*, Mungo Park and his search for the Niger, Henry Morton Stanley and the exploration of Africa, the nineteenth-century reporter Nellie Bly (the intrepid Englishwoman who toured Africa in the late nineteenth century), and the Swedish explorer Salomon Andree. Also covered are the Antarctica explorer Shackelton, the famed anthropologist Margaret Mead, Thor Heyerdahl's journey on the raft *Kon-Tiki*, the lion's champion Joy Adamson, and Arlene Blum's team and its climb of Annapurna. Illustrations and photographs in sepia tones. The short articles can be used one at a time in many different settings. Each contains learning materials, word games, and explanatory notes. For units in history, geography, cultural history, and women's studies. *Subjects*: Biography—Collective; Readers for New Literates.

Blau, Melinda. *What Ever Happened to Amelia Earhart?* Austin, TX: Steck-Vaughn, 1992. Unsolved Mystery Series. Hardcover $24.26 (ISBN 0–8172–1957–1); paper $11.42 (ISBN 0–8114–6868–2). Fry Reading Level 4+. Interest Level Grade 5–Adult.

Biography of a pacesetter and record setter in early aviation, who disappeared over the Pacific Ocean in an attempt to fly solo around the world in a small plane. Covers her childhood and her family's financial woes that kept them moving, her adolescent and college years, and World War I. Discusses her solo flight across the Atlantic and the mysterious purposes ascribed to the last flight. Color drawings and black and white and color photographs. For units on women, flying, adventure, geography, and history or for recreational reading. *Subjects*: Earhart, Amelia, 1898–1937; Air Pilots.

Burnford, Sheila. *The Incredible Journey.* New York: Bantam. Paper $4.50 (ISBN 0–440–2267–8L) Fry Reading Level 6. Interest Level Grade 5–Adult.

A true adventure of three pets that journeyed across Canada to return to their home and owners. Lots of danger and excitement as the two dogs and one cat seek out their beloved family. Travel in the wilderness. For units in geography, determination, perseverance, and character and for recreational reading. Students may already be familiar with the movie version. *Subjects*: Cats; Dogs.

Collins, Jim. *The Bermuda Triangle.* Austin, TX: Steck-Vaughn, 1992. Unsolved Mysteries Series. Hardcover $24.26 (ISBN 0–8172–1050–4); paper $11.46 (ISBN 0–8114–6851–8). Fry Reading Level 4+. Interest Level Grade 5–Adult.

About one of the best-known and well-documented mystery areas. Talks about the unexplained accidents and losses of ships and planes in this area of the Atlantic Ocean between Florida and Bermuda. Tells about the missing flight of five bombers, Columbus's experience there, and people who have survived strange occurrences there. Notes theories, such as a hole in the sea or the sky, and tries to pinpoint what the triangle is. Drawings and photographs in black and white and color. For units on popular culture, geography, adventure, and legends and myths and for recreational reading. *Subject*: Bermuda Triangle.

*Contemporary Reader*, Volume 1, Number I. Chicago: Contemporary Books, 1984. Contemporary Reader Series. Hardcover $5.95 (ISBN 0–8092–3462–0). Fry Reading Level 3+. Interest Level Grade 4–Adult.

Contains material on the life and work of the artist Fernando Botero, the study of color, ghosts, maple sugar, and maple syrup. Also looks at caves and snakes, Egyptian wonders, budgeting, Ellis Island, the Arctic, and pants as clothing. The articles range from eight to twelve pages in length, and each contains pictures and illustrations, usually in black and white, but some are in color. Captioned photos, glossary. Each article has questions for answering, and the paragraphs are numbered for easy identification. Excellent for use piecemeal. For units on art, science, food, history, life skills, psychology, and cultural history and for fun reading. *Subject*: Readers for New Literates.

Gallagher, I. J. *The Case of the Ancient Astronauts.* Austin, TX: Steck-Vaughn, 1992. Unsolved Mystery Series. Hardcover $24.26 (ISBN 0–8172–1059–8); paper $11.42 (ISBN 0–8114–6854–2). Fry Reading Level 4+. Interest Level Grade 5–Adult.

Talks about the possibilities of early space travelers and UFOs visiting ancient civilizations. Looks at some ancient maps, some peculiar legends, and some Mayan mysteries, as well as Easter Island. Discusses the famous land markings in Peru. Black and white and color illustrations and photographs. For units on history, popular culture, archaeology, geography, and mythology and for recreational reading. *Subjects*: Interplanetary Voyages; Civilization— Ancient; Man—Prehistoric.

Ganeri, Anita. *The Search for Tombs*. Austin, TX: Raintree/Steck-Vaughn, 1998. Treasure Hunters Series. Hardcover $24.97 (ISBN 0–8172–4839–0). Fry Reading Level 4+. Interest Level Grade 5–Adult.

Archaeology for beginners. Can be used in sections or all as a piece as needed. Informative look at searches for prehistoric graves and royal tombs. Looks at the pharaohs and their curses, Agamemnon, Chinese royal tombs, the Maya, ship graveyards, and others. Includes some of the legends as well as unsolved mysteries about tombs and their exploration. Color illustrations and photographs. Simple maps, glossary, index, bibliography. For units in art, death and dying, customs of countries, archaeology, history, and geography and for recreational reading. *Subjects*: Tombs; Archaeology.

Klotter, James C. *History Mysteries*. Lexington: University Press of Kentucky, 1989. New Books for New Readers Series. Hardcover $5.58 (ISBN 0–8138–0903–5). Fry Reading Level 4+. Interest Level Grade 5–Adult.

History has always contained mysteries, and some of these mysteries have contributed to legends over time. The four history mysteries here let the reader play detective on some unsolved historical mysteries: the disappearance of James Harrod, the leader of the first settlers into Kentucky; the murder of the famed Indian chief Tecumseh; the case of "Honest Dick" Tate, a Kentucky politician who lived a double life; and the mystery pertaining to William Goebel, the son of German immigrants. It contains political corruption, murder, and missing facts. Good stories to teach critical and analytical thinking and can instruct on the never-changing face and facets of politics. Clues and pointers for possible conclusions. Black and white illustrations. Bibliography. For units on history, politics, and Native Americans. Particularly useful in Kentucky, Indiana, and Ohio. *Subjects*: Kentucky—History—Miscellaneous; Curiosities and Wonders; Readers for New Literates.

Kudalis, Eric. *Dracula and Other Vampire Stories*. Minneapolis: Capstone Press, 1994. Classic Monster Stories Series. Hardcover $19.00 (ISBN 1–56065–212–8). Fry Reading Level 4. Interest Level Grade 5–Adult.

Tells the tale of the vampire Dracula; explores the many superstitions and legends surrounding vampires; gives a very brief background on Bram Stoker, who created the Dracula story; and talks about Vlad the Impaler, the actual ruler from Wallachia in Romania on which much of the Dracula legend is based. Discusses vampires in books and movies and even covers vampire bats. Uses pictures from the various Dracula movies and black and white and color photographs. Easy to read. Good index, glossary, and a bibliography with books on Dracula movies, bats, and Romania. For units on popular culture, history, superstitions, geography, and biology and for recreational reading. *Subject*: Vampires.

Kudalis, Eric. *Stories of Mummies and the Living Dead*. Minneapolis, MN: Capstone Press, 1994. Classic Monster Stories Series. Hardcover $19.00 (ISBN 1–56065–214–4). Fry Reading Level 4. Interest Level Grade 5–Adult.

Tells the classic mummy story as retold endless times in the movies and includes other mummy tales. Explains what a mummy is, how they were created and how science is still exploring them, and their history. Black and white and color photographs and illustrations. Glossary, index, bibliography. For units in popular culture and history and for recreational reading. *Subject*: Mummies.

Lawless, Joann A. *Mysteries of the Mind*. Austin, TX: Steck-Vaughn, 1992. Unsolved Mysteries Series. Hardcover $24.26 (ISBN 8071–1066–0); paper $11.42 (ISBN 0–8114–6859–3). Fry Reading Level 4+. Interest Level Grade 5–Adult.

Covers mental telepathy, touch communication, unusual mental powers, telekinesis, and clairvoyance. Talks about ESP, the future, sleep mysteries, and people known as healers. Relates tales about the "sixth sense." Color and black and white illustrations, black and white photographs. For classes in science, psychology, popular culture, and health and for recreational reading. *Subject*: Psychical Research.

McMullen, David. *Atlantis: The Missing Continent*. Austin, TX: Steck-Vaughn. 1992. Unsolved Mysteries Series. Hardcover $24.26 (ISBN 0–8172–1047–4); paper $11.42 (ISBN 0–8114–6850–X). Fry Reading Level 4+. Interest Level Grade 5–Adult.

About the Atlantis of legend and lore, believed to lie off the west coast of Africa. Contains myth, fiction, speculation, and facts from ancient and early writers. Notes people who throughout the ages have had remarkably similar dreams about Atlantis as a city. Includes the dreams of the famed novelist Taylor Caldwell and the American seer Edgar Cayce. Illustrations and photographs in black and white and color. For units on myths and legends, the paranormal, the unexplained, geography, and the ancient world and for recreational reading. *Subject*: Atlantis.

Robinson, Minnie Mae, with Dee Yurdock. *Minnie Mae: My Story*. Grand Rapids, MI: 1996. Open Door Books Series. Paper $3.95 (ISBN 1–56212–181–2). Fry Reading Level 4+. Interest Level Grade 6–Adult.

The story of Minnie Mae in her own words: Minnie Mae is an ordinary person who as an adult felt the need to further her education, and this is her story as she lived it—her life in Alabama, her catch-as-catch-can schooling, and her need to learn to read as an adult. Provides a good look at the life of an African American in the poor, rural section of a southern community. Highlights her religious roots and the religious roots of her family. For reinforcement for older adults who are returning to learning, cultural history, social history, and inspirational reading. *Subjects*: Robinson, Minnie Mae, 1923–; Literacy Programs—United States; Reading (Adult Education)—United States; Volunteer Workers in Education—United States; Biography.

Swinburne, Laurence, and Irene Swinburne. *The Deadly Diamonds*. Austin, TX: Steck-Vaughn, 1992. Unsolved Mysteries Series. Hardcover $24.26 (ISBN 0–8172–1064–4); paper $11.42 (ISBN 0–8114–6856–9). Fry Reading Level 4+. Interest Level Grade 5–Adult.

A brief look at the history and horrendous luck surrounding and attributed to the Regent diamond, the Hope diamond, and other famous diamonds. Includes the tale of Alexander the Great and the diamonds in India, the hapless owners of the Regent, and the magnificent but bad luck Hope. For units in popular culture, science, and geography and for recreational reading. *Subject*: Diamonds.

Tanaka, Shelly. *Disaster of the Hindenberg*. New York: Scholastic, Time Quest Books, 1993. Hardcover $16.95 (ISBN 0–590–45750–0). Fry Reading Level 7+. Interest Level Grade 7–Adult.

Covers all points of views of the tragedy and creates a kind of docudrama. Details the planning and engineering that went into the ship, as well as the publicity that surrounded its voyage and the hints of sabotage that surfaced after the explosion in New Jersey. For more advanced readers. Oversized, packed with illustrations in color and black and white that ably enhance the informative text. For units on popular history, disasters, and airships. *Subjects*: Disasters; *Hindenberg* Disaster; Travel—Airships.

Wilcox, Tamara. *Mysterious Detectives: Psychics*. Austin, TX: Steck-Vaughn, 1992. Unsolved Mysteries Series. Hardcover $24.26 (ISBN 0–8172–1061–X); paper $14.94 (ISBN 0–8114–6860–7). Fry Reading Level 4+. Interest Level Grade 5–Adult.

About how psychics have helped solve crimes throughout the ages. Discusses Peter Hurkos, the Dutch psychic who claims to use his sense of touch and a sixth sense to know things; another Dutch psychic, Marius Dykshoorn, as well as the tracer of lost persons, Gerard Croiset; Chicago sleuth Irene Hughes and her involvement with police cases; as well as a group in America known as the Psi Squad. For classes in psychology and popular culture, for units on crime and criminals; and for recreational reading. *Subjects*: Parapsychology; Criminal Investigations.

Wolfe, Tom. *The Right Stuff*. New York: Literacy Volunteers of New York City, 1991. Writers Voices Series. Paper $3.50 (ISBN 0–929631–31–5). Fry Reading Level 5+. Interest Level Grade 6–Adult.

A simplified and extracted piece of the work about the first American astronauts. The selection tells about John Glenn, the first man to go around the earth in space. Has material about the qualities needed for the astronauts, a short biography of the author, a brief history of the manned space program, and notes for study, with a chronology of early space travel. Mass market paperback size is attractive to readers. For classes in science, space exploration, psychology, history, and popular culture and for recreational reading. *Subjects*: Space; Manned Space Flight, Glenn, John.

## FICTION

Attema, Martha. *A Time to Choose*. Custer, WA: Orca Book Publishers, 1995. Paper $6.95 (ISBN 1–55143–045–2). Fry Reading Level 7. Interest Level Grade 5–Adult.

The story, set in the Netherlands in 1944, when the country has been occupied by the Nazis for several years, is about a young man whose father is a collaborator with the enemy. The girl he loves is a member of the Dutch resistance. The adventures of Johannes as he tries to instill trust in his motives, as well as reclaim honor for his family, are based on actual events. Looks at sacrifice, courage, love, betrayal, and making choices. For units on history, life skills, and psychology. *Subjects*: World War, 1939–1945—Fiction; World War, 1939–1945—Netherlands—Fiction.

Barnes, Creighton, and Sarah Creighton. *Exit for Two*. Columbia, SC: Educational Development Laboratories, 1990. Midnight Thriller Series. Hardcover $14.94 (ISBN 1–55855–689–3). Fry Reading Level 4+. Interest Level Grade 5–Adult.

Contains three thriller and horror-type short stories. "Deep Freeze" is about a magic show that involves the death of the villain; "Exit for Two" tells of a thing created by a crazed doctor that is killing gang leaders; "The Wonder Drug" tells what bizarre things can happen when a man tries to cure baldness. Well-developed plots. No illustrations. Can be read as entire book or in sections. For literature classes and recreational reading. *Subject*: Short Stories—Thrillers—Fiction.

Benchley, Peter. *Selected from Jaws.* Syracuse, NY: Signal Hill, 1990. Imprint of New Readers Press. Writers' Voices Series. Paper $3.50 (ISBN 0–929631–14–5). Fry Reading Level 4–5. Interest Level Grade 5–Adult.

An adapted version of the thriller *Jaws* that maintains the flavor and essence of the famed story and movie while providing an easy read. Mass market paperback format makes it attractive to teens. Tells of the shark's initial attack and its eventual capture. Besides the selections from the original story, the book contains a brief author biography, maps of the places covered, a brief history of sharks, information about the movie, and a study guide to help promote understanding and discussion. For units on animals, popular culture, biology, and literature and for supplemental reading for entertainment. *Subject*: Sharks—Fiction.

Carbone, Sonny. *Three Shots in the Night.* New York: Literacy Volunteers of New York City, 1992. New Writers' Voice Series. Paper $3.50 (ISBN 0–929631–65–X). Fry Reading Level 4+. Interest Level Grade 9–Adult.

This story, written by a person learning to read as an adult, provides an effective approach to learning English. Short and fast-paced mystery set in New York tells how a detective uses reasoning and thinking to solve a murder case. Mass market paperback format makes the book attractive to readers. For classes in reading and writing and for recreational reading. *Subjects*: Mysteries—Fiction; Murder—Fiction.

Cebulash, Mel. *Knockout Punch.* Syracuse, NY: New Readers Press, 1993. Paper $4.25 (ISBN 1–56420–009–6); tape (ISBN 1–56420–009–4). Fry Reading Level 3–5. Interest Level Grade 5–Adult.

One of the series of Sully Gomez mysteries set in California. Gomez is a Hispanic American detective who takes on cases for poor people who need his expert help. He becomes involved in this case when a young boxer he knows is in a fight that is supposed to be fixed. The character and personality of Gomez are established and the setting of the book is created with ease. Characters seem real. Vocabulary can be understood by those fairly new to English. Line drawings add faces to the characters. Read-along tape is excellent for reinforcing language learning. For readers who like detective stories and stories with happy endings. Has universal appeal but appeals especially to Hispanic readers because of its hero and the area in which he works and lives. For supplementary reading and English language classes. *Subjects*:

Sports—Boxing—Fiction; Hispanic Americans—Fiction; Detective Stories—
Fiction.

Cebulash, Mel. *Sully Gomez Mysteries*. Syracuse, NY: New Readers Press, 1993. Sully
Gomez Series. Paper $4.25 tape $10.10. Fry Reading Level 3–5. Interest Level Grade 7–
Adult.

All of these delightful stories feature a Hispanic detective who lives in Los
Angeles, who uses street smarts, common sense, and a caring nature to solve
problems that range from illegal immigrants who want to be legal, to fixed
sporting events involving a boxer to a gang-related problem, to some handgun
troubles. Most of his clients are people in his neighborhood who need help.
Easy-to-read short stories geared to new readers. Will appeal to ESL students
because they can relate to the incidents as well as the people involved, sports
fans, mystery fans, and youths. Particularly appealing to Hispanic immigrants
and to those in California. For classes in reading, writing, popular culture,
and life skills and for recreational reading. Also available on tapes for read-
along experiences.
   *Dirty Money*. (ISBN 1–56420–002–7); tape (ISBN 1–56420–003–5).
   *Knockout Punch*. (ISBN 1–56420–008–6); tape (ISBN 1–56420–008–6).
   *Set to Explode*. (ISBN 1–56420–004–3); tape (ISBN 1–56420–005–1).
   *Sucker for a Redhead*. (ISBN 1–56420–006–X); tape
(ISBN 1–56420–007–8). *Subjects*: Mysteries—Fiction; Detectives—Fiction.

Clark, Mary Higgins. *Selected from Lost Angels*. Syracuse, NY: Signal Hill, 1990. Writers'
Voices Series. Paper $3.95 (ISBN 092963113–7). Fry Reading Level 4. Interest Level
Grade 7–Adult.

Selected and adapted from a short story written by this popular author of
suspense stories. It tells of a mother's search for her daughter, kidnapped by
her father. Takes place in Chicago and New York. Contains a short biography
of the author as well as a brief article about parental kidnapping of children.
Paperback format attractive to readers. Material for study and discussion included. For classes in reading, life skills, family problems, and geography.
*Subjects*: Short Stories; Kidnapping—Fiction.

Golding, William. *Lord of the Flies*. New York: Putnam. Paper $6.95
(ISBN 0–399–50148–7). Fry Reading Level 7+. Interest Level Grade 7–Adult.

This modern classic is an adventure story that tells of the aftermath of a
plane crash that puts a group of school children on a deserted island. Their
struggle to survive uncovers a frightening look at the darker side of human
nature. A parable of the times. "Lord of the Flies" is a euphemism for the

devil. For advanced readers. For English classes, psychology, sociology, and popular culture. *Subject*: Survival—Fiction.

Greenburg, Dan. *A Ghost Named Wanda*. New York: Grosset and Dunlap. Zack Files Series. Hardcover $11.99 (ISBN 0–448–41290–X). Fry Reading Level 4. Interest Level Grade 4–9.

Zack is a ten-year-old boy who has adventures of interest to young readers of both genders. His parents are divorced, and he spends half his time with each parent. In this tale of the supernatural, a ghost named Wanda has taken up residence in his father's apartment. Covers father-son relationships, ingenuity, and original thinking. For units on family, teaching reading, and for fun reading depending on the cultural reaction to ghosts. *Subjects*: Supernatural—Fiction; Ghosts—Fiction.

Greenburg, Dan. *Great-Grandpa's in the Litter Box*. New York: Grosset and Dunlap. Zack Files Series. Hardcover $11.99 (ISBN 0–448–41289–6); paper $3.50 (ISBN 0–448–41260–8). Fry Reading Level 4. Interest Level Grade 4–9.

Story of what happens when Zack's father lets him get a cat—not the kitten he planned on, but a cat who talks to him and claims to be his long-dead Great-Grandfather Julius. Zack learns that family is family. Book is amusing and fun. It also teaches about family, some cultural history, and a little Jewish tradition. For units on family, pets, cultural history, popular culture, and relationships and for recreational reading. *Subjects*: Cats—Fiction; Reincarnation—Fiction; Great-Grandfathers—Fiction; Supernatural—Fiction.

Greenburg, Dan. *Through the Medicine Cabinet*. New York: Grosset and Dunlap. Zack Files Series. Hardcover $11.98 (ISBN 0–448–41291–8); paper $3.50 (ISBN 0–448–4126–4). Fry Reading Level 4. Interest Level Grade 4–9.

Zack has more supernatural adventures. This time it involves a parallel universe. Manages to cover orthodontics, writers, divorced parents, sports, and science fiction. Fun reading that can be used in several curriculum areas, including learning to read better. *Subject*: Supernatural—Fiction.

Greenburg, Dan. *Zap! I'm a Mind Reader*. New York: Grosset and Dunlap. Zack Files Series. Hardcover $11.99 (ISBN 0–448–41292–6); paper $3.95 (ISBN 0–448–41263–2). Fry Reading Level 4. Interest Level Grade 4–9.

The adventures of Zack continue with ESP and the supernatural. This adventure is the culmination of an electrifying science experiment. Covers the closeness of fathers and sons. Provides peer reinforcement for young readers. For units in popular culture, science classes, and family living and for recreational reading. *Subjects*: Extrasensory perception—Fiction; Supernatural—Fiction.

Holder, Andre. *Fatal Beauty*. Syracuse, NY: New Readers Press, 1993. New Writers' Voices Series. Paper $3.50 (ISBN 0-1-56853-003-X). Fry Reading Level 3. Interest Level Grade 7–Adult.

A French-born detective living in New York assumes the persona of an international playboy to entice and trap a deadly widow who has both money and murder on her mind. Easy-reading book written by an adult new reader and writer for a literacy series that provides effective material for teaching reading of English. Short and simple sentences. Mass market paperback format makes the material attractive to use. For classes in reading, writing, and popular culture. *Subject*: Detectives—Fiction.

Keown, Don. *The Creature in the Forest*. Novato, CA: High Noon Books, 1994. Scoop Doogan Series. Paper $3.95 (ISBN 0-87879-436-0). Fry Reading Level 3+. Interest Level Grade 7–12.

Story of Skip Malone, a high school senior who has an after-school job with the ace reporter for the *Big City Times* and the adventures that are part of this association. They cover reports of a strange and scary creature that has been frightening visitors to a state of recreational area. Now they have to find out what the creature in the forest really is and unmask it if they can. For teaching reading and for recreational reading. *Subjects*: Newspapers—Fiction; Mysteries—Fiction.

Leroux, Gaston. *The Phantom of the Opera*. Adapted by Kate McMullen. New York: Random House, 1989. Bullseye Chiller Series. Paper $5.99 (ISBN 0-394-83847-5). Fry Reading Level 4+. Interest Level Grade 6–Adult.

An easy-to-read retelling of the classic tale that has been a hit in movies and on the stage. A disfigured musical genius lives in tunnels beneath the opera house in Paris and falls in love with a beautiful opera star. His desperation to fulfill his unrequited love leads him into terrifying acts and deeds. Tells of the horrors of rejection. Black and white block drawings. Information about the adapter and illustrator included. For literature classes, units on popular culture and psychology, and recreational reading. *Subject*: Horror Stories.

Lynch, Chris. *Iceman*. New York: HarperCollins, 1994. Hardcover $19.89 (ISBN 0-06-023341-9). Fry Reading Level 6+. Interest Level Grade 6–12.

Story of a fourteen-year-old who truly wants to love his parents, who seem incapable of showing warmth to him. He suppresses his anger and rage and lets it surface when he plays hockey. Known as the Iceman to the opponents and as the "animal" to his teammates who shun him because of his out-of-control behavior. He finds a friend with a taciturn employee at a local mortuary. Covers life-from-death motifs, parental problems, teen emotional needs, generational blunders. Since hockey in one form or another is an international sport, this tale will be understood by students from many backgrounds. For units in psychology, family life, problem solving, and sports and for recreational reading. *Subjects*: Hockey—Fiction; Families—Fiction.

Miller, Julano. *Canyon Rescue*. Novato, CA: High Noon Books, 1985. Life Line Series. Paper $3.00 (ISBN 0–87879–486–7). Fry Reading Level 3+. Interest Level Grade 5–Adult.

Fast-paced story of a rescue of a baby who fell down a cliff. Deals with courage, bravery, and adventure. Easy and short reading. Black and white line drawings. Use for life skills and fun reading for most ages. *Subject*: Rescues—Fiction.

Miller, Julano. *Flying Hospital*. Novato, CA: High Noon Books, 1985. Life Line Series. Paper $3.00 (ISBN 0–87879–489–1). Fry Reading Level 3+. Interest Level Grade 5–Adult.

Story of a pilot who flies a hospital helicopter. Deals with a rescue of a person who had a water mishap. Covers courage, bravery, dares, peer pressure, illnesses, and rescues. Easy reading with black and white line drawings. For units in life skills and peer counseling and for pleasure reading. *Subjects*: Rescues—Fiction; Accidents—Fiction; Helicopters—Fiction.

Miller, Julano. *Hi-Jack!* Novato, CA: High Noon Books, 1985. Life Line Series. Paper $3.00 (ISBN 0–87879–488–3). Fry Reading Level 3+. Interest Level Grade 5–Adult.

Another in the Life Line Helicopter books that deals with adventure, adversity, and courage. This involves a criminal hijacking and the way it is handled. Easy to read. Black and white illustrations. For life skills and fun reading for all ages. *Subjects*: Hijackings—Fiction; Crime and Criminals—Fiction; Rescues—Fiction.

Mosher, Richard. *The Taxi Navigator*. New York: Philomel Books, Grosset & Dunlap Group, 1996. Hardcover $15.95 (ISBN 0–399–23104–8). Fry Reading Level 5+. Interest Level Grade 5–10.

The story of a boy whose banker mother and lawyer father are growing increasingly estranged. Kid Kyle finds solace and help with his taxicab-driving uncle and some eccentric friends. Includes roller skating witches, piano playing, and some peculiar star gazing. Copes with divorce, death, grief, and being different. Adventure and friendship come from strange places. Amusing and off-center. For units in life skills and personal development and for pleasure reading. *Subjects*: Uncles—Fiction; Taxicabs—Fiction; Family Problems—Fiction; Friendship—Fiction; Death—Fiction; Grief—Fiction; New York (NY)—Fiction.

Poe, Edgar Allan. *Tales of Edgar Allan Poe*. Adapted by Diana Stewart. Austin, TX: Steck-Vaughn, 1991. Raintree Short Classics Series. Hardcover $11.92 (ISBN 0–8172–1662–6); paper $3.50 (ISBN 0–8114–6841–0). Fry Reading Level 4. Interest Level Grade 5–Adult.

Simplified and adapted tales from Poe include "The Masque of the Red Death," "The Cask of Amontillado," "The Pit and the Pendulum," "The Tell-Tale Heart," and "Hop-Frog." Color illustrations add to the setting and enhance the atmosphere. For classes in literature and popular culture and for recreational reading. *Subjects*: Horror Stories; Short Stories.

Prowse, Philip. *L.A. Detective*. Portsmouth, NH: Heinemann International, 1993. Guided Readers Series. Paper $2.95 (ISBN 0–435–27160–1). Fry Reading Level 2. Interest Level Grade 5–Adult.

Done in comic book and graphic novel style in full color, this is an easy way to tackle reading English as a second language. The Los Angeles detective has to deal with gangs and a kidnapping. Use for classes in reading and units on gang culture and social problems. *Subjects*: Detectives—Fiction; Gangs—Fiction; Kidnapping—Fiction; Graphic Novels.

Rorry, Ginny. *Dolphin Sky*. New York: G. P. Putnam's Sons, 1996. Hardcover $16.95 (ISBN 0–399–299–5–1). Fry Reading Level 6+. Interest Level Grade 6–12.

Dyslexia in a twelve-year-old girl creates school and personal problems. Befriending dolphins and helping in their rescue helps her. Set in and near the Florida Everglades. Covers abuse of animals as well as the psychological abuse of a slow learner or one who is different. For better students but can be used to demystify differences among students. Map showing location of Everglades and general vicinity. For life skills, personal development, science, ethics, geography, and popular culture and for extra-credit reading. *Subjects*: Dolphins—Fiction; Animals—Treatment—Fiction; Dyslexia—Fiction; Everglades (Fla.)—Fiction.

Sans Souci, Robert D., ed. *Even More Short and Shivery: Thirty Spine Tingling Tales*. New York: Doubleday (Bantam Doubleday Dell), 1997. Hardcover $14.95 (ISBN 0–395–32252–6). Fry Reading Level 5+. Interest Level Grade 5–Adult.

Contains thirty classic and contemporary tales of horror and terror from all over the world, including Mexico, Poland, China, and the Philippines. Some of the chillers are "Guests from Gibbett Island," "The Skull That Spoke," and "The Dancing Dead." Short stories for easy reading. Some illustrations. For units in popular culture, folklore, holidays such as Halloween, and reading and for recreational reading. *Subjects*: Horror Stories; Short Stories.

Stewart, Winnie. *Night on 'Gator Creek*. Syracuse, NY: New Readers Press, 1990. Sundown Books Series. Paper $3.95 (ISBN 0–88336–215–5). Fry Reading Level 4–5. Interest Level Grade 5–Adult.

Based on a true story, this is an account of courage and love in the face of terror and adversity. Story of young Mattie and what happens when camping out with his grandparents in their part of Florida near Tallahassee. Covers the lifestyle of a youth who lives with grandparents because his parents have divorced and remarried. Describes a life that involves flea markets, fishing, trading, and family involvement. Realistic in its treatment of death and funerals. For units on family, death, and nature, and regional for Florida. *Subjects*: Florida—Fiction; Accidents—Fiction; Death—Fiction; Lifestyles—Fiction.

Taylor, Theodore. *The Weirdo*. New York: Avon. Paper $4.50 (ISBN 0–380–72017). Fry Reading Level 6+. Interest Level Grade 7–12.

About a girl who finds a dead body in a swamp and sees another getting dumped there and her developing friendship with a bear tracker who lives in an eerie, gothic southern swamp. The loner gets his nickname, Weirdo, from a tragically scarred face. Tells of their search for the lurking murderer. Shades of Frankenstein with a little mystery tossed in. For better readers. For units in geography, environment, and psychology and recreational reading. *Subjects*: Mystery Stories—Fiction; Murder—Fiction; Friendship—Fiction.

Trembath, Don. *A Fly Named Alfred*. Custer, WA: Orca Book Publishers, 1997. Paper $6.95 (ISBN 1–55143–083–5). Fry Reading Level 6. Interest Level Grade 6–10.

The further adventures of Harper Winslow, a problem high school student. Winslow was introduced in *The Tuesday Cafe*, also a good read. The book is titled after the column that Winslow writes for the school paper, and the column is what gets him into trouble again with the school bully. A case of mistaken and unknown identity livens up the school. For units in journalism, life skills, psychology, and writing and for recreational reading. *Subjects*: High Schools—Fiction; School Newspapers—Fiction.

Wells, H. G. *The Time Machine*. Adapted by Betty Ren Wright. Austin, TX: Steck-Vaughn, 1991. Raintree Short Classics. Hardcover $11.92 (ISBN 0–8172–1675–8); paper $3.50 (ISBN 0–8114–6842–9). Fry Reading Level 4. Interest Level Grade 5–Adult.

A simplified and adapted version of a time traveler into the future from an earlier era who discovers that the world is divided into two races. This classic science fiction is enhanced by the color illustrations that reflect the ideas of the author. Glossary. For literature classes, units on popular culture, and recreational reading. *Subject*: Science Fiction.

# 2

# Biographies

These biographies were selected to provide supplementary reading materials for many areas of the curriculum and to represent our multicultural society. Biographies can provide readers with a personalized information about the history of a country, the struggle of a minority, the music of an era, the social life of the time, and a sense of the time. These were chosen for the information they contain, reader appeal, and cultural depiction. They can be used for classes in social studies, communication, history, and language arts, as well as for recreational reading for both young adults and adults.

## NONFICTION

Billings, Charlene. *Christa McAuliffe: Pioneer Space Teacher.* Hillside, NJ: Enslow Publishing, 1986. Hardcover $11.92 (ISBN 0–89490–148–6). Fry Reading Level 4+. Interest Level Grade 5–Adult.

Tells of McAuliffe's life before her selection as the first private citizen to go into space. Written as a tribute to her after the shuttle disaster that claimed her life as well as those of the other astronauts on board the *Challenger*.

Covers her training as an astronaut and the disaster. Black and white pictures. Well indexed. *Subjects*: McAuliffe, Christa, 1948–1986; Astronauts; Teachers; *Challenger* (Spacecraft).

Billings, Melissa Stone, and Henry Billings. *Winners: Nobel Prize.* Austin, TX: Steck-Vaughn Company, 1993. Winners Series. Paper $5.58 (ISBN 0–8114–4781–2). Fry Reading Level 5+. Interest Level Grade 5–Adult.

Explains the origin and the history of the Nobel Prize and lists the six areas in which prizes are awarded. Includes profiles of Marie Curie, Albert Einstein,

Alexander Fleming, Emily Greene Balch, Albert Luthuli, Nelly Sachs, Alexander Solzhenitsyn, Betty Williams and Mairead Corrigan, Gabriel Garcia Marquez, Barbara McClintock, Wole Soyinka, and Augn San Suu Kyi. Workbook-type format with questions and their answers and a glossary. Black and white illustrations. Pulp paper. Use for classes in reading and units on gang culture and social problems. *Subjects*: Biography, Collective; Awards and Prizes—Nobel.

Billings, Melissa Stone, and Henry Billings. *Winners: Presidential Medal of Freedom*. Austin, TX: Steck-Vaughn, 1994. Winners Series. Paper $5.95 (ISBN 0-8114-4791-X). Fry Reading Level 5 +. Interest Level Grade 5–Adult.

About the medal awarded by the president of the United States for achievement in education, science, entertainment, and public service. This selection of modern awards covers eleven individual citations as well as one group citation given to the crew of *Apollo 13* for performing a space rescue. Musicians, politicians, humanitarians, an oceanographer, an architect, and an actress are among those included (Pablo Casals, Dr. Martin Luther King, Luis Muñoz Marin, Lena Edwards, Jacques Cousteau, Pearl Bailey, I. M. Pei, and Audrey Hepburn among others). Since it is not necessary to be an American to receive this highest award, the heritages of the winners include Chinese, Spanish, French, Native American, Puerto Rican, African-American, and Dutch. Workbook format with about seven pages of black and white pictures, information, and questions for discussions for each person or group. Pertinent facts are pulled out and highlighted. Vocabulary studies included. Glossary and answers for the questions included. For multicultural classes, music, art, history, government, popular culture, recreational reading, and teaching reading. *Subject*: Presidential Medal of Freedom.

Carrillo, Louis. *Edward James Olmos*. Austin, TX: Raintree/Steck-Vaughn, 1997. Contemporary Hispanic American Biography Series. Hardcover $24.26 (ISBN 0-8172-3989-8). Fry Reading Level 4–6. Interest Level Grade 5–Adult.

Excellent look at the life and career of a Hispanic American who transformed himself from a shy Chicano from East Los Angeles into an award-winning actor, an advocate of youth, and an icon for Hispanics in the United States. Color and black and white photographs. Lists dates in his life. Index. For units in theater, television, popular culture, ethnic diversity, and life skills. *Subjects*: Olmos, Edward James; Actors and Actresses; Hispanic Americans—Biography.

Chrisman, Abbott. *David Farragut*. Austin, TX: Steck-Vaughn Company, 1991. Raintree Hispanic Stories Series. English and Spanish. Hardcover $15.33 (ISBN 0-8172-2904-3); paper $3.75 (ISBN 0-8114-6754-6). Fry Reading Level 5+. Interest Level Grade 5–Adult.

The story of America's first admiral whose sea captain father was from the Spanish island of Minorca and whose mother was an American. After both parents died, Farragut was brought up by an American naval officer and his family. Covers his life as a young sailor, his rise through the ranks, and the naval battles during the Revolutionary War and the American Civil War. Farragut is known for the quotation, "Damn the torpedoes! Full speed ahead!" Half color illustrations, half text. The text is in both English and Spanish, as is the brief glossary. For history, social studies, reading, and language classes. *Subjects*: Farragut, David Glasgow, 1801–1870; Admirals; Spanish Language Materials—Bilingual.

Chrisman, Abbott. *Hernando de Soto*. Austin, TX: Steck-Vaughn Company, 1991. Raintree Hispanic Stories Series. English and Spanish. Hardcover $15.33 (ISBN 0–8172–2903–5); $3.75 paper (ISBN 0–8114–6753–8). Fry Reading Level 5+. Interest Level Grade 5–Adult.

About the Spanish explorer who led the first European expedition to reach the Mississippi River. Covers his youth in what is now Panama; his soldiering for his patron, Pedrarias; the beheading of Balboa; the fight with his own countryman, Cortes; the conquest of the Incas with Pizarro; the return to Spain; his marriage; and his return to the New World as a conquistador. Half text, half color illustrations. Text in both English and Spanish. Excellent for classes in history, social studies, reading, and language. *Subjects*: Soto, Hernando de, ca. 1500–1542; Explorers; Spanish Language Materials—Bilingual.

Collins, David R. *Farmworker's Friend: The Story of Cesar Chavez*. Minneapolis, MN: Carolrhoda Books, 1996. Paper $5.95 (ISBN 1–57505–031–5); hardcover $17.50 (ISBN 0–87614–892–4). Fry Reading Level 4–6. Interest Level Grade 4–Adult.

The story of the son of an Arizona shopkeeper who became the champion of farm laborers. The experiences of Chavez's family as farm laborers formed the basis that drove Chavez throughout his life to get equitable treatment and pay for farmworkers. Known as the instigator of the lettuce boycott in the 1970s and later the grape boycott, he was both labor organizer and political activist. Black and white photographs flesh out the story of his fight for and with the union. Extensive bibliography. Use for units on agriculture, labor, social justice, social conditions, cultural diversity, Mexican Americans, or migrant workers. *Subjects*: Chavez, Cesar, 1927–; Labor Leaders; Mexican Americans—Biography; Migrant Labor.

Collins, David R. *Eng and Chang: The Original Siamese Twins*. Morristown, NJ: Silver Burdett, 1994. People in Focus Series. Paper $7.95 (ISBN 0–382–24719–1); hardcover $13.95 (ISBN 0–87518–602–5). Fry Reading Level 6–8. Interest Level Grade 6–Adult.

Explains where, why, and how the term *Siamese twins* came to be. Eng and Chang were the first Siamese twins to become public figures. This readable book with black and white illustrations and photographs tells the remarkable and curious story of these brothers and how they managed to live.

It shows how nineteenth-century society dealt with an anomaly of nature and that sensationalism is not the invention of our era. Also provides a glimpse at the quality of life before medical science could sometimes remedy a mistake of nature. Well indexed, attractive format. Excellent book for health classes, classes teaching sensitivity and tolerance, and for recreational reading. *Subjects*: Biography; Ethnic Groups; Siamese Twins.

Cox, Clinton. *Mark Twain: America's Humorist, Dreamer, Prophet, a Biography.* New York: Scholastic Press, 1995. Hardcover $14.95 (ISBN 0–590–45642–9). Fry Reading Level 5. Interest Level Grade 5–Adult.

About the multifaceted man who wrote *Huck Finn* and *Tom Sawyer* and why he chose the pseudonym that he did. Covers his life and his penchant for travel. Shows the dark as well as the humorous side to his writing. For classes in literature and popular culture. *Subjects*: Clemens, Samuel L.—Biography; Twain, Mark (pseudonym)—Biography; Authors—American.

Davidson, Sue. *Heart in Politics: Jeanette Rankin and Patsy T. Mink.* Seattle, WA: Seal Press, 1994. Women Who Dares Series. Paper $9.95 (ISBN 1–878–067–53–2). Fry Reading Level 8. Interest Level Grade 9–Adult.

Biographies of two members of the U.S. Congress before the feminist era who worked for women's rights and world peace. Shows the lives of two very different women and the effect they had on the country and the lives of other women. For units on women's studies, politics and government, and popular history and for teaching role models. *Subjects*: Mink, Patsy T.—Biography; Rankin, Jeanette—Biography; United States—Congress—Women; United States—History; Women's Studies—United States.

Dunlop, Eileen. *Tales of St. Patrick.* New York: Holiday House, 1996. Hardcover $15.95 (ISBN 0–8234–1218–0). Fry Reading Level 4–6. Interest Level Grade 5–Adult.

The patron saint of Ireland and the fifth century he lived in are recreated in this fictionalized biography. Stories are taken from Patrick's own writings, ancient sources, and legends. The son of privileged parents in Britain, Patrick was captured and sold into slavery in Ireland. The book tells of his escape and journey home, his religious studies and quest, and his return to Ireland to convert it to Christianity. Contains difficult words with no guide to pronunciation, but the story carries the book. *Subjects*: Patrick, Saint—Fiction; Ireland—History—Fiction.

Ferris, Jeri. *What I Had Was Singing.* Minneapolis, MN: Carolrhoda Books, 1994. Trailblazers Series. Paper $6.95 (ISBN 0–87614–634–5); hardcover $17.50 (ISBN 87614–818–6). Fry Reading Level 8+. Interest Level Grade 8–Adult.

Two decades before Martin Luther King's march on Washington, D.C., opera singer Marian Anderson was advancing the cause of African Americans through her magnificent voice. First lady Eleanor Roosevelt became Anderson's champion and defeated the Daughters of the American Revolution in their attempt to prevent her from presenting a concert in the nation's capital. This inspiring biography explains Anderson's courage and perseverance in pursuing a career in opera in an era when African Americans were not welcomed into the world of serious music. Well illustrated, index. Will appeal more to girls and women, but boys and men would also enjoy it. For supplementary reading in music classes as well as in social studies, history, and classes dealing with cultural diversity. *Subjects*: Anderson, Marian; Afro-Americans in Music—Women; Civil Rights; Music.

Glendinning, Richard and Sally Glendinning. *The Ringling Brothers: Circus Family.* New York: Chelsea House Publishers, 1991. Discover Biographies Series. Hardcover $14.95 (ISBN 0–7910–1468–1). Fry Reading Level 3+. Interest Level Grade 5–Adult.

Line drawings and multicolored drawings illustrate this easy-to-read story of the five brothers who grew up to be the premier circus people in America. Tells of their early amateur shows and their own days as performers, their hard work and determination, and their creation of the "Greatest Show on Earth" and making the name Ringling synonymous with circus. Creates dialogue and becomes a biographical docudrama. For the lower grades and beginning readers of English. *Subjects*: Circuses; Ringling Brothers—Biography.

Guernsey, Jo Ann Bren. *Hillary Rodham Clinton: A New Kind of First Lady.* Minneapolis, MN: Lerner Publications, 1993. Achiever Series. Hardcover $13.13 (ISBN 0–87614–2875–4); paper $6.96 (ISBN 0–87614–9650–4). Fry Reading Level 8. Interest Level Grade 8–12.

Looks at the life of one of America's first ladies and her role in the administration. Considers how personal politics change in life and what opportunities are available for bright and well-educated women. For advanced students. For units on women's studies, role models, politics, and popular culture. *Subjects*: Clinton, Hillary Rodham—Biography; Presidents—United States—Wives.

Guzzetti, Paula. *A Family Called Bronte.* Morristown, NJ: Silver Burdett Press, 1994. People in Focus Series. Hardcover $25.80 (ISBN 0–87518–592–4). Fry Reading Level 8. Interest Level Grade 9–Adult.

Biography of an eccentric and talented English family of writers that will be of interest to those who may have read or at least are familiar with the sisters' writings. Gives a background in literature and helps explain some familiar stories. Shows the lifestyles of the times. Time line, useful bibliography. For classes in literature, English literature, and popular culture. Can be used with movies made from some of the books. *Subjects*: Brontë, Charlotte—Biography; Brontë, Emily—Biography; Brontë Family—Biography; Literature—English.

Hoobler, Dorothy, and Thomas Hoobler. *African Portraits.* Austin, TX: Raintree/Steck-Vaughn, 1993. Images Across the Ages Series. Hardcover $15.96 (ISBN 0–8114–6378–8). Fry Reading Level 7–8. Interest Level Grade 7–Adult.

Short biographies of African leaders spanning the centuries from the pharaohs to Miriam Makeba and ranging in geography from the Nile to the Congo to the Cape. Because of its cultural diversity, can be a supplement for current events and history classes. The variety of people profiled provide role models for boys and girls. *Subjects*: Biography—Collective; Political Science.

Hughes, Libby. *Colin Powell: A Man of Quality.* Parsippany, NJ: Dillon Press, 1996. People in Focus Book Series. Paper $6.05 (ISBN 0–382–39261–2); hardcover $25.80 (ISBN 0–382–39260–4). Fry Reading Level 4–6. Interest Level Grade 5–Adult.

Tells the life of Colin Powell, son of Jamaican immigrant parents, from his youth in the South Bronx in New York to his position of national prominence in the 1990s. Covers his career during two tours in Vietnam, his Pentagon years, his years as a national security adviser and chairman of the Joint Chiefs of Staff, and the overseeing of the Operation Desert Storm, plus his emergence as a political public figure. An inspiring look at a figure Americans consider a hero. Family life as well as professional life is well represented. Black and white photographs. Includes advice to young people from Powell. Lists important dates and events in Powell's life; bibliography of books, periodicals, speeches, and media. Use for units on African Americans, Jamaican immigrants, armed forces, history, political science, world conflict, and current events. Excellent for role model study. *Subjects*: Powell, Colin; Afro-Americans—Generals—Biography; United States Army—Biography.

Kramer, Barbara. *Ken Griffey, Junior: All-Around Star.* Minneapolis, MN: Lerner Publications Company, 1996. Sports Achievers Biographies Series. Paper $5.95 (ISBN 0–8225–9729–2); hardcover $14.21 (ISBN 0–8225–2887–8). Fry Reading Level 4–6. Interest Level Grade 4–Adult.

Color and black and white photographs supplement the life story of an all-around, all-star baseball player. Traces Griffey's life as the son of a major league baseball player to his all-star status. Tells of his youthful suicide attempt and his overcoming injuries. Looks at the family life of star athletes. Inspirational biography. Use for units on sports, baseball, African Americans, biography, contemporary life, and role modeling. *Subjects*: Griffey, Ken—Biography, Afro-Americans—Biography; Baseball Players.

Krohn, Katherine. *Marilyn Monroe: Norma Jeane's Dream*. Minneapolis, MN: Lerner Publications Company, 1997. Newspaper Biographies Series. Hardcover $16.95 (ISBN 0–8225–4930–1). Fry Reading Level 7. Interest Level Grade 7–Adult.

Black and white and color photographs add to this story of the life of an American film icon. Covers her early life, career, marriages, and death. Concise, nonspeculative, matter-of-fact coverage. Bibliography of newspapers, magazines, and books; list of films; author's sources, author information. For units on biography, popular culture, theater, movies, and history. *Subjects*: Monroe, Marilyn, 1926–1962; Actors and Actresses; Women—Biography.

Ling, Bettina. *Maya Lin*. Austin, TX: Raintree/Steck-Vaughn, 1997. Contemporary Asian Americans Biography Series. Hardcover $24.26 (ISBN 0–8172–3992–8). Fry Reading Level 4–6. Interest Level Grade 5–Adult.

Describes the life and work of the talented Ohio-born architect and sculptor whose designs were chosen for the Vietnam War Memorial in Washington, D.C., and the Civil Rights Memorial in Montgomery, Alabama. Color and black and white photographs. List of important dates, glossary, bibliography, indexes. For units on women and girls, art, architecture, ethnic diversity, history, and popular culture. *Subjects*: Lin, Maya Ying; Architects; Sculptors; Chinese-Americans—Biography.

Lorbiecki, Marybeth. *Of Things Natural and Free*. Minneapolis, MN: Carolrhoda Books, 1993. Creative Minds Series. Hardcover $11.21 (ISBN 0–87614–97–X). Fry Reading Level 6. Interest Level Grade 6–Adult.

A biography of Aldo Leopold, pioneer in the field of conservation. Although well known by his colleagues, he is not well known to the public. This informative biography discusses his determination to educate the government as well as the public about the need to preserve and protect the environment and about the importance of ecosystems. Black and white illustrations and photographs. Bibliography on the environmental movement over the past seventy-five years, well indexed. For units on nature, the environment, geography, and social studies. *Subjects*: Leopold, Aldo; Biography; Conservation; Environment; Nature.

McPherson, Stephanie Sammartine. *Ordinary Genius: The Story of Albert Einstein*. Minneapolis, MN: Carolrhoda Books, 1995. Hardcover $19.95 (ISBN 0–87614–1478–0). Fry Reading Level 5. Interest Level Grade 5–Adult.

Looks at the personal life of the compassionate man who was also a consummate scientific researcher and the drive that compelled him in his work to expand the knowledge in mathematics and physics. Looks at his theories that had an impact on changing the world. For units on refugees, discrimination, mathematics, physics, science, and popular culture. *Subject*: Einstein, Albert—Biography.

McPherson, Stephanie Sammartine. *Peace and Bread: The Story of Jane Addams.* Minneapolis, MN: Carolrhoda Books, 1993. Trailblazers Series. Hardcover $17.50 (ISBN 0–87614–792–9). Fry Reading Level 8+. Interest Level Grade 8–Adult.

The story of the social worker and founder of Hull-House in Chicago, who received the Nobel Prize for peace. Provides insight into the life of the poor in America in the early twentieth century. Hull-House was a place where immigrants needing help could go to learn English, learn about their new country, and help obtain information necessary for surviving. Black and white photographs and illustrations. Index. Excellent for classes in social studies, history, and cultural diversity. *Subjects*: Addams, Jane; Biography; Feminism; Hull-House, Chicago, Illinois.

O'Connor, Barbara. *Barefoot Dancer: The Story of Isadora Duncan.* Minneapolis, MN: Carolrhoda Books, 1994. Trailblazer Series. Hardcover $17.50 (ISBN 0–86714–807–0). Fry Reading Level 8+. Interest Level Grade 7–Adult.

An even-handed approach to the eccentric and eclectic life of this avantgarde dancer. Discusses her life and its influence on modern dance and provides a good look at the hedonistic life of that era. For advanced readers. Interesting to women. For units on popular culture, popular and cultural history, dance and theater, and women's studies. *Subjects*: Duncan, Isadora—Biography; Dancers—Women.

Patrick-Wexler, Diane. *Toni Morrison.* Austin, TX: Steck-Vaughn Company, 1997. Contemporary African American Biography Series. Hardcover $24.26 (ISBN 0–8172–3987–1). Fry Reading Level 4–6. Interest Level Grade 6–Adult.

Covers the life of the first African American woman writer to win the Nobel Prize in literature. Informative and entertaining. Well illustrated in black and white and color. List of important dates, glossary, index. For classes in literature, popular culture, women, and ethnic diversity and for general reading. *Subjects*: Morrison, Toni; Afro-Americans—Biography; Authors—American; Women—Biography.

Patrick-Wexler, Diane. *Walter Dean Myers.* Austin, TX: Steck-Vaughn Company, 1996. Contemporary African American Biography Series. Hardcover $24.86 (ISBN 0–8172–3979–0); paper (0–8114–9796–8). Fry Reading Level 3–6. Interest Level Grade 4–Adult.

About one of the most popular African American authors of books for young people. Shows how many of his stories evolved from his life. Myers's own troubles in school with speech and pronunciation prepared him for writing for today's youth. Black and white and color photographs illustrate this informative book. Time line of Myers's life, glossary, bibliography. For units on literature, biography, African Americans, speech, and role modeling. *Subjects*: Myers, Walter Dean; Authors—American; Afro-Americans—Biography.

Perez, Frank, and Ann Weil. *Raul Julia*. Austin, TX: Raintree Steck-Vaughn, 1996. Contemporary American Series. Hardcover $15.98 (ISBN 0–8172–3984–7). Fry Reading Level 4–5. Interest Level Grade 5–Adult.

Covers the life of the much-admired Hispanic actor and his life before and after his success on the screen and the stage. Excellent illustrations. Short bibliography, glossary, time line of his life. For classes in cultural diversity, speech, theater, and popular culture. *Subjects*: Julia, Raul—Biography; Actors and Actresses—Biography.

Potts, Steve. *Andrew Jackson, A Photo-Illustrated Biography*. Mankato, MN: Bridgestone Books, 1996. Read and Discover Photo-Illustrated Biographies Series. Hardcover $14.59 (ISBN 1–56065–455–4). Fry Reading Level 3–4. Interest Level Grade 4–Adult.

Brief biography of the seventh president of the United States. Covers his boyhood in the Carolinas, his rough treatment at the hands of the British during the Revolutionary War, how he gambled away his inheritance, decided to study law, and moved west into the territory that would become Tennessee. Looks at his life as a soldier, how his war exploits made him a hero to the common man and got him elected as president twice, and his Indian policy that forced many Native Americans to relocate west in a tragic journey known as the Trail of Tears. Half text, half black and white illustration. Quotes, dates, words to know, more books to read, useful addresses, Internet sites. Easy reading. For social studies or history units. *Subjects*: Jackson, Andrew, 1767–1845; Presidents—United States—Biography.

Potts, Steve. *Franklin D. Roosevelt: A Photo-Illustrated Biography*. Mankato, MN: Bridgestone Books, 1996. Read and Discover Photo-Illustrated Biographies Series. Hardcover $14.59 (ISBN 1–56065–453–8). Fry Reading Level 3–4. Interest Level Grade 4–Adult.

A brief biography of the thirty-second president of the United States that covers all of his terms as well as his famous relatives and his bout with polio, thus showing how people can overcome disabilities. Discusses his time as governor of New York State, his political career, and the Great Depression and World War II. Archival pictures depict his life. Balance of text and pictures. Quotes, dates, glossary, bibliography, and addresses and Internet sites. Easy reader. For social studies and history units. *Subjects*: Roosevelt, Franklin D. (Franklin Delano), 1882–1945; Presidents—United States—Biography.

Potts, Steve. *John F. Kennedy: A Photo-Illustrated Biography.* Mankato, MN: Bridgestone
Books, 1996. Read and Discover Photo-Illustrated Series. Hardcover $14.59
(ISBN 1-56065-454-6). Fry Reading Level 3-4. Interest Level Grade 4-Adult.

Brief and easy-to-read biography of the thirty-fifth president of the United
States. Gives family background and tells about his school years. Discusses
his status as a war hero, his political career, his presidential campaign, and
his presidency. Illustrates determination and goal setting. Quotes, important
dates, a glossary, brief bibliography, and useful addresses and sites on the
Internet. Half illustration in black and white, half text. For units in social
studies, history, and comparative religion. *Subjects*: Kennedy, John F. (John
Fitzgerald), 1917-1963; Presidents—United States—Biography.

Potts, Steve. *Theodore Roosevelt: A Photo-Illustrated Biography.* Mankato, MN: Bridgestone
Books, 1996. Read and Discover Photo-Illustrated Biography Series. Hardcover $14.59
(ISBN 1-56065-452-X). Fry Reading Level 3-4. Interest Level Grade 4-Adult.

Easy-to-read and brief biography of the twenty-sixth president of the United
States. Discusses the Roosevelt family, the health problems that sent Teddy
out West, his personal triumphs and tragedies, and his desire to help people.
A writer, an outdoorsman, a civil servant, and a family man, he became a hero
during the Spanish-American War. Discusses the ensuing career in politics
and his Nobel Prize. Illustrates the ability to overcome adversity and promotes
personal courage. Quotes, important dates, archival photographs, glossary, addresses and Internet sites. For history or social study units. *Subjects*: Roosevelt, Theodore, 1858-1919; Presidents—United States—Biography.

Rediger, Pat. *Great African Americans in Music.* New York: Crabtree Publishing Company,
1996. Outstanding African American Series. Hardcover $23.97 (ISBN 0-86505-800-8);
paper $7.95 (ISBN 0-86505-814-8). Fry Reading Level 4+. Interest Level Grade 4-Adult.

Easy-to-read and colorful magazine format with short pieces about popular
musicians: Aretha Franklin, Ray Charles, Hammer, Nat King Cole, Ella Fitzgerald, Sarah Vaughan, Stevie Wonder, Chuck Berry, Natalie Cole, Thomas
Dorsey, Whitney Houston, Janet Jackson, and Charlie Pride. Profiles include
accomplishments, special interest, a personality profile, and obstacles each had
to overcome. Color and black and white photographs. Special information is
highlighted with colored bullets. For career guidance, inspirational reading,
and supplemental reading for social studies. *Subjects*: Musicians; Afro-
Americans—Biography.

Rodriguez, Janel. *Nely Galan.* Austin, TX: Raintree/Steck-Vaughn, 1997. Contemporary
Hispanic Americans Biography Series. Hardcover $24.26 (ISBN 0-8172-3991-X). Fry
Reading Level 4-6. Interest Level Grade 7-Adult.

Covers the exciting and often glamorous life of a young Cuban-American
woman as she went from high school student, to editor of a magazine, to the

president of her own production company. Also tells of her family's escape from Cuba and eventual resettlement in New Jersey and shows how she began to rely on television to learn her second language. Highly readable book that traces her journey from a student to entertainer to business woman and eventually to a Hispanic community leader. Well illustrated in color and black and white. Timely information. Lists important dates. Glossary, useful bibliography. For units on women and girls, history, television, careers and work, ethnic diversity, popular culture, and social studies and for recreational reading. *Subjects*: Galan, Nely, 1963–; Television Producers and Directors; Cuban Americans—Biography; Women—Biography.

St. George, Judith. *To See with the Heart: The Life of Sitting Bull.* New York: G. P. Putnam's Sons, 1996. Hardcover $17.95 (ISBN 0–399–22930–2). Fry Reading Level 7. Interest Level Grade 7–Adult.

The life of Sitting Bull covered from youth up to his funeral in 1890. The history of the Hunkpapa Sioux is discussed, and there is good coverage of Indian life in the 1800s and the Indian wars on the Great Plains. Legendary people such as Chief Crazy Horse, George Crook, Shave Head, and White Bull also make up parts of this biography. Maps are the only black and white illustrations. *Subjects*: Sitting Bull; Dakota Indians; Hunkpapa Indians.

Savage, Jeff. *Julie Krone: Unstoppable Jockey.* Minneapolis, MN: Lerner Publications Company, 1996. Achievers Series. Hardcover $14.96 (ISBN 0–8225–2888–6); paper $5.95 (ISBN 0–8225–9728–4). Fry Reading Level 6. Interest Level Grade 6–Adult.

Good treatment of the winningest woman jockey of all times. Covers the accomplishments of a female who is successful in this historically male-dominated profession. Talks about the money mechanics of racing and details how to advance in the jockey system. Lots of action that is covered in black and white and color photographs. Career highlights, glossary of racing terms. Use for units in sports, biography, career study, and role models. *Subjects*: Krone, Julie; Jockeys; Women—Biography.

Schwartz, Michael. *LaDonna Harris.* Austin, TX: Raintree/Steck-Vaughn Publications, 1997. Contemporary Native Americans Biography Series. Hardcover $24.26 (ISBN 0–8172–3995–2). Fry Reading Level 4–6. Interest Level Grade 7–Adult.

A powerful story of the woman from Oklahoma of Comanche and Irish ancestry who worked most of her life to better the life for Native Americans. Touches on some of the history of Indian policies as well as living conditions in the 1930s when Harris was growing up, as well as her life as the wife of a senator, a mother, and a civil rights worker. Tells how one determined person can make a difference. Dates provide an overview on the civil rights and the Native American rights struggles. Color and black and white photographs.

Index. For history, civil rights, Native Americans, social studies, women, and popular culture. *Subjects*: Harris, LaDonna; Comanche Indians—Biography; Indians of North America—Oklahoma—Biography.


Tan, Sheri. *Seiji Ozawa*. Austin, TX: Raintree/Steck-Vaughn Publications, 1997. Contemporary Asian American Biographies Series. Hardcover $24.26 (ISBN 0–8172–3993–6). Fry Reading Level 4–6. Interest Level Grade 6–Adult.

Biography of the Grammy-winning conductor who is a citizen of both the United States and Japan. Born in the Japanese-occupied Chinese province of Manchuria in the 1930s in a pacifist family set the tone for this unusual boy, who returned to Japan with his parents in 1944 and was there for the end of World War II. Tells of his studies in Paris and France, his association in New York with Leonard Bernstein, and his musical accomplishments. Well illustrated in color and black and white. Bibliography, important dates, glossary. For units in music, history, ethnic diversity, social studies, and popular culture. *Subjects*: Ozawa, Seiji, 1935–; Conductors (Music); Japanese Americans—Biography.


Turk, Ruth. *Ray Charles: Soul Man*. Minneapolis, MN: Lerner Publications Company, 1996. Newsmakers Series. Hardcover $17.96 (ISBN 0–8225–4928–X). Fry Reading Level 5. Interest Level Grade 5–Adult.

Beginning to play at age four, Ray Charles spent his life as a musician. Overcoming blindness, addictions, and racism, he is widely considered the father of soul music. Combining jazz, blues, and gospel has made his long career a major force in American music. Segregation mandated that the white and black students, although they could not see each other, were separated in the school for the blind, where he was schooled after he lost his sight to youth-onset glaucoma. Black and white and color photographs illustrate the rise of his career and show other musicians of the era. Discography, bibliography. For units on visual impairments, music and musicians, African Americans, education, and biography. *Subjects*: Charles, Ray; Singers; Afro-Americans—Biography; Blind.


Vare, Ethlie Ann. *Adventurous Spirit*. Minneapolis, MN: Carolrhoda Books, 1992. Hardcover $14.95 (ISBN 0–87614–733–3). Fry Reading Level 2+. Interest Level Grade 5–Adult.

The story of the first woman to be graduated from the Massachusetts Institute of Technology, class of 1873. Being accepted into the university and attending classes took perseverance and courage because some male faculty members resented her intrusion, and some of her classmates let her know that her presence was unwelcome. This strong-willed woman used her education as a chemist to aid her in her fight for better living conditions for all through her work in public health. Richards was a pioneer for public health through clean air, sanitation, and hot lunches for school children and launched the science of ecology. Especially appealing to girls and women and used in career guidance counseling. Black and white illustrations and photographs. Index, glossary. For health units and social studies. *Subjects*: Richards, Ellen; Public Health; Women in Medicine.

Vernon, Roland. *Introducing Bach*. Parsippany, NJ: Silver Burdett Press, 1996. Introducing . . . Series. Hardcover $11.92 (ISBN 0–382–39157–8). Fry Reading Level Grade 6–7. Interest Level Grade 6–Adult.

Vernon, Roland. *Introducing Beethoven*. Parsippany, NJ: Silver Burdett Press, 1996. Introducing . . . Series. Hardcover $11.92 (ISBN 0–382–39154–3). Fry Reading Level 6–7. Interest Level Grade 6–Adult.

Both books are biographies of famed and classic musicians and composers that also cover the life and culture of their times. Fully illustrated, with excellent time lines, useful glossaries, and other suggested reading. For units in music, European history and culture, family, and overcoming disabilities. *Subjects*: Bach, Johann Sebastian—Biography; Beethoven, Ludwig von—Biography; Composers.

Weidt, Maryann N. *Revolutionary Poet: A Story about Phillis Wheatley*. Minneapolis, MN: Carolrhoda Books, 1997. Creative Minds Biography Series. Hardcover $14.59 (ISBN 1–57505–037–4). Fry Reading Level 4+. Interest Level Grade 5–Adult.

The story of the famed poet who arrived in Boston as a child slave in 1761. Her purchasers, the Wheatleys, taught her to read and write, and her talent for poetry was nurtured. Her poems expressed the call for freedom and shows slavery as it existed in Boston in colonial America. The black and white illustrations add a sense of place and time and reality to the story. Easy to read and highly informative. Index, useful bibliography. For units on American history, slavery in America, literature, African American literature, black history, ethnic diversity, music, and cultural history. *Subjects*: Wheatley, Phillis, 1753–1784; Poets—American; Slaves; Afro-Americans—Biography; Women—Biography.

# 3

# Career, Workplace, Life Skills, and Parenting

This chapter features fiction and nonfiction that provide insights into work situations, home life, and interpersonal relationships. Topics include medical care, physical and mental abuse, date rape, language skills, education, job searches, parenting, marriage, and life skills. Some materials here are applicable to other members of an ESL family.

## NONFICTION

Bratman, Fred. *Becoming a Citizen: Adopting a New Home*. Austin, TX: Steck-Vaughn Company, 1993. Good Citizenship Library Series. Hardcover $17.29 (ISBN 08–8114–7345–6); paper $6.95 (ISBN 0–8114–5582). Fry Reading Level 3–4. Interest Level Grade 4–Adult.

Discusses immigration law, the laws creating citizenship, the court system, and citizenship here and in other countries. Describes the waves of immigration to this country. Notes which states have high rates of immigration and which groups are settling where. Color and black and white photographs, and charts. Glossary, index, brief bibliography. For citizenship and history classes and with social studies units. Helpful for ESL students. *Subjects*: United States—Emigration and Immigration—History; Citizenship—United States.

Clayman, Charles B. *The Human Body: An Illustrated Guide to Its Structure, Function & Disorders*. New York: Dorling Kindersley, 1995. Hardcover $29.95 (ISBN 1–56458–992–7). Fry Reading Level 8. Interest Level Grade 7–Adult.

A basic reference for health, science, and sex education classes. Provides complete coverage of the human body and explains health functions. Answers medical questions and is very well illustrated. Use for units on health, biology, science, and life skills. Not a book for beginners but a useful one. *Subjects*: Anatomy—Human; Body—Human;

Fargo, Jean. *Discovering Words*. New York: Literacy Volunteers of America, 1992. Paper $3.50 (ISBN 0–929631–66–8). Fry Reading Level 4+. Interest Level Grade 5–Adult.

A spirited book covering 1500 years or so of the English language. Traces the origins of words and phrases as they came into spoken language and traces the migration and melding of the words into our present-day usage. Excellent for teachers as well as students. Variable reading level. For teaching writing and reading and explaining the vagaries of American English to ESL students of all ages. *Subjects*: Language and Languages—English; English Language—Study and Teaching; Word Origins.

Freeman, Daniel B. *Speaking of Survival*. New York: Oxford University Press, 1982. Paper $23.82 (ISBN 0–19–503110–5). Fry Reading Level 5–8+. Interest Level Grade 7–Adult.

Although this book was designed for ESL adults at the high beginning or low intermediate level, it can be extremely useful for high school students at the same level. Provides lessons in survival skills in many areas of daily life: dealing with doctors, hospitals, dentists, housing, fire, robbery, and jobs. Includes information on post office procedure, telephone usage, and how to use public and private transportation. Tackles skills in shopping for food, clothing, and furniture. Dealing with all levels of schools is covered, as is dealing with repairs of all kinds. Illustrations are used to explain the text. Textbook-style presentation of materials. Lots of good study opportunities presented. For units on life skills, family living, home repairs, and dealing with people. *Subjects*: English Language—Textbooks for Foreigners.

Gilbert, Judy B. *Clear Speech: Pronunciation and Listening Comprehension in North American English*. New York: Cambridge University Press, 1993. 2d ed. Teacher's resource book $11.95 (ISBN 0–521–42116–0); student's book $10.95 (ISBN 0–521–42118–7); cassette set $14.95 (ISBN 0–521–42117–9). Fry Reading Level 7–Adult. Interest Level Grade 9–Adult.

This set will be of use in classrooms where students are concentrating on learning and listening to North American English. Primarily written for adult learners, it will appeal to older and more prepared students. Textbook approach with exercises and tests. For classes in reading, speech, and learning English. *Subject*: English Language—Study and Teaching.

Glassman, Bruce. *Everything You Need to Know about Step-families.* New York: Rosen Publishing Group, 1991. Need to Know Library. Paper $12.95 (ISBN 0–8114–3045–6). Fry Reading Level 4+. Interest Level Grade 4–12.

Discusses the problems and adjustments involved in having only one parent in a family, what happens when that parent remarries, and the problems that blended families often face. Discusses change brought on by death or divorce. Specifically deals with teens in stepfamilies and looks at stepfamilies or blended families of varied ethnic backgrounds. Color and black and white photographs illustrate the text and some of the problems presented. For units on family, life skills, and conduct of life and for counseling and guidance. *Subjects*: Stepfamilies; Single-Parent Family; Remarriage.

Gruber, Edward C. *Improving Your Reading with Cartoon Strips.* New York: Educational Design, 1994. Hardcover $15.24 (ISBN 0–87694–212–5). Fry Reading Level 1–5+. Interest Level Grade 5–Adult.

Includes popular and well-known comic strips. Each page features a different cartoon and questions to answer, with a section to introduce words reader should know. Answers are provided for each question for self-teaching. Oversize format makes easy reading. Comics are black and white. Excellent for reading classes. *Subjects*: English Language—Study and Teaching; Reading—Study and Teaching.

Hammerslough, Jane. *Everything You Need to Know about Teen Motherhood.* Rev. ed. New York: Rosen Publishing Group, 1992. Need to Know Library Series. Hardcover $12.95 (ISBN 0–8114–3047–2). Fry Reading Level 4. Interest Level Grade 6–12.

An easy-to-read book that discusses the practical aspects of becoming a teenage mother: what to do to prepare for motherhood, the delivery, and the first few months of baby's life; the psychological as well as physical aspects; and practical advice for other parenting and budgeting skills. Well illustrated with color and black and white photographs and graphics. Includes frequently asked questions. Glossary, bibliography, list of organizations that can provide more information. Practical information for parenting and life skills classes. *Subjects*: Teenage Mothers—United States; Teen Parenting; Pregnancy.

Heller, Ruth. *Behind the Mask: A Book about Prepositions.* New York: Grosset and Dunlap, 1995. Hardcover $16.95 (ISBN 0–448–41123–7). Fry Reading Level 3–4. Interest Level Grade 5–Adult.

Although this book aims at the more juvenile market, the poetic and colorful presentation of prepositions successfully disguises language learning in a really fun and meaningful manner. Can be read independently or used in a classroom setting. This author has also written books on other parts of speech. For language arts and English language classes for the ESL student as a catchy way to learn grammar. *Subjects*: English Language—Study and Teaching; English Language—Grammar; Prepositions.

Hirschy, Margaret W., and Patricia L. Hirschy. *The Way to U.S. Citizenship*. New rev. ed. Carlsbad, CA: Dominie Press, 1997 Hardcover $14,94 (ISBN 1–56270–972–0). Fry Reading Level 6–8+. Interest Level Grade 7–Adult.

Basically a U.S. history and government workbook designed for adult ESL but also very useful in a high school classroom setting. Comprehensible for beginning as well as intermediate readers, the book provides vital knowledge of the history and political workings of the United States. Recognizes that lack of English is not lack of knowledge or intelligence. Provides repetitive exercises for learning and for group as well as individual instruction. Integrates language and content. Contains maps, pictures, graphs, charts, illustrations, and examples to explain the text. For classes in political science, reading, history, social studies, government, and life skills as well as for preparation for the INS tests. *Subject*: Citizenship—United States.

Kenel, Dr. Frank C., and Beverly Vaillancourt. *Studying for a Driver's License*. Maywood, NJ: Peoples Publishing Groups, 1994. Drivers Education Series. Hardcover $13.00 (ISBN 1–56256–208–8). Fry Reading Level 8. Interest Level Grade 9–Adult.

Oversized book packed with materials to help new readers of English pass the driver's exam. Covers signs, laws, road markings, and information about vehicles and provides hints on taking the test. Pictures, illustrations, exercises. One caveat is that the type size is rather small. Excellent for classes in driver's training and life skills. *Subjects*: Automobile Driving; Driver's Licenses—Tests and Preparations.

Lindsay, Jeanne Brunelli, and Warren Lindsay. *Teen Dads: Rights, Responsibilities and Joys*. Buena Park, CA: Morning Glory Press, 1993. Hardcover $15.95 (ISBN 0–930934–78–4); paper $9.96 (ISBN 0–90934–77–6). Fry Reading Level 6. Interest Level Grade 7–Adult.

The title gives an accurate description. Well illustrated with black and white photographs of teen dads of several ethnic backgrounds. Easy to understand and basic, with some statements by the dads. Written in an objective, nonjudgmental style. Deftly written. For classes on sexuality, parenting, and life skills. Useful for teenagers before they become fathers. Excellent in classes that include students who are parents. *Subjects*: Teen Parenting; Conduct of Life.

Lindsay, Warren, and Jean Brunelli. *Your Pregnancy and NewBorn Journey.* Buena Park, CA: Morning Glory Press, 1992. Teen Parenting Series. Hardback $15.95 (ISBN 0–930934–62–8); paper $9.95 (ISBN 0–930934–61–X). Fry Reading Level 3. Interest Level Grade 5–Adult.

Good book for teenage parents who have toddlers. Graphics and layout make the book easy to read and comprehend, with material presented in a nonjudgmental way. Personal quotes from young parents give immediacy and reality to the contents. A good choice for the collection and for parenting and family living classes. Even useful in families where teens are expected to function as surrogate parents. *Subjects*: Teen Parenting; Conduct of Life.

Lundgren, Mary Beth. *Getting to Know Computers.* Cleveland, OH: Project: LEARN, 1997. Paper $8.50. No ISBN. Fry Reading Level 3. Interest Level Grade 5–Adult.

Available as a controlled vocabulary book on skill level 3 and in a generic version that is easy to use but has an enlarged vocabulary. Well-written and concise introduction to computers and how to use them for all users. Good black and white graphics. Extensive vocabulary list. Excellent for use in computer classes or any life skill class, business course, or any other class or setting that requires computer literacy. *Subject*: Computers.

Marecek, Mary. *Breaking Free from Partner Abuse.* Buena Park, CA: Morning Glory Press, 1993. Paper $7.95 (ISBN 0–90934–74–1). Fry Reading Level 6. Interest Level Grade 6–Adult.

Although adult in theme, it is applicable to many young women in school because of date abuse or family abuse, and it could aid in promoting understanding of and coping with abuse by one's parents. The firsthand accounts are compelling and realistically written. Easy vocabulary. Includes workable guidelines for action and help. Useful for students dealing with this problem and in social studies classes or classes on family living. *Subjects*: Abused Children; Abusive Relationships; Spousal Abuse.

Mernit, Susan. *Everything You Need to Know about Changing Schools.* New York: Rosen Publishing Group, 1992. Need to Know Library Series. Hardcover $12.95 (ISBN 0–8239–1326–0). Fry Reading Level 5. Interest Level Grade 5–12.

Provides guidance to students on how to cope with moving from one school to another, as well as how to handle problems arising from it: Covers differences in classes, loss of friends, and the feeling of alienation that comes from having to learn to fit in. Easy to adapt for foreign students ESL learners. Black and white and color photographs. Easy to read and understand. Glossary, index, books for further reading, suggested sources of help. For life skills units, guidance, and support use. *Subject*: Transfer Students.

Moore, Mamie. *Make Way for August.* New York: Literacy Volunteers of America, 1991. Paper $3.58 (ISBN 0–929631–36–6). Fry Reading Level 2–3. Interest Level Grade 4–Adult.

A true story of a family living in an apartment in New York and their adventures with their pet guinea pig will appeal to many ages. Easy-to-read, humorous, and emotional. Black and white photographs. For classes in reading, life skills, and family relationship and for recreational reading. *Subjects*: Animals as Pets; Family Relationships.

Mosenfelder, Donn, and Maureen Sloan. *Beginning ESL Book One: Survival at School.* New York: Educational Design, 1992. Paper $8.50 (ISBN 0–87694–427–6). Fry Reading Level 3+. Interest Level Grade 6–12.

A workbook-style book for use in any class to help with school survival skills in communication. Teaches greetings and farewells, numbers; names for teachers, room numbers, and alphabet; terms for family living; days and dates and clock time; forms and maps. Black and white drawings illustrate the words and concepts. Slangy terms are used. *Subjects*: English—Study and Teaching; English as a Second Language; Literacy.

Murphy, Raymond. *Basic Grammar in Use: Reference and Practice for Students of English.* New York: Cambridge University Press, 1993. Student's book $14.94 (ISBN 0–521–42606–5); answer key $14.84 (ISBN 0–521–42607–3). Fry Reading Level 5–Adult. Interest Level Grade 7–Adult.

Based on the British text *Essential Grammar in Use*, this book has been prepared for average beginning to low-intermediate students, with exercises geared to the beginning level of learning English. The 106 units contain the same number of points in English grammar. Explanations are simple and short. Material can be used in any order as needed and with individual or group sessions. For classes in reading, learning English, and grammar. *Subjects*: English Language—Textbooks for Foreign Speakers; English Language—Grammar.

Now Hiring Series. Morristown, NJ: Silver Burdett Press, 1994. Hardcover $14.95 each. Fry Reading Level 6–8. Interest Level Grade 6–Adult.
  Bonner, Staci. *Careers in Sports.* (ISBN 0–89686–789–7).
  Crisfield, Deborah. *Careers in Travel.* (ISBN 0–89686–790–0).
  Marshall, Mary Ann. *Careers in Music.* (ISBN 0–89686–793–5).
  Weeks, Jessica Vitkus. *Careers in Television.* (ISBN 0–89686–783–8).

These books cover getting employment in all phases of the field. Singing, engineering, selling, and writing are part of the coverage in music careers. Sports careers include all the behind-the-scenes careers such as manager, agent, and trainer Cruise ships, travel agents, and tour guides are a part of the career world in travel. Television does the on-camera as well as the behind-the-scenes production jobs. Excellent for guidance counselors, vocational education, and students needing to learn about employment in America. *Subjects*: Career Guidance; Employment.

Palmer, Ezra. *Everything You Need to Know about Discrimination*. New York: Rosen Publishing Group, 1990. Need to Know Library Series. Hardcover $12.95 (ISBN 0–8114–3039–1). Fry Reading Level 4+. Interest Level Grade 5–Adult.

Covers prejudice in such areas as religion, race and nationality, sex, and physical disabilities and discusses how it can lead to job discrimination. Covers housing and general treatment in current society. Defines discrimination and covers individual rights. Discusses stereotypes and how they are used in the media and how they are perceived in society. Illustrated with black and white and color photographs. Glossary, index, bibliography, addresses of national groups that can provide information and help. Excellent for use with minority and ESL students in guidance, for psychology units, and for units in popular culture and social studies. Good for life skills use and career preparation. *Subjects*: Prejudices; Discrimination; Toleration.

Pollock, Sudie. *Will the Dollars Stretch? Teen Parents Living on Their Own*. Buena Park, CA: Morning Glory Press. Paper $6.95 (ISBN 1–88535609). Fry Reading Level 5+. Interest Level Grade 7–12.

Explains check writing and banking step by step, complete with the appropriate forms, discusses the problems of single teen parents as well as couples; covers jobs and working at home; and tells how to prepare and survive on a budget. The budgets are for time as well as money. For use in guidance situations before and after pregnancy and/or marriage. Can be used as a supplement for units in math, consumer economics, building relationships, parenting, and independent study. *Subjects*: Marriage—Teenage; Life Skills; Budgeting; Parenting; Consumer Economics.

*Preparation for Citizenship*. Austin, TX: Steck-Vaughn Company, 1995. Paper $5.94 (ISBN 0–8114–7987–0). Fry Reading Level 4+. Interest Level Grade 5–Adult.

A workbook used to prepare for citizenship with concise information for ESL students on the symbols, history, government, and holidays of the United States. Includes the Pledge of Allegiance, a study of the flag, a discussion of the Constitution, and commentary on several wars (Revolutionary, Civil, World Wars I and II, and Vietnam). The branches of federal government are covered, as are states and their capitals, and our political system is included. Time line, world map, special section for the teacher. For classes in citizenship, history, and social studies. *Subject*: Citizenship—United States.

Ralbovsky, Marianne, ed. FYI Series. Syracuse, NY: New Readers Press, 1994. Paper
$5.95 each. Fry Reading Level 3–5. Interest Level Grade 5–Adult.
  *About AIDS.* (ISBN 1–56420–0190–1).
  *About Alcohol and Other Drugs.* (ISBN 1–56420–05–9).
  *About Cancer.* (ISBN 0–56420–017–5).
  *Eating Right.* (ISBN 56420–021–3).
  *Getting Fit.* (ISBN 0–56420–023–X).
  *Getting Good Health Care.* (ISBN 0–56420–029–9).
  *Managing Stress.* (ISBN 0–56420–025–6).
  *Staying Well.* (ISBN 0–56420–027–3).

Well-written books with easy-to-understand language that should be very
usable for ESL students. Covers subjects that will be explored in classes on
sexuality, health, and life skills: drugs, stress, alcohol, AIDS, fitness, and nu-
trition. I think that this is one of the most succinct books on AIDS, and I
have recommended it for all age levels. Can be used in guidance sessions and
offered for guidance or supplementary reading. Adequate and pertinent illustrations. Timely. *Subjects*: AIDS; Alcoholism; Drugs; Fitness and Health; Nu-
trition; Stress; Wellness.

Rediger, Pat. *Great African Americans in Entertainment.* New York: Crabtree Publishing
Company, 1996. Outstanding African American Series. Hardcover $23.47
(ISBN 0–86505–799–0); paper $7.95 (ISBN 0–86505–813–X). Fry Reading Level 4+.
Interest Level Grade 4–Adult.

Colorful and easy-to-read magazine format of brief biographies of notable
African American entertainers: Bill Cosby, Spike Lee, Whoopi Goldberg, Jo-
sephine Baker, Harry Belafonte, Sammy Davis, Jr., Sidney Poitier, Pearl Bailey, Dick Gregory, James Earl Jones, Diana Ross, and Tina Turner. Several
of these people have ties to other countries, such as France, West Indies, and
Canada. Gives accomplishments, obstacles overcome, and personal histories.
Useful in career guidance and social studies and as inspiration. *Subjects*: Entertainers; Singers; Afro-Americans—Biography.

Risso, Mario. *Safari Grammar.* Lincolnwood, IL: Passport Books, 1989. Safari Series. Paper
$5.95 (ISBN 0–8442–5466–5). Fry Reading Level 5+. Interest Level Grade 6–Adult.

Cartoons and humor help students make the journey through "Grammar-
land" and learn the rules of grammar, with guidance from Jungle Jack. Exercises for practice. Black and white cartoon-style drawings. Excellent for
teaching reading and writing and for classes in English grammar. *Subject*:
Grammar.

Risso, Mario. *Safari Punctuation.* Lincolnwood, IL: Passport Books, 1990. Safari Series.
Paper $5.95 (ISBN 0–8442–5467–3). Fry Reading Level 5+. Interest Level Grade 6–Adult.

To explore the rules of punctuation, the intrepid explorer Jungle Jack sets
out to explore the hills and valleys of Punctuation Country. Helps students

use punctuation well to write clearly and concisely. Black and white cartoons illustrate the text. Exercises for practice. For classes in learning English, writing, and life skills. *Subjects*: Punctuation; Grammar.

St. Pierre, Stephanie. *Everything You Need to Know When a Parent Is Out of Work.* New York: Rosen Publishing Group, 1991. Need to Know Library Series. Hardcover $12.95 (ISBN 0–8114–3049–9). Fry Reading Level 4+. Interest Level Grade 6–12.

Dicusses reasons that a parent can lose a job, how families can learn to cope, and how to manage during the hard times. Covers immediate effects on the family and long-term unemployment and discusses what can and cannot be done and how to get help for special problems. Particularly important for students whose parents may have language barriers at work. Black and white and color photographs. Bibliographical references, index. For units on work, life skill classes, and classes in family problems. *Subject*: Unemployment.

Shuker, Nancy. *Everything You Need to Know about an Alcoholic Parent.* Rev. ed. New York: Rosen Publishing Group, 1993. Need to Know Library Series. Hardcover $12.95 (ISBN 0–8114–3036–7). Fry Reading Level 4+. Interest Level Grade 5–12.

Advice and help on how to deal with a parent or parents who are alcoholics. Notes warning signs, the effects on the family, and how to cope with emergencies. Discusses what students can do for themselves and for the parents. Glossary, index, bibliography, list of places for help. Black and white and color photographs. For units on family, life skills, coping, health, and psychology. *Subjects*: Alcoholism; Children of Alcoholics.

Spies, Karen. *Everything You Need to Know About Grieving.* Rev. ed. New York: Rosen Publishing Group, 1993. Need to Know Library Series. Hardcover $12.95 (ISBN 0–8239–1617–0). Fry Reading Level 4+. Interest Level Grade 6–Adult.

Examines grief and its effect on the lives of all people: ways to grieve, learning to talk about death, what happens after death, and how to recover from grief. Discusses the deaths of parents, relatives, and friends. Good starting point for discussion of grief and how it is handled in different cultures. Color and black and white photographs. Glossary, index, brief bibliography, list of places to go for help. For units in psychology, life skills, personal development, popular culture, and guidance. *Subject*: Bereavement.

Taylor, Barbara. *Everything You Need to Know about AIDS.* New York: Rosen Publishing Group, 1988. Need to Know Library Series. Hardcover $12.95 (ISBN 0–8239–7). Fry Reading Level 4+. Interest Level Grade 5–Adult.

Discusses AIDS: its history, causes, transmission, treatment, and what can be done to protect against the disease. Color and black and white photographs.

Good question and answer section, glossary, bibliography. For classes on health and hygiene, life skills, and sex education and for guidance. *Subject*: AIDS.

Thomas, Alicia. *Everything You Need to Know about Romantic Breakup*. New York: Rosen Publishing Group, 1990. Need to Know Library Series. Hardcover $12.95 (ISBN 0–814–3044–8). Fry Reading Level 4+. Interest Level Grade 7–12.

Discusses the real emotional trauma felt when a romantic relationship ends. Useful in explaining local mores and customs to people of different cultures. Offers advice on how to handle and face feelings, how to let go in good grace, ways to beat the blues, how to move on with life, and where to get help. Black and white and color photographs. Glossary, suggested readings. For units in life skills and coping, popular culture, social studies, and psychology and for guidance. *Subjects*: Dating; Separation; Love.

## FICTION

Altman, Linda Jacobs. *Nobody Wants Annie*. Syracuse, NY: New Readers Press, 1990. Sundown Book Series. Hardcover $3.95 (ISBN 0–88336–209–0). Fry Reading Level 3–4. Interest Level Grade 7–Adult.

Story of an eighteen-year-old girl who has no work experience and whose personality and persona are off-putting to prospective employers. Deals with personality, attitude, honesty, being different, and working with problem children. Black and white line drawings. For units in life skills, psychology, career preparation, and reading. *Subject*: Career Guidance—Fiction.

Barnett, Cynthia. *Ben's Gift*. Syracuse, NY: Signal Hill, 1990. Sundown Books Series. Hardcover $3.95 (ISBN 0–88336–210–4). Fry Reading Level 3–4. Interest Level Grade 7–Adult.

Deals with the plight of an adult with cerebral palsy who has been cared for by his mother, who has just died. Shows how he makes a life for himself and deals with self-respect and self-esteem as well as expectations. Black and white illustrations. For units in health, psychology, and life skills; for counseling about self-esteem; and for reading classes. *Subjects*: Cerebral Palsy—Fiction; Self-Esteem—Fiction.

Bosley, Judith A. *Don't Sell Me Short*. Syracuse, NY: Signal Hill, 1990. Sundown Books Series. Hardcover $3.95 (ISBN 0–88336–205–8). Fry Reading Level 3–4. Interest Level Grade 9–Adult.

Deals with the plight of an adult male who does not succeed in school or the armed services because of learning problems and low test scores. Shows how hard he tries to make a go of life, not be known as a "loser," and not be taken advantage of by unscrupulous people. Shows how he uses his strengths to make a good life. Happy ending and a love story as well. Black and white line drawings. For classes in life skills, career guidance, and psychology and for units in self-esteem. *Subjects*: Learning Disabled—Fiction; Death—Fiction.

Christian, Mary Blount, *Just Once*. Syracuse, NY: New Readers Press, 1990. Sundown Book Series. Hardcover $3.95 (ISBN 0–88336–208–2). Fry Reading Level 3–4. Interest Level Grade 7–Adult.

Deals with married life and lack of money and job loss; covers excessive drinking and spousal abuse, as well as possible child battering; delves into pride, self-esteem, and enabling a co-dependency; and covers therapy and counseling. A slice of family life that many may be familiar with. Black and white line drawings. For units on counseling, life skills, self-esteem, and family problems, as well as supplemental readings. *Subjects*: Family Life—Fiction; Spousal Abuse—Fiction; Job Loss—Fiction; Counseling—Fiction.

Coret, Harriette. *In and Out the Windows*. Syracuse, NY: New Readers Press, 1990. Sundown Books Series. Hardcover $3.95 (ISBN 0–88336–201–5). Fry Reading Level 3–4. Interest Level Grade 7–Adult.

Story of a seventeen-year-old girl who develops schizophrenia. Details her life in and out of hospitals, with her family and with her friends; discusses the condition and its treatment; and offers ways that people can cope with the disease. Black and white line drawings. For units on health, mental health, life skills, interpersonal relationships, prejudice, family life, and self-esteem and for recreational reading. *Subjects*: Schizophrenia—Fiction; Mental Health—Fiction.

Dailey, Janet. *Riding High*. Syracuse, NY: Signal Hill, 1994. Janet Dailey's Love Scenes Series. Paper $3.50 (ISBN 1–56420–098–1). Fry Reading Level 4+. Interest Level Grade 7–Adult.

Easy-to-read romance story by best-selling romance author, with a mass market paperback look that appeals to young women. Story of a rancher who teaches a movie star how to ride a horse. For units in reading, popular culture, and life skills and for recreational reading. More books available in this series. *Subject*: Readers for New Literates.

Goethel, Jan. *Shared Umbrella Series. Set 1.* Eau Claire, WI: Chippawa Valley Publishing, 1997. Paper $16.00 set. Fry Level 1. Interest Level Grade 7–Adult.
*Carmen's Day.* (ISBN 1–885474–02–4).
*Go to Work Fred.* (ISBN 1–885474–01–6).
*A Holiday for Mee.* (ISBN 1–885474–03–2).
*Picture Dictionary and Guide for Tutors.* (ISBN 1–885474–04–0).

Ostensibly for adults, this very easy-to-read material will appeal to all learners of English. Carmen tackles the problems of a single mother supporting two young children and gives a baby sitter good advice on how to unstick a child from a glass jar. Fred deals with car troubles and the concept of punctuality. Mee learns about American holidays the hard way. Amusing cartoonstyle graphics that add to the story. Separate dictionary and tutor guide. For teaching reading, life skills, and family units. *Subjects*: Life Skills—Fiction; Holidays.

Goldstein, Edith. *People.* Columbia, SC: Education Development Laboratories, 1991. EDL GO Series, Book 1. Paper $23.82 (ISBN 0–070319421–2). Fry Reading Level 5+. Interest Level Grade 5–Adult.

Collection of short stories, each one to two pages in lengths about people who have problems, need help, or are doing things on their own. Each story has a brief extract to give its gist. Mass market paperback size. Study questions and answers. Line drawing. illustrations. For units on work, career choices, life skills, problem solving, and personal decisions. *Subjects*: Life Skills—Fiction; Employment—Fiction; Personal Development—Fiction.

Laubach, Frank C., Elizabeth Mooney Kirk, and Robert S. Laubach. *City Living.* Syracuse, NY: New Readers Press, 1991. Laubach Way to Reading Series. Paper $2.95 (ISBN 0–88336–922–2). Fry Reading Level 2. Interest Level Grade 6–Adult.

Seven short stories. Very easy reading with simple words and sentences. This works with the Laubach Skill Book 2 and deals with short vowel sounds. Word list. For classes in reading, spelling, and life skills. *Subjects*: Reading; Short Stories.

Levoy, Myron. *A Shadow Like a Leopard.* New York: HarperCollins, 1994. Hardcover $17.84 (ISBN 0–06–440458–7). Fry Reading Level 6. Interest Level Grade 5–12.

Ramon Santiago is fourteen years old; his mother is in the hospital and his father is in jail. His knife and pen become his survival tools in Hell's Kitchen—the knife to impress the gang and make them believe he is macho and the pen because he wants to write. A foiled holdup of a wheelchair-bound artist gives Ramon a new friend and the hope of becoming a writer. For units in psychology, life skills, and working with troubled youth and for recreational reading. *Subject*: Gangs—Fiction.

*Real Life Stories: The Shopping Adventure*. Roslyn, NY: Berrent Publications, 1994. Paper $6.95 (ISBN 1-55743-750-5). Fry Reading Level 3+. Interest Level Grade 6–Adult.

Very short story about a Chinese-American woman and her young son on a shopping trip and the problems that befall them. The ethnic background seems almost incidental. Talks about getting separated from parents and what to do. The nine-page booklet includes discussion possibilities. For teaching responsibility, especially in family living units. *Subjects*: Life Skills—Fiction; Shopping—Fiction; Parenting—Fiction.

Reiff, Tana. *Beauty and the Business*. Belmont, CA: Lake Publishing Company, 1994. Working for Myself Series. Paper $6.95 (ISBN 1-56103-903-9). Fry Reading Level 3–5. Interest Level Grade 6–Adult.

Deals with a young woman who has a flair for working with hair and decides to become a professional hair stylist. The book follows her step by step as she gets her GED, pursues her goal by attending beauty school, works in a big shop, and finally gets to work in her own home with her own shop. Teaches how to get along with people, how to prioritize, and how to set goals. Shows appropriate behavior and how to behave in relationships with others. Inspirational and instructional, as well as fun to read. Easy to read. Mass market paperback format attractive. For supplementary reading for career guidance and life skills classes. *Subjects*: Cosmetology—Fiction; Education—Fiction; Hairdresser—Fiction; Self-employed—Fiction.

Reiff, Tana. *Cooking for a Crowd*. Belmont, CA: Lake Publishing Company, 1994. Working for Myself Series. Paper $6.95 (ISBN 1-56103-908-X). Fry Reading Level 3–5. Interest Level Grade 6–Adult.

The feel of a paperback novel may make this attractive as supplemental reading for classes in life skills, career guidance, and home economics. The story of a young, divorced mother who has three children to support and needs work that she can do immediately. She decides to use her cooking skills and become a caterer. Follows her career from the beginning. Shows how planning is needed and how the city or state has certain requirements that need to be met. Shows importance of responsibility and hard work to building a successful business. Talks about family life in a one-parent situation and some universal problems that can occur in any language. For teaching self-esteem and self-confidence and how to get along with others. *Subjects*: Catering—Fiction; Cookery—Fiction; Self-employed—Fiction; Single Parenting—Fiction.

Reiff, Tana. *The Green Team*. Belmont, CA: Lake Publishing Company, 1994. Working for Myself Series. Paper $6.95 (ISBN 1–56013–906–3). Fry Reading Level 3–5. Interest Level Grade 6–Adult.

An easy reader about a young man who parlayed a part-time lawn mowing service into a full-time yard maintenance business with employees. Shows how perseverance and hard work can produce results and provides plenty of tips about lawn maintenance as well as how to start and run the business. Teaches respect and how to get along with others. The ethnic connection is Spanish. Supplemental reading for career and life skills units and for building self-esteem and confidence. *Subjects*: Lawn and Garden Care—Fiction; Self-employed—Fiction; Yard Maintenance—Fiction.

Reiff, Tana. *Handy All Around*. Belmont, CA: Lake Publishing Company, 1994. Working for Myself Series. Paper $6.95 (ISBN 1–56103–907–1). Fry Reading Level 3–5. Interest Level Grade 6–Adult.

Easy-to-read story about how Wayne raised helping out to a learning process and became a sought-after handyman. Teaches responsibility, collaboration, persevering, and problem solving. Tells a good story as it teaches how to start up a small business and win trust and discusses some of the requirements for being self-employed. An intergenerational as well as a multicultural slant. For units in life skills, career planning, and consumer education. *Subjects*: Handyman—Fiction; Self-employed—Fiction; Service Business—Fiction.

Reiff, Tana. Work Tales Series. Belmont, CA: Fearon Janus, 1991. Fry Reading Level 0–4. Interest Level Grade 7–Adult.
  *The Easy Way*. Paper $3.56 (ISBN 0–8224–7153–1).
  *Fighting Words*. Paper $3.56 (ISBN 0–8224–7156–2).
  *Handle with Care*. Paper $3.56 (ISBN 0–8224–7151–1).
  *Help When Needed*. Paper $3.56 (ISBN 0–8224–7155–8).
  *The Rip-Offs*. Paper $3.56 (ISBN 0–8224–7160–4).
  *The Road to Somewhere*. Paper $3.56 (ISBN 0–8224–7154–Y).
  *A Robot Instead*. Paper $3.56 (ISBN 0–8224–7156–6).
  *The Saw That Talked*. Paper $3.56 (ISBN 0–8224–7152–3).

A very easy-to-read series dealing with problems encountered in the workplace: drugs, personality clashes, illiteracy, inappropriate behavior, crime, learning and education, accidents, and sex discrimination. Workplace settings include factories, delivery, retail, hotels, services, and health care. Excellent for both sexes. Discussion questions after each chapter. Ethnic groups included are African Americans, Filipinos, and Hispanics. For learning to read, vocational guidance, problem solving, and supplemental reading. *Subjects*: Conduct of Life—Fiction; Workplace—Fiction.

Reynolds, Marilyn. *Beyond Dreams*. Buena Park, CA: Morning Glory Press, 1995. True-to-Life Series. Paper $8.95 (ISBN 1–885356–00–5). Fry Reading Level 7+. Interest Level Grade 7–Adult.

Short stories for young adults that speak to both sexes about problems encountered in life and how they can be handled. Timely topics include abuse, failure in school, racism, accidents, and relationships. Thoughtful and objectively written. Can be used to show that there are universal problems encountered by all sexes and races and ethnic groups. For supplemental reading, in social problems classes, and for psychology or life skill classes. *Subjects*: Conduct of Life—Fiction; High Schools—Fiction; Racism—Fiction.

Reynolds, Marilyn. *But What about Me?* Buena Park, CA: Morning Glory Press, 1996. True-to-Life Series from Hamilton High. Hardcover $24.95 (ISBN 1–885356–11–0); paper, $8.95 (ISBN 1–88536–10–2). Fry Reading Level 7+. Interest Level Grade 7–Adult.

The story of how a young woman who has always been a serious student can get her life messed up because of a bad relationship. Adolescents have more than their share of pressures and serious problems and that is what this novel is all about: premarital sex, drugs, death, trouble with the law, and acquaintance rape. Family relationships, good and bad, are highlighted. Some education about the humane treatment of animals is a subplot. Ethnic background does not matter in this story that has universal application. Promotes the concept of respect for self, education, pride, and responsibility. For supplementary reading for units on life skills, family living, career guidance, and conduct of life. *Subjects*: Conduct of Life—Fiction; High Schools—Fiction.

Watson, Jude. *Brides of Wildcat County: Tempestuous Opal's Story*. New York: Aladdin Paperbacks, 1996. Brides of Wildcat County Series. Paper $3.95 (ISBN 0–689–81023–7). Fry Reading Level 5+. Interest Level Grade 5–Adult.

Historical romance and adventure set in California. A former slave has her own business and is planning to be married when the son of her former owner appears, bringing trouble and fear into her life. Mass market paperback format. For units in American history, popular history, and African American history and for recreational reading. *Subjects*: Afro-Americans—Fiction; Frontier and Pioneer Life—California—Fiction; California—Fiction.

Wenger, Christine. *The Lady and the Cowboy*. Syracuse, NY: Signal Hill, 1997. Janet Dailey's Love Scenes Series. Paper $3.50 (ISBN 1–56853–029–3). Fry Reading Level 4+. Interest Level Grade 7–Adult.

Ranching in Wyoming takes a back seat to the love story in this adaptation of a Janet Dailey romance. Mass market paperback format makes it attractive to adolescent and adult readers, usually women. Easy to read. *Subjects*: Readers for New Literates; Cowboys—Fiction.

# 4

# Folktales, Myths, Poetry, and Classics

This is a potpourri of literature, folktales, and poetry from all times and from all over the world. It includes classics, modern classics, myths and legends of all areas and eras, fantasy, and science fiction as well as romance.

## FOLKTALES, MYTHS, AND POETRY

Abdullah, Omanii. *I Wanna Be the Kinda Father My Mother Was: Poems by Omanii Abdullah.* Syracuse, NY: New Readers Press, 1993. Paper $3.95 (ISBN 0–88336–33–0); $12.95 tape (ISBN 0–88336–623–1). Fry Reading Level 4+. Interest Level Grade 5–Adult.

Powerful poems that are fun to read aloud and will help with language usage. Particularly useful for black males, black pride, relationships, and feelings. Helps attack stereotypes. The book includes tributes to black heroes, known and unknown. Slang, street talk, and strong language. Black and white illustrations with an African-American theme. For literature, speech, family, and social science classes. *Subject*: Poetry—African American.

Davenport, Tom, and Mary Carden. *From the Brothers Grimm.* Fort Atkinson, WI: Highsmith Press, 1992. Hardcover $12.95 (ISBN 0–917846–20–6). Fry Reading Level 3+. Interest Level Grade 5–Adult.

A modern retelling of Grimm's fairy tales that will reward both teacher and students. These modern versions work well in conjunction with the old ones for a look at where we have been and where we are going. For classes on ethnic diversity, literature, and cultural history and as recreational reading. *Subject*: Fairy Tales.

DeSpain, Pleasant. *Eleven Nature Tales: A Multicultural Journey.* Little Rock, AR: August House, 1996. World Storytelling Series. Hardcover $14.95 (ISBN 0–87483–447–3); $7.95 paper (ISBN 0–87483–458–9). Fry Reading Level 5+. Interest Level Grade 4–Adult.

Retells traditional tales and folklore stories from Zaire, Canada, the Fiji islands, Kazakhstan, Australia, China, Portugal, and America. The stories from Canada are from the Algonquin Indians; the Australian tale is from the Aborigines; the American tales are from the Tlingit Indians, the Quinault, and the Cherokee. All deal with the natural elements and show relationships of all things natural. Explanatory notes for each story include motif and author's notes, as well as connections to other similar tales. For classes in science, nature, ecology, environment, multiculturalism, and literature and for recreational reading. Good for reading aloud. *Subjects*: Tales: Folklore; Storytelling—Collections.

Erlbach, Arlene. *Teddy Bears.* Minneapolis, MN: Carolrhoda Books, 1997. Household History Series. Hardcover $16.95 (ISBN 1–57505–019–6); paper $7.95 (ISBN 1–57505–222–9). Fry Reading Level 5+. Interest Level Grade 5–Adult.

A well-illustrated look at the history and lore of teddy bears that explains why bears, originally created to be a boys' toy, are favorites of all people, young and old. Explains the popularity of bears and their value as a collectible. Shows how teddy bears are used by doctors, dentists, social workers, and psychologists to reduce fear and inspire trust. Also discusses the history of toys around the world. Color and black and white illustrations and photographs. Glossary, index. For units on popular culture, history, and psychology. *Subject*: Teddy Bears.

Forrest, Heather. *Wonder Tales from Around the World.* Little Rock, AR: August House, 1995. World Storytelling Series. Hardcover $26.95 (ISBN 0–87483–421–X); paper $17.95 (ISBN 0–87483–422–8). Fry Reading Level 5+. Interest Level Grade 5–Adult.

Easy-to-read collection of twenty-seven folktales from all over the world: China, West Africa, Norway, Siberia, Japan, Germany, Iceland, India, United States, Indonesia, Australia, Kenya, England, Greece, Canada, France, Finland Japan, Ecuador, Russia, ancient Babylon, and Eastern Europe. Nonrealistic and magical stories with a touch of poetry cover a range of human emotion. Good overcomes evil, justice prevails, and love wins out in these tales of good with a sense of universal morality. Black and white illustration. For units on cultural diversity, literature, social history, and teaching values and for recreational and extra reading. Good to read aloud. Author's notes with sources and brief history of story. *Subject*: Tales: Folklore.

Gordon, Ruth, Selector. *Pierced by a Ray of Sun: Poems about the Times We Feel Alone.* New York: HarperCollins, 1995. Hardcover $15.95 (ISBN 0–06–012613–2). Fry Reading Level 6. Interest Level Grade 6–12.

Poems that voice the common feelings of many adolescents: alienation, worry, depression, and Angst. Includes works of poets from many cultures and many times, ancient to modern. For units in psychology, reading, literature, problem solving, and life skills and for recreational reading. *Subject*: Poetry, Collections.

Horowitz, Anthony. *Myths and Legends.* New York: Kingfisher Books, 1994. Story Library Series. Paper $6.95 (ISBN 1–85697–975–X). Fry Reading Level 6. Interest Level Grade 5– Adult.

Thirty-five stories from around the world: ancient Greek myths (the bulk of the book), plus Egyptian, Babylonian, English, Celtic, Anglo-Saxon, Norse, Indian, Chinese, American Indian, Inca, Eskimo, Polynesian and West African tales. Stories of famous heroes (Beowulf, Hercules, Perseus, King Arthur) and villains or monsters (Grendel, Cyclops, the Minotaur). Index of characters also serves as a brief biographical source for each. Black and white illustrations. For units for history, religion, multiculturalism, and social history and for recreational reading. Good to read aloud. *Subjects*: Mythology; Folklore.

May, Jim. *The Farm on Nippersink Creek; Stories from a Midwestern Childhood.* Little Rock, AR: August House, 1994. American Story Telling Series. Hardcover $17.95 (ISBN 0–87483–339–6). Fry Reading Level 5+. Interest Level Grade 5–Adult.

Tells of growing up in the Midwest in the era between Truman and Kennedy. These stories, told by a professional storyteller, capture the essence of rural Illinois life and make it understandable to a new generation of children from another place and time. Each story can be used separately. Can be read alone or aloud. Covers small town politics, childhood terrors, storms, holidays, family, religion, animals, and much more. Contains humor, wonder and serious thought. No illustrations. For classes in reading, social science, and American history. *Subjects*: Country Life—Illinois—Biography.

Radin, Ruth Yaffe. *From the Wooded Hill.* Syracuse, NY: New Readers Press, 1993. Paper $3.00 (ISBN 0–88336–039–X). Fry Reading Level 1–3+. Interest Level Grade 5–Adult.

Radin, Ruth Yaffe. *Morning Streets.* Syracuse, NY: New Readers Press, 1993. Paper $3.00 (ISBN 0–88336–040–3). Fry Reading Level 1–3+. Interest Level Grade 5–Adult.

These two books need to be used as a set. They contrast the early morning charms of the country and the early morning sights and sounds of the city in poetry. Easy to read and easy to understand. Well illustrated. For units in poetry, literature, and self-expression and for recreational reading. These read well aloud. *Subject*: Poetry.

Radin, Ruth Yaffe. *Sky Bridges and Other Poems*. Syracuse, NY: New Readers Press, 1993. Paper $3.50 (ISBN 0–8836–642–X). Fry Reading Level 1–3+. Interest Level Grade 5–Adult.

Lighthearted poems with appeal to readers at all levels and ages. Easy-to-read and easy-to-understand poems about life and places. Excellent for beginning readers of English. For units on reading, literature, poetry, and popular culture and for as recreational reading. *Subject*: Poetry.

Reiff, Tana. *Adventures*. Syracuse, NY: New Readers Press, 1993. Timeless Tales Series. Paper $3.50 (ISBN 0–88336–458–1). Fry Reading Level 2+. Interest Level Grade 4–Adult.

Contains the stories of Gilgamesh, the Babylonian king who was part human and part god and wanted to live forever; the minute Tom Thumb; the adventurous Sinbad of the Arabian nights; the Mayan twin brothers; and Jason and the Argonauts on their search for the golden fleece. Very easy to read; can be used for early ESL students. Black and white illustrations. For classes in reading, multiculturalism, and history and for recreational reading. *Subject*: Adventure Stories—Cross-Cultural Studies.

Reiff, Tana. *Fables*. Syracuse, NY: New Readers Press, 1991. Timeless Tales Series. Paper $3.50 (ISBN 0–88336–270–8). Fry Reading Level 2+. Interest Level Grade 4–Adult.

Retelling of sixteen fables of Aesop from early Greece. Fables can be used to teach lessons of morality and values and to illustrate traits in people. Black and white illustrations. Easy to read. For units on multiculturalism, reading, literature, social history, and nature. *Subjects*: Fables—Aesop; Fables—Cross-cultural Studies.

Reiff, Tana. *Folktales*. Syracuse, NY: New Readers Press, 1991. Timeless Tales Series. Paper $3.50 (ISBN 0–88336–272–4). Fry Reading Level 2+. Interest Level Grade 4–Adult.

Nine folktales retold in an easy-to-read manner. Tells what folktales are and how they came to be. Stories from China, England, India, Vietnam, Kenya, Italy, the Middle East, and other areas. For units on teaching values, multiculturalism, and reading and for recreational reading and reading aloud. *Subject*: Folktales—Cross-Cultural Studies.

Reiff, Tana. *Legends*. Syracuse, NY: New Readers Press, 1991. Timeless Tales Series. Paper $3.50 (ISBN 0–88336–273–4). Fry Reading Level 2+. Interest Level Grade 4–Adult.

Nine legends from around the world, about both real people (Johnny Appleseed, Robin Hood) and magical little people. Some are about animals. Easy to read with black and white illustrations. For popular history, teaching of values, reading, and multiculturalism and for recreational reading. *Subjects*: Myths and Legends—Cross-Cultural Studies; Tall Tales—Cross-Cultural Studies.

Reiff, Tana. *Love Stories*. Syracuse, NY: New Readers Press, 1993. Timeless Tales Series. Paper $3.50 (ISBN 0-88336-462-X). Fry Reading Level 2+. Interest Level Grade 4–Adult.

Six of the most famous love stories of all time retold in an easy-reading collection. Includes several countries. Couples include Cupid and Psyche, Beauty and the Beast, and Romeo and Juliet. Black and white illustrations. For reading and literature classes, as well as units on multiculturalism, popular history, and social history and to teach relationships. *Subject*: Love stories—Cross-Cultural Studies.

Reiff, Tana. *Myths*. Syracuse, NY: New Readers Press, 1991. Timeless Tales Series. Paper $3.50 (ISBN 0-88336-272-4). Fry Reading Level 2+. Interest Level Grade 4–Adult.

Eight Greek myths as well as an explanation of myths and how all countries have them and create new ones. Includes stories about Pandora, Midas, Narcissus and Echo, Helen of Troy, Achilles, Oedipus, and Daedalus. Useful in teaching morality and values and for explaining some of the phrases in English. Good to use as a base for cultural literacy. For reading, religion, popular history, and recreational reading. *Subject*: Myths and Legends—Greek.

Reiff, Tana. *Tales of Wonder*. Syracuse, NY: New Readers Press, 1993. Timeless Tales Series. Paper $3.50 (ISBN 0-88336-459-X). Fry Reading Level 2+. Interest Level Grade 4–Adult.

Ten wonder tales from around the world retold in easy-to-read language. Includes an explanation of wonder tales and how they are used to teach lessons about life. Includes the Firebird from Russia, the Magic Eagle from Venezuela, and the Thunderbird from the Winnebago Indians of America, as well as others. Black and white illustrations. For teaching reading, multiculturalism, and values and for recreational reading. *Subjects*: Fantastic Fiction; Folklore—Cross-Cultural Studies; Folktales—Cross-Cultural Studies.

Reiff, Tana. *Tall Tales*. Syracuse, NY: New Readers Press, 1993. Timeless Tales Series. Paper $3.50 (ISBN 0-88336-463-8). Fry Reading Level 2+. Interest Level Grade 4–Adult.

The stories of Paul Bunyan, Pecos Bill, John Henry, and Stormalong the Sailor, as well as tales from Ireland, Burma, and Syria. Gives an explanation of tall tales. For units on literature, popular culture, cultural literacy, how to read, social history, and multiculturalism. *Subject*: Tall Tales—Cross-Cultural Studies.

Roberts, Willa Davis. *The Girl with the Silver Eyes*. New York: Scholastic. Paper $4.50 (ISBN 0–590–44248–1). Fry Reading Level 5+. Interest Level Grade 5–9.

For younger readers. Young girl has the ability to make things move when she merely thinks about them. A hook for the reader. Teaches about being different. Can be used as a springboard for a discussion of the power of the mind, the paranormal, and the power to believe. For units in reading, popular culture, and psychology and for recreational reading. *Subjects*: Unexplained Phenomenon—Fiction; Telekinesis—Fiction.

Sherman, Josepha. *Once Upon a Galaxy: Folktales, Fantasy and Science Fiction*. Little Rock, AR: August House, 1995. American Storytelling Series. Hardcover $19.95 (ISBN 0–87483–386–6); paper $9.95 (ISBN 0–87483–387–6). Fry Reading Level 5+. Interest Level Grade 5–Adult.

Anthology of fifty original folktales that are the basis for much popular literature throughout history. These tales from around the world are tied in with modern science fiction, fantasy, and cartoons. Norse mythology and tricksters provide ancestors for Tolkien's people and Bugs Bunny. Some of these tales are purportedly the basis for later stories such as Star Trek, Superman and Star Wars. Includes myths and legends from ancient Greece, the Ukraine, Hawaii, Russia, Finland, Turkey, Poland, Great Britain, Japan, and Ireland. Folktales from ancient Akkad, ancient Persia, France, Estonia, Egypt, North American Indians, the Ulger people of China, the people of Ghana, and from Chile. Bibliography, extensive collection of notes for each chapter. A few black and white illustrations. For units on ethnic diversity, social studies, popular history, literature, and history. Can be used as whole book or chapter by chapter. *Subjects*: Tales; Mythology; Folklore; Storytelling.

Sherman, Josepha. *Trickster Tales: Forty Folk Stories from Around the World*. Little Rock, AR: August House, 1996. World Storytelling Series. Paper $18.95 (ISBN 0–87483–450–3). Fry Reading Level 5+. Interest Level Grade 5–Adult.

Tricksters have always been a part of all countries' cultures. Today we have Bugs Bunny, Bart Simpson, and Wile E. Coyote. Bre'r Rabbit, Raven, Fox, Coyote, Anansi, and the leprechaun are the traditional tricksters. Forty different world cultures are represented, including Botswana, China, Eastern Europe, Morocco, Central and South America, the Creole, African American, Native American, Mozambique, and Jamaica. Extensive bibliography and chapter notes with motifs, story history, and explanation. For units on multiculturalism, history, popular culture, and culture literacy and recreational reading. *Subjects*: Trickster—Cross-Cultural Studies; Tales—Cross-Cultural Studies.

Suter, Joanne. *African*. Belmont, CA: Fearon/Janus, 1992. World Myths and Legends Series. Paper $7.32 (ISBN 0–8224–4639). Fry Reading Level 3+. Interest Level Grade 5–Adult.

Retelling of African myths and legends that are easy to read. These stories have their roots in the oral traditions with the groups of people in Africa who lived south of the Sahara Desert. Shows how ancient peoples provided order in their world. Includes religious tales as well as those about animals with human qualities. Tales of the Yoruba, Krachi, Ibibio, and Dagomba are included. Black and white illustrations. For classes in history, popular culture, literature, and multiculturalism and for recreational reading. *Subject*: Myths and Legends—African.

Suter, Joanne. *Ancient Middle East*. Belmont, CA: Fearon/Janus, 1992. World Myths and Legends Series. Paper $7.32 (ISBN 0–8224–4642–1). Fry Reading Level 3+. Interest Level Grade 5–Adult.

Tales of creation, evil brothers, and others from the oral tradition of the past. Includes tales from Sumeria, Babylonia, and ancient Egypt. Tales from the Old Testament will appear similar. For units in religion, history, and popular culture. Fine for ethnic diversity. *Subject*: Myths and Legends—Ancient Middle East.

Suter, Joanne. *Celtic*. Belmont, CA: Fearon/Janus, 1992. World Myths and Legends Series. Paper $7.32 (ISBN 0–8224–4637–5). Fry Reading Level 3+. Interest Level Grade 5–Adult.

Retells Celtic tales and gives a brief history of the Celts and the lands where they lived. Relates stories of gods and heroes, the legends of King Arthur and other folk heroes, and tales of the Otherworld. Includes Jack the Giant-Killer, tales of Cuchulain, and Finn Mac Cool. Pronunciation guide. For multiculturalism, literature, reading, popular culture, and cultural literacy. *Subject*: Myths and Legends—Celtic.

Suter, Joanne. *Far Eastern*. Belmont, CA: Fearon/Janus, 1992. World Myths and Legends Series. Paper $7.32 (ISBN 0–8224–4638–5). Fry Reading Level 3+. Interest Level Grade 5–Adult.

Tales from ancient Japan and China well retold. Excellent tales to use to understand the cultural literacy of other nations. For classes in literature, reading, history, and religion. *Subject*: Myths and Legends—Far Eastern.

Suter, Joanne. *Greek and Roman*. Belmont, CA: Fearon/Janus, 1992. World Myths and Legends Series. Paper $7.32 (ISBN 0–8224–4636–7). Fry Reading Level 3+. Interest Level Grade 5–Adult.

Brief history of Greek and Roman mythology. Includes creation stories, the stories of mortals who make mistakes such as Arachne, love stories, heroes and their adventures, and stories from history. Includes stories of Pygmalion, Theseus, and Romulus and Remus. Black and white illustrations. Questions for study with each story. Pronunciation guide. For history, religion, popular culture, literature, and recreational reading, as well as for multicultural units. *Subjects*: Myths and Legends—Greek; Myths and Legends—Roman.

Suter, Joanne. *Native American*. Belmont, CA: Fearon/Janus, 1992. World Myths and Legends Series. Paper $7.32 (ISBN 0–8224-4640–5). Fry Reading Level 3+. Interest Level Grade 5–Adult.

Common themes from all the Indians of the Americas, ranging from the Indians in Alaska to the Aztecs and others in South and Central America. Includes trickster, creation themes, and uses and meaning of the stars and astronomy. For units in literature, popular history, ethnic diversity, cultural literacy, and religion and for recreational reading. *Subject*: Myths and Legends—Native American.

Suter, Joanne. *Norse*. Belmont, CA: Fearon/Janus, 1992. World Myths and Legends Series. Paper $7.32 (ISBN 0–8224–4638–3). Fry Reading Level 3+. Interest Level Grade 5–Adult.

Some not-so-familiar tales from Norse mythology, including Odin. Includes tales from several northern European countries. For classes in literature, popular culture, religion, geography, and ethnic diversity. Useful in cultural literacy as a study of word origin and recreational reading. *Subject*: Myths and Legends—Norse.

Suter, Joanne. *Regional American*. Belmont, CA: Fearon/Janus, 1992. World Myths and Legends Series. Paper $7.32 (ISBN 0–8224–4641–3). Fry Reading Level 3+. Interest Level Grade 5–Adult.

Covers both the heroes and the villains of American mythology. An easy-to-read retelling of familiar stories. For units in popular culture, popular history, and literature and for recreational reading. *Subject*: Myths and Legends—American, Regional.

Yolen, Jane. *Here There Be Unicorns*. New York: Harcourt Brace, 1994. Hardcover $16.95 (ISBN 0–15–209902–6). Fry Reading Level 6. Interest Level Grade 5–Adult.

A collection of poems, stories, and songs about unicorns show that this mythical beast is popular in and with all cultures. Creates imagery for the eyes and minds. Magical look at how to catch unicorns, feed them, and divine the magic of their horns. For recreational reading, popular culture, and literature. *Subject*: Unicorns—Fiction.

York, Joanne, and Tom McGreevey. *Movie Westerns*. Minneapolis, MN: Lerner Books, 1994. Silver Screen Series. Hardcover $19.95 (ISBN 0–8225–1643–8). Fry Reading Level 7. Interest Level Grade 10–Adult.

A well-written and profusely illustrated popular history of western movies from 1903 up to the early 1990s. Provides an excellent look at popular American culture as seen on the screen throughout the century and how America has perceived its various cultural minorities throughout the century. For classes in popular culture and cultural history and for recreational reading. *Subject*: Movies.

Zindel, Paul. *Loch*. New York: HarperCollins, 1994. Hardcover $75.00 (ISBN 0–6–024542–5). Fry Reading Level 6. Interest Level Grade 6–10.

Is the Loch Ness Monster real or myth? Loch Perkins is fifteen years old and knows the truth because he has seen Nessie himself. Loch's father is using sonar and other scientific equipment to search for the legend, but Loch literally stumbles across one of Nessie's young. Will Loch provide the proof to the world that Nessie and the creatures live and possibly ensure their extinction? Or will he remain silent in order to save the ancient animals? A lesson in doing the right thing. For recreational reading, popular culture, and problem solving. *Subjects*: Loch Ness Monster—Fiction; Fantasy.

## CLASSIC AND MODERN FICTION

Armstrong, William. *Sounder*. New York: HarperCollins, 1969. Hardcover $11.92 (ISBN 0–06–020144–4). Fry Reading Level 6+. Interest Level Grade 6–Adult.

A book about a boy and a dog that provides a rare and poignant look at the life of a poor African family of sharecropping farmers in the American South of the nineteenth century. A sensitive portrayal of emotion and faith. The book has garnered many awards and may been seen on video. Also available on cassette. For units on history, black history, family life, and problem solving and for recreational reading. *Subjects*: American South—History—Fiction; Dogs—Fiction.

Barron, T. A. *The Lost Years of Merlin*. New York: Philomel Books, 1996. Hardcover $19.95 (ISBN 0–399–23018–1). Fry Reading Level 6. Interest Level Grade 5–Adult.

The story of a young boy who is washed ashore in ancient Wales. He has no identity. This tale tells how the lad learns the lore of the Celts, Druids, and even more ancient peoples on the journey to find his true name and homeland. A look at the early life of the greatest wizard of all time, Merlin. For advanced readers because of its length. Black and white illustrations. For literature, popular culture, reading, and recreational reading. *Subjects*: Merlin (Legendary Character)—Fiction; Wizards—Fiction; Fantasy.

Brontë, Charlotte. *Jane Eyre*. Adapted by Diana Stewart. Austin, TX: Raintree Steck-Vaughn, 1991. Raintree Short Classics Series. Hardcover $24.26 (ISBN 0–8172–1661–8); paper $11.92 (ISBN 0–8114–6830–5). Fry Reading Level 4. Interest Level Grade 6–Adult.

Retells in very easy-to-read and simple language the events leading up to and following the arrival of Jane at the country estate owned by the enigmatic and mysterious Mr. Rochester. Provides a basis for understanding the story as a whole. Provides an introduction to the classic that is known through books and movies and video. Brief glossary. Excellent illustrations. For classes in literature, for recreational reading, and for cultural literacy. *Subject*: Gothic Novel.

Chaucer, Geoffrey. *The Canterbury Tales*. Adapted by Diana Stewart. Austin, TX: Raintree Steck-Vaughn, 1991. Raintree Short Classics Series. Hardcover $24.26 (ISBN 0–8172–1666–9); paper $11.92 (ISBN 0–8114–6821–6). Fry Reading Level 4. Interest Level Grade 6–Adult.

An easy-to-read retelling in simple language for easy comprehension. This version contains an introduction that tells about Chaucer and his work, as well as some useful biographical material. Included in the collection are the Prologue, the Wife of Bath's Tale, the Pardoner's Tale, and the Canon Yeoman's Tale. Excellent full-page and full-color illustrations. For literature classes, recreational reading, and cultural literacy. *Subjects*: Middle Ages—Fiction; England—Fiction; Short Stories.

Dickens, Charles. *A Christmas Carol*. New York: DK Publications, 1997. Eyewitness Classics Series. Hardcover $14.95 (ISBN 0–7894–2070–8). Fry Reading Level 5. Interest Level Grade 5–12.

A retelling of the classic Dickens Christmas holiday tale set in England. This tale, with its lavish and colorful illustrations, will help readers from other cultures understand some of the traditional customs of the Christmas season and their origins. Teaches lessons in living. Provides background information about the story and its setting. For units on holidays and customs, literature, popular culture, and origins of phrases. *Subjects*: Christmas—Fiction; Victorian England—Fiction.

Dickens, Charles. *Great Expectations*. Adapted by Jan Gleiter. Austin, TX: Raintree Steck-Vaughn, 1991. Raintree Short Classics Series. Hardcover $24.26 (ISBN 0–8172–2762–8); paper $11.92 (ISBN 0–8114–6823–2). Fry Reading Level 4. Interest Level Grade 5–Adult.

A simple and easy-to-read retelling of the story of a young English orphan who is given a great deal of money by an unknown benefactor. This enables him to lead a life as a "gentleman" and thus fulfill his great expectations. Covers his adventures en route. With an afterword to finish the tale and a glossary to help with some of the vocabulary of the era. Excellent full-color illustration. For units in English literature, English history, classics, recreational reading, and cultural literacy. *Subjects*: Orphans—Fiction; England—Fiction.

Eagle, Gertrude, Editor. *More Stories 1*. Syracuse, NY: New Readers Press, 1991. Laubach Way to Reading Series. Paper $3.00 (ISBN 0–88336–926–5). Fry Reading Level 1. Interest Level Grade 4–Adult.

Very easy stories to help beginning readers learn to read. Works on sounds and names of the letters of the English alphabet. Very short sentences and lots of repetitive sounds and words. Black and white line drawings illustrate each lesson. For classes for learning to read and learning to write. *Subject*: Reading.

Farley, Walter. *The Black Stallion*. New York: Random House. Paper $4.50 (ISBN 0–679–81343–8). Fry Reading Level 7. Interest Level Grade 7–Adult.

A classic tale about a boy and a wild stallion he finds on a desert island and tames. Teaches resiliency, responsibility, courage, and trust. For classes in literature and social customs and for recreational reading. *Subjects*: Horses—Fiction; Shipwrecks—Fiction.

Gipson, Fred. *Old Yeller*. New York: HarperCollins, 1956. Paper $5.50 (ISBN 0–06–440382–3). Fry Reading Level 5+. Interest Level Grade 5–Adult.

A heart-warming tale, set in the wild Texas frontier of the Old West, about a youth and his family and the wily stray dog that adopts them. Fine writing and a strong emotional impact. For units in American history, family life, and popular culture and for recreational reading. *Subjects*: Dogs—Fiction; Texas—History—Fiction.

Guy, Rosa. *The Friends*. New York: Bantam. Paper $3.99 (ISBN 0–553–27326–4). Fry Reading Level 5+. Interest Level Grade 6–12.

Tells of the problems of a black girl who moves from the West Indies to Harlem. Language and setting are realistic. About love, death, and friendship.

Powerful. For units on ethnic diversity, popular culture, social studies, and problem solving. *Subjects*: West Indian Americans—Fiction; Harlem—Fiction.

Hijuelos, Oscar. *Selected from The Mambo Kings Play Songs of Love*. New York: Literacy Volunteers of New York City, 1992. Writers' Voices Series. Paper $3.50 (ISBN 0–929631–53–6). Fry Reading Level 5. Interest Level Grade 6–Adult.

Selected passages from the modern novel about Cuban American musicians in New York in the 1950s. Mass market paperback format is attractive to adolescent as well as adult readers. Brief biography of the author, a Cuban American. For classes in reading, literature, popular culture, social history, and ethnic diversity and for recreational reading. *Subjects*: Cuban-Americans—Fiction; Musicians—Fiction.

Homer. *The Iliad*. Adapted by Diana Stewart. Austin, TX: Raintree Steck-Vaughn, 1991. Raintree Short Classics Series. Hardcover $26.24 (ISBN 0–8172 01663–4); paper $11.92 (ISBN 0–8114–6828–3). Fry Reading Level 4. Interest Level Grade 5–Adult.

Retelling in easy-to-read, simple language of the events of the war between Greece and the city-state of Troy. Focuses mainly on the quarrel between Achilles and Agamemnon. Includes the duel between Paris and Menelaus, the gift for Achilles, Patroclus in the battle, and the death of Hector. Excellent full-page and full-color illustrations. Glossary of proper names in the story. For classes in Greek history or mythology, and world literature and for recreational reading and cultural literacy. *Subjects*: Myths and Legends, Greek; Troy—Fiction.

Homer. *The Odyssey*. Adapted by Diana Stewart. Austin, TX: Raintree Steck-Vaughn, 1991. Raintree Short Classics. Hardcover $24.26 (ISBN 0–8172–1654–5); paper $11.52 (ISBN 0–8114–6835–6). Fry Reading Level 4. Interest Level Grade 5–Adult.

Simple and easy-to-read retelling of five episodes in the classic story of Odysseus: the voyage from Troy to Ithaca, his landing in Phaeacia, his bout with the Cyclops, his adventure with Circe, his men's foolish behavior, and his return to Ithaca. Color illustrations. Glossary of proper names and some of the terms used. For classes in literature, mythology, Greek culture, and cultural literacy. *Subject*: Myths and Legends, Greek.

Jacques, Brian. *The Great Redwall Feast*. New York: Philomel Books, 1996. Hardcover $18.95 (ISBN 0–399–22707–5). Fry Reading Level 4+. Interest Level Grade 2–10.

Delightful fantasy set in England. Animals are the main characters in the Redwall series, with stories for all ages and reading levels. This poem story tells of the animals' (mice, hares, otters, moles, and others) planning a surprise feast for the abbot of Redwall. Delightfully illustrated in color. This book reads well aloud. For literature and reading and for recreational reading. For those who like animals and fantasy. *Subjects*: Parties—Fiction; Animals—Fiction; Stories in Rhyme; Fantasy.

Jacques, Brian. *Martin the Warrior.* New York: Philomel Books, 1993. Redwall Series. Hardcover $17.95 (ISBN 0–399–22670–2). Fry Reading Level 6. Interest Level Grade 6– Adult.

From the Redwall fantasy series. Martin is a mouse warrior imprisoned with several of his companions by a tyrant. They must be rescued from slave labor and make their way back home. Battles, dangers, and adventure. For recreational reading and literature. *Subjects*: Fantasy; Animals—Fiction.

Kipling, Rudyard. *The Jungle Book.* New York: Viking, 1997. Whole Story Series. Hardcover $22.99 (ISBN 0–67–86919–8); paper $14.99 (0–67–86797–7). Fry Reading Level 7. Interest Level Grade 6–Adult.

Classic tales from India by an English author. Many students will be familiar with the Disney movie version. An extremely high use of black and white and color illustrations, which include maps, engravings, and paintings as well as photographs. Informative sidebar captions with contemporary facts about history, science, life, social customs, and geography. Complete and unabridged text. For units in history, literature, reading, and popular history and for recreational reading. *Subject*: India—Fiction.

Lawlor, Laurie. *Little Women: A Novel Based on the Motion Picture Screen Play by Robin Swicord from the Novel by Louisa May Alcott.* New York: Minstrel, Pocket Books, 1994. Paper $3.99 (ISBN 0–671–51902–6). Fry Reading Level 5+. Interest Level Grade 5–12.

A contemporary rewriting of the classic aimed at modern teens. Simplified language in a condensed book. About the life of the March sisters in New England: their struggle with poverty, their quarrels, their crushes, their love of theater and plays, and their coming of age. Girls like it. For classes in literature, popular culture, and history, and for recreational reading. *Subject*: Families—Fiction.

Lester, Julius. *Othello: A Novel.* New York: Scholastic, 1995. Hardcover $12.95 (ISBN 0590–41967–6). Fry Reading Level 5. Interest Level Grade 5–Adult.

Shakespearean Othello by an acclaimed African American author of books for young people. Introductory material to prepare for the retelling. For classes in literature and popular culture and for recreational reading. *Subject*: Classics—Fiction.

London, Jack. *The Call of the Wild*. Adapted by Lillian Nordlicht. Austin, TX: Raintree Steck-Vaughn, 1991. Raintree Short Classics Series. Hardcover $17.92 (ISBN 0–8172–1656–1); paper $11.92 (ISBN 8114–6820–8). Fry Reading Level 4. Interest Level Grade 5–Adult.

An easy-to-read adaptation of the adventure classic about an unusual dog, part St. Bernard and part Scotch shepherd, who is taken by force to Alaska, where he becomes a leader of a pack of wolves. Excellent color illustrations. Brief glossary. For literature classes; to teach classics; and for units on animals, travel, American literature, and cultural literacy. *Subjects*: Dogs—Fiction; Alaska—Fiction.

Mansfield, Katherine. *The Doll's House and Other Stories*. New York: Penguin English, 1991. Simply Stories Series. Paper $3.50 (ISBN 0–14–081035–8). Fry Reading Level 7+. Interest Level Grade 10–Adult.

Short stories about the turn of the century for the intermediate to advanced learner of English. Mansfield was a New Zealand native who studied in England and traveled a great deal for her health. These stories, set in New Zealand and England, are at times funny, sad, and cruel but always witty. Retold by Ann Ward. Black and white line drawings. Book suggests dictionary use by printing some words in darker ink that may be unfamiliar to the reader. Exercises to be done by the student. For more advanced literature units dealing with short stories, and for recreational reading. *Subjects*: Short Stories; New Zealand—Fiction; England—Fiction.

Melville, Herman. *Moby Dick*. Belmont, CA: Fearon Education, 1991. Pacemaker Classic Series. Paper $3.85 (ISBN 0–8224–9350–0). Fry Reading Level 4+. Interest Level Grade 8–Adult.

A retelling of the tale of man against whale with its adventure story and moral implications that retains the flavor of the telling by Ishmael. Covers the entire story. Black and white line drawings to illustrate and explain the story. People may be acquainted with the story through the classic movie. For classes in literature, psychology, geography, and history and for recreational reading and popular culture. *Subjects*: Whales—Fiction; Sea Stories—Fiction.

Orwell, George. *Animal Farm*. New York: NAL, 1996. Paper $5.95 (ISBN 0–451–52634–1). Fry Reading Level 7. Interest Level Grade 7–Adult.

The classic political satire, written as an allegory set in a farmyard with animals rather vividly and aptly portraying the characters. Wise and compassionate. An illuminating attack on totalitarianism, a subject in which some of students might already be well versed. Shows a different way of looking at things. For units in literature, political science, government, and popular culture and for recreational reading. *Subjects*: Totalitarianism—Fiction; Animals—Fiction.

Schaefer, Jack. *Shane*. Portsmouth, NH: Heinemann International, 1992. Guided Readers Series. Paper $5.00 (ISBN 0–435–27227–6). Fry Reading Level 5. Interest Level Grade 4–Adult.

A simplified version for intermediate readers of the classic western story. Tells of a young lad and his family in the American West and the effect that the arrival of a mysterious stranger has on their lives. Has a basic vocabulary of 1,600 words. Makes cultural backgrounds explicit. Glossary, study guide for points to understand, list of materials on same reading level from this publisher. For units in reading, literature, American history, and popular culture and for recreational reading. Could be used with the movie of the same name to illustrate popular history and American traditions. *Subjects*: American West—Fiction; Strangers—Fiction.

Scott, Walter, Sir. *Ivanhoe*. Adapted by Jan Gleiter. Austin, TX: Raintree Steck-Vaughn, 1991. Raintree Short Classics Series. Hardcover $24.26 (ISBN 0–8172–2765–8); paper $11.92 (ISBN 0–8114–6829–1). Fry Reading Level 4. Interest Level Grade 6–Adult.

A simplified retelling of the story of the adventures of the Saxon knight of the twelfth century. Mainly about 1194, the year that Richard the Lionhearted returned from the Third Crusade. Students may already be familiar with the movie or video version. Lovely color illustrations. Short glossary. For classes in English literature and English history and for recreational reading and cultural literacy. *Subjects*: Great Britain—History—Richard I—Fiction; Knights and Knighthood—Fiction.

Sewell, Anna. *Black Beauty*. New York: Signet, 1986. Signet Classic. Paper $3.95 (ISBN 0–4515–205–64). Fry Reading Level 5+. Interest Level Grade 5–Adult.

The horse story classic that started them all. First published in 1877, this story of the purebred horse who through a series of misfortunes ended up as a nearly rejected work horse is sentimental and sad (but it has a happy ending) and is the forerunner of many animal stories. For units on animals, literature, recreational reading, and social history. *Subjects*: Horses—Fiction; Animals—Fiction.

Shakespeare, William. *Hamlet*. Adapted by Kathleen Thompson and Michael Nowak.
Austin, TX: Raintree Steck-Vaughn, 1991. Raintree Short Classics Series. Hardcover $24.26
(ISBN 0–8172–2764–4); paper $11.92 (ISBN 0–8114–625–9). Fry Reading Level 4.
Interest Level Grade 6–Adult.

Simple retelling in play format of the tragic story of the Prince of Denmark.
Cast of characters and their relations to one another, glossary. For classes in
English literature, European history, theater, and cultural literacy and for
recreational reading. Colorful illustrations. *Subjects*: Princes—Fiction; Murder—Fiction; Revenge—Fiction.

Shakespeare, William. *A Midsummer Night's Dream*. Adapted by Diana Stewart. Austin, TX:
Raintree Steck-Vaughn, 1991. Raintree Short Classic Series. Hardcover $24.26
(ISBN 0–8172–1689–4); paper $11.92 (ISBN 0–8114–6833–X). Fry Reading Level 4.
Interest Level Grade 6–Adult.

An adaptation of the fey play in which fairy creatures meddle with the lives
of humans who are wandering about an enchanted woods. The results are
often humorous and droll. Done in play format. Lists a cast of characters with
the relationships noted. Delightfully amusing color illustrations, as well as a
glossary. For classes in English literature, classics, theater, and cultural literacy. *Subject*: Fairies—Drama—Plays.

Shakespeare, William. *Romeo and Juliet*. Adapted by Diana Stewart. Austin, TX: Raintree
Steck-Vaughn, 1991. Raintree Short Classics Series. Hardcover $24.26
(ISBN 0–8172–4653–7); paper $11.92 (ISBN 0–8114–6838–0). Fry Reading Level 4.
Interest Level Grade 5–Adult.

A simple retelling in play format of the tragic and ill-fated love affair of two
young people. The story is known throughout the world from plays, adaptations, films, and videos. This easy-to-read text shows how love can be de-
stroyed by family feuds and hatred. Introduction explains how plays were
presented in the era of Shakespeare. Illustrations. Cast of characters and relationships, glossary. For classes in literature, theater, family relationships, and
cultural literacy and for recreational reading. *Subjects*: Death—Fiction; Suicide, Teen Age—Fiction.

Shelley, Mary Wollstonecraft. *Frankenstein*. Adapted by Diana Stewart. Austin, TX: Raintree
Steck-Vaughn, 1991. Raintree Short Classic Series. Hardcover $24.26
(ISBN 0–8172–1674–X); paper $11.92 (ISBN 0–8114–6822–4). Fry Reading Level 4.
Interest Level Grade 5–Adult.

A prologue sets the stage for this simple and easy-to-read retelling of the
horror classic about the monster who was supposed to be a help to man but
was scorned for his ugliness, and took revenge on his creator and other hu-

mans. Known to students through many films and videos. For classes in literature, cultural literacy, reading, and interpersonal relationships. *Subjects*: Monsters—Fiction; Horror Stories.

Steinbeck, John. *The Pearl*. New York: Scholastic. Paper $4.95 (ISBN 0–14–017737–X). Fry Reading Level 6+. Interest Level Grade 7–Adult.

A pearl found by a poor Mexican family brings tragedy instead of the hoped-for good luck. Teaches values. For recreational reading as well as classes in literature and ethnic diversity. *Subject*: Pearls—Fiction.

Stevenson, Robert Louis. *Treasure Island*. New York: Viking, 1997. Whole Story Series. Hardcover $23.99 (ISBN 0–670–86920–1); paper $15.99 (ISBN 0–670–86795–0). Fry Reading Level 6+. Interest Level Grade 6–Adult.

The complete and unabridged text of the original story is explained and enhanced by the use of sidebar captions that contain information about contemporary science, history, life and customs, and geography. Color and black and white illustrations include maps, engravings, and painting. Students may be familiar with this story of treasure and pirates through the movies. For classes in literature, reading, and popular culture and for recreational reading. *Subjects*: Buried Treasure—Fiction; Pirates—Fiction.

Swift, Jonathan. *Gulliver's Travels*. Austin, TX: Austin, TX: Raintree Steck-Vaughn, 1991. Paper $14.94. (ISBN 0–8114–6824–0). Fry Reading Level 4+. Interest Level Grade 6–Adult.

Simplified and abbreviated version of the English classic satire. Trade paper size. Many color illustrations. Glossary. For classes in reading, literature, social studies, and cultural literacy and for recreational reading. *Subjects*: Fantasy; Fiction.

Twain, Mark, pseud. *Huckleberry Finn*. Adapted by June Edwards. Austin, TX: Raintree Steck-Vaughn, 1991. Raintree Short Classics Series. Hardcover $17.95 (ISBN 0–8172–1651–0); paper $1.25 (ISBN 0–8114–6826–7). Fry Reading Level 4. Interest Level Grade 5–Adult.

Nineteenth-century tale about a young lad from the center of America and his adventures. Can be used to explain attitudes and how they change in society. Easy to read and simple language. Color illustrations. Glossary. For classes in cultural literacy, popular culture, literature, geography, history, and social studies and for recreational reading. *Subjects*: Mississippi River—Fiction; Missouri—Fiction.

Twain, Mark, pseud. *Tom Sawyer*. Adapted by June Edwards. Austin, TX: Raintree Steck-Vaughn, 1991. Raintree Short Classics Series. Hardcover $17.95 (ISBN 0–8172–165–0); paper $1.25 (ISBN 0–8114–6843–7). Fry Reading Level 4. Interest Level Grade 5–Adult.

An easy-to-read, simplified version of the American classic tale of a nineteenth-century boy who lives along the Mississippi River and gets into a lot of scrapes and adventures with his pal Huck Finn and his friend Becky Thatcher. In the episodes included here, they run away from home, witness a murder, and find treasure in a cave. Colorful illustrations give faces to the characters and set the stage for the era through their clothing. For units in American literature, popular culture, cultural literacy, and history and for recreational reading. *Subjects*: Mississippi River—Fiction; Missouri—Fiction.

Verne, Jules. *Around the World in Eighty Days*. New York: Viking, 1997. Whole Story Series. Hardcover $23.99 (ISBN 0–670–86917–1); paper $15.99 (ISBN 0–670–86793–4). Fry Reading Level 6+. Interest Level Grade 6–Adult.

This speedy trip for its time introduced the whole world to readers. Now readers can understand its importance as a classic with this full-text version. Fact-filled sidebar captions explain contemporary history, life and customs, geography, and science. French author. Over 300 illustrations in color and black and white, including maps. For classes in reading, literature, and geography and for recreational reading. *Subject*: Travel—Fiction.

Verne, Jules. *20,000 Leagues under the Sea*. Adapted by Lillian Nordlicht. Austin, TX: Raintree Steck-Vaughn, 1991. Raintree Short Classics. Hardcover $1.25 (ISBN 0–8172–1652–9); paper (ISBN 0–8114–6848–1). Fry Reading Level 4. Interest Level Grade 5–Adult.

Simple sentences in this easy-to-read and -understand version of the famous nineteenth-century science-fiction adventure featuring an electric submarine with the very eccentric Captain Nemo in command. An underseas world is depicted that anticipated many later scientific achievements. Rich color illustrations. Glossary. For units in literature, and science and for recreational reading. *Subjects*: Sea Stories—Fiction; Science Fiction; Submarines—Fiction.

Wilde, Oscar. *The Picture of Dorian Gray*. Portsmouth, NH: Heinemann International, 1993. Heinemann Guided Readers Series. Paper $5.00 (ISBN 0–435–27213–6). Fry Reading Level 5. Interest Level Grade 6–Adult.

Abbreviated and simplified version of the English literary classic of the man who never seems to grow old. It is the tale of a man who sold his soul to the devil for vanity and who is evil behind the facade of beauty. This book is at the elementary reading level and supposes a vocabulary of approximately

1,100 words. Points to understand in the study guides, notes about the author. Cassette recording available. Could be used with the movie version for literature classes. For classes in literature and reading and for recreational reading. *Subjects*: Fantasy.

# 5

# Ethnic Diversity

Each ethnic group brings its own history, customs, celebrations, and lifestyle to the classroom as well as to this country. It is important for all students to know the background of their fellow students. This chapter contains materials on lifestyles, people, celebrations, countries, and cooking. It covers people outside the United States, ethnic groups who have been in this country for a long time, and ethnic groups who are relative newcomers.

## NONFICTION

Brady, April. *Kwanzaa Karamu: Cooking and Crafts for a Kwanzaa Feast.* Minneapolis, MN: Carolrhoda Books, 1995. Hardcover $14.95 (ISBN 0–87614–842–9); paper $6.95 (ISBN 0–87614–633–7). Fry Reading Level 3. Interest Level Grade 5–Adult.

Brief background to the African American celebration, tasty recipes that are easy to make, and an artful presentation of simple craft activities. Very easy to read and use. Excellent for units on holidays. *Subject*: Holidays—African American.

Braine, Susan. *Drumbeat–Heartbeat: A Celebration of the Powwow.* Minneapolis, MN: Lerner, 1995. We are Still Here Series. Hardcover $19.95 (ISBN 0–8225–2656–5). Fry Reading Level 5–6. Interest Level Grade 5–Adult.

All ages can enjoy and appreciate this celebration of Native American culture told in words and colorful pictures in the context of the 1990s. Informative and excellent for current affairs and cultural diversity units. *Subjects*: Native Americans—Customs; Native Americans—Powwows.

Burckhardt, Ann. *The People of Africa and Their Food.* Mankato, MN: Capstone Press, 1996. Multicultural Cookbook Series. Hardcover $18.40 (ISBN 1–56065–434–1). Fry Reading Level 4+. Interest Level Grade 4–Adult.

Facts about Africa and brief information about the countries. Discusses the importance of the market for cooking and socializing in African countries; explores celebrations, including Kwanzaa, even though it was started by an American in 1966; and gives recipes for main dishes, side dishes, soups, salads, desserts, and beverages. Metric measurements are converted for the recipes. Food and celebrations are Americanized. Color photographs. *Subjects*: Cookery, African; Food Habits, Africa; Africa, Social Life and Customs.

Burckhardt, Ann. *The People of China and Their Food.* Mankato, MN: Capstone Press, 1996. Multicultural Cookbook Series. Hardcover $18.40 (ISBN 1–56065–433–3). Fry Reading Level 4+. Interest Level Grade 4–Adult.

Contains brief facts about China that include a relief map and a verbal picture of Chinese markets. Description of the typical celebration of the Chinese New Year. Easy recipes, with measurements explained. Colorful pictures of well-presented foods. Bibliography, useful addresses and Internet sites. For domestic science classes and helpful at home. *Subjects*: Cookery, Chinese; Food Habits, China; China, Social Life and Customs.

Burckhardt, Ann. *The People of Mexico and Their Food.* Mankato, MN: Capstone Press, 1996. Multicultural Cookbook Series. Hardcover $18.40 $ (ISBN 1–56065–432–5). Fry Reading Level 4+. Interest Level Grade 4–Adult.

Mexican food has achieved great popularity across the United States, and this book makes it easy for all to cook. Learning some words in Spanish starts the book, along with brief facts about the country and a look at the open-air markets, the *mercado*. Cinco de Mayo is the celebration highlighted, with a description and history. Foods highlighted include basics (corn, beans, peppers, tomatoes, avocados, beef, cheese, and herbs). Recipes for such favorites as fajitas, tacos, enchiladas, tortilla chips, and Mexican wedding cakes. Colorful pictures illustrate costumes for musicians and dancers. For cooking and social studies classes. *Subjects*: Cookery, Mexican; Food Habits, Mexico; Mexico, Social Life and Customs.

Burckhardt, Ann. *The People of Russia and Their Food.* Mankato, MN: Capstone Press, 1996. Multicultural Cookbook Series. Hardcover $18.40 (ISBN 1–56065–432–5). Fry Reading Level 4+. Interest Level Grade 4–Adult.

Facts about Russia include marketing habits and foods such as root crops and sour cream. Russian Orthodox Easter, with its egg coloring, is the celebration highlighted. Main dishes show the uses of cabbage, fillings, and meats with side dishes using grains such as buckwheat and root crops such as potatoes. Borscht and Easter sweet bread are featured. Guidelines for kitchen safety included. Recipes can be done in cooking classes, and foods can be discussed in social studies classes. Color pictures of the food and the people. Relief map of Russia. *Subjects*: Cookery—Russian; Food Habits—Russia (Federation); Russia (Federation)—Social Life and Customs.

Cappelloni, Nancy. *Ethnic Cooking the Microwave Way*. Minneapolis, MN: Lerner, 1994. Easy Menu Ethnic Cookbook Series. Paper $5.95 (ISBN 0–8225–9660–1); hardcover $14.95 (ISBN 0–8335–0929–6). Fry Reading Level 5. Interest Level Grade 5–Adult.

Carefully done book with easy-to-follow recipes that can be of use to those learning to cope with a microwave in a different language. Recipes from several countries, with tips for utensils and a useful primer on how a microwave works and how to use it. Fun for a unit on food preparation or social studies. *Subject*: Cookery—Ethnic.

Chrisman, Abbott. *Luis Muñoz Marin*. Austin, TX: Steck-Vaughn Company, 1991. Raintree Hispanic Stories Series. English and Spanish. Hardcover $15.33 (ISBN 0–8172–2907–8); paper $3.75 (ISBN 0–8114–6760–8). Fry Reading Level 5+. Interest Level Grade 5–Adult.

Biography of the Puerto Rican leader who worked to improve the living conditions for his compatriots and was their governor from 1949 to 1965. Covers how Puerto Rico gained its independence, only to fall to the United States in the Spanish American War; the long struggle of the Puerto Rican people for political stability, which saw social reforms and cultural renewal culminating in their electing Muñoz Marin governor in 1952 and their decision to become a commonwealth in 1952; and Muñoz Marin's life. Half text, half color illustrations. Text in both Spanish and English. Good for social studies, history, civics, reading, and language classes. *Subjects*: Muñoz Marin, Luis, 1898–; Governors; Puerto Rico—Politics and Government; Spanish Language Materials—Bilingual.

Chung, Okwha. *Cooking the Korean Way*. Minneapolis, MN: Lerner, 1988. Easy Menu Ethnic Cookbooks Series. Hardcover $15.95 (ISBN 0–8225–0921–0). Fry Reading Level 5. Interest level Grade 5–Adult.

Gives a brief overview of Korea and its history; provides a map showing where foodstuffs are produced; and discusses foods, holidays, and celebrations. Cooking safety is discussed, as well as the cooking utensils needed for Korean cooking. Cooking terms and special ingredients are explained. There is a lesson on how to eat with chopsticks. There are suggested food combinations for meals and a pronunciation guide with the Korean word plus the American way to say the Korean word. Recipe for kimchi, noodles, bean sprouts, dumplings, tofu, and simmered meats. Color photographs present the food beautifully. Black and white drawings show how to do some of the recipes. For cooking classes and social studies classes. *Subjects*: Cookery, Korean; Korea—Social Life and Customs.

Codye, Corinn. *Luis W. Alvarez.* Austin, TX: Steck-Vaughn Company, 1991. Raintree Hispanic Stories. Hardcover $15.33 (ISBN 0–8172–3376–8); paper $3.75 (ISBN 0–8114–6750–3). English and Spanish. Fry Reading Level 5+. Interest Level Grade 5–Adult.

Story of the life of one of the scientists who worked on the atomic bomb and was the Nobel Prize winner for physics in 1968. Covers his student days at the University of Chicago, where he began his career in physics and worked with the geiger counter to measure cosmic rays; his work with the cyclotron at the University of California at Berkeley and of the radar developed during World War II; his time at Los Alamos working on the development of the atomic bomb and his being on the flight when the bomb was dropped; and how he and his scientist son came to the conclusion that a large meteor or asteroid from space had struck the earth and caused the extinction of the dinosaurs. Fine color illustrations make up half of the book. Half of the text is in Spanish. For classes in science, social studies, and history as well as extra credit reading in all classes. *Subjects*: Alvarez, Luis W., 1911–1988; Physicists; Spanish Language Materials—Bilingual.

Codye, Corinn. *Queen Isabella I.* Austin, TX: Steck Vaughn Company, 1991. Raintree Hispanic Stories Series. English and Spanish. Hardcover $15.33 (ISBN 0–18172–3380); paper $3.75 (ISBN 0–8114–6758–9). Fry Reading Level 5+. Interest Level Grade 5–Adult.

Life of the queen of Spain who made it possible for Christopher Columbus to search for a way to the orient. Explains how this queen's strong Roman Catholic faith led to the expulsion from Spain of Jews who would not convert and Muslims. Romantic view of the marriage of Ferdinand and Isabella and their rise to the throne. Tells of the creation of a national police force and a national army to protect it and laws and courts to govern. Color illustration. Text in Spanish and English. For classes in history, social studies, and language. *Subjects*: Isabella I, Queen of Spain, 1451–1504; Kings, Queens, Rulers, etc.; Spain—History, Spanish Language Materials—Bilingual.

Codye, Corinn. *Vilma Martinez.* Austin, TX: Steck-Vaughn Company, 1991. Raintree Hispanic Stories Series. English and Spanish. Hardcover $15.33 (ISBN 0–8172–3382–2); paper $3.75 (ISBN 0–8114–6762–7). Fry Reading Level 5+. Interest Level Grade 5–Adult.

Examines the life on a contemporary woman lawyer who has won many landmark civil rights cases. Traces her life from a poor child in Texas to her life in private practice law in Los Angeles. Highlights the discrimination against Mexican Americans and her perseverance to get the best education available. Covers her determination to become and succeed as a lawyer; her work up through the ranks in civil rights to the founding of the Mexican-American Legal Defense and Educational Fund; her fight to include Mexican Americans in the Voting Rights Act of 1975; and her fight for bilingualism at school, at work, and in the voting booth. Excellent to bolster the self-images of young women, particularly Mexican ones. *Subjects*: Martinez, Vilma; Women Lawyers—United States—Biography; Civil Rights Workers; Spanish Language Materials—Bilingual.

Coronado, Rosa. *Cooking the Mexican Way.* Minneapolis, MN: Lerner Publications Company, 1982. Easy Menu Ethnic Cookbook Series. Hardcover $14.95 (ISBN 0–8225–0907–5); paper (ISBN 0–825–9614–8). Fry Reading Level 5+. Interest Level Grade 5–Adult.

Information about the land and peoples of Mexico. Explains the utensils needed and the special ingredients and cooking terms used. Presents a full meal, as well as dishes for each meal of the day. Metric conversion, index, and safety tips. Includes recipes for Mexican hot chocolate, refried beans, tortillas with beef, and red snapper with lime. Colorful with easy-to-read format. Color and black and white illustrations. For social studies and life skills classes, home economics, and units on ethnic diversity. Useful at home also. *Subjects*: Cookery—Mexican; Mexico—Social Life and Customs.

de Varona, Frank. *Bernardo de Galvez.* Austin, TX: Steck-Vaughn Company, 1991. Hispanic Stories Series. English and Spanish. Hardcover $15.33 (ISBN 0–8172–3379–2); paper $3.75 (ISBN 0-8114-6756-2). Fry Reading Level 5+. Interest Level Grade 5–Adult.

Biography of the Spanish governor in the New World who raised an army of seven thousand soldiers to drive the British from the Mississippi River valley during the American Revolutionary War. Covers his childhood in Spain, life in France, and stint in the Louisiana Territory. His command of the French language made Galvez a popular governor and helped him marry a daughter of a leader of the French community of New Orleans. One of the lesser-known fighters for the American cause. For classes in history, social studies, and languages. *Subjects*: Galvez, Bernardo de, 1746–1786; Governors; United States—History—Revolution, 1775–1783; Spanish Language Materials—Bilingual.

Gleiter, Jan. *Benito Juarez.* Austin, TX: Steck-Vaughn Company, 1991. Raintree Hispanic Stories Series. English and Spanish. Hardcover $15.33 (ISBN 0–8172–3381–4); paper $3.75 (ISBN 0–8114–6759–7). Fry Reading Level 5+. Interest Level Grade 5–Adult.

Biography of the nineteenth-century president of Mexico who during his tenure separated church and state, established religious tolerance, and redistributed land, His Zapotec Indian heritage ensured that he would experience discrimination and second-class citizenship. Perseverance and hard work earned him a law degree and the right to argue cases before the highest courts. Covers the monetary and personal abuse of the church against the poor and uneducated, the political corruption of the time, the political strife that made him a political president as well as hero of the people, wars with the United States and European countries that invaded to get payment of a debt, and civil wars. Half color illustrations, half text. Text in English and Spanish. For social studies, history, and language units. *Subjects*: Juarez, Benito, 1806–1872; Mexico—History—1821–1872; Presidents—Mexico.

Gleiter, Jan. *Diego Rivera*. Austin, TX: Steck-Vaughn Company, 1991. Raintree Hispanic Stories Series. English and Spanish. Hardcover $15.33 (ISBN 0–8172–2908–6); paper $3.75 (ISBN 0–8114–6764–3). Fry Reading Level 5+. Interest Level Grade 5–Adult.

Traces the life of the Mexican artist from his sickly childhood through his schooling, where he advanced rapidly. Beginning to draw in great detail even before he had any formal education, he entered the San Carlo School of Fine Arts when he was thirteen. Shows the growth of his talent and his political bent through the paintings of workers, particularly as depicted in the murals for which he is famous. Half text, half color illustration. Text in both English and Spanish. For classes in art, language, social studies, history, and political science. *Subjects*: Rivera, Diego, 1886–1957; Artists—Mexico—Biography; Spanish Language Materials—Bilingual.

Gleiter, Jan. *José Martí*. Austin, TX: Steck-Vaughn Company, 1991. Hispanic Stories Series. English and Spanish. Hardcover $15.33 (ISBN 0–8172–2906–X); paper $3.75 (ISBN 0–8114–6761–9). Fry Reading Level 5+. Interest Level Grade 5–Adult.

Biography of the famed Cuban patriot who worked to free his country from Spain. Explores his work as an author and journalist and the importance he played in Cuban life. His dedication to his county can inspire other Hispanics. As a youth his writings in a revolutionary newspaper landed him in prison. Tells of his belief in and love of freedom that made him a political exile from Cuba almost all of his life. Bits of poetry included. Half text, half color illustrations. Text in English and Spanish. For literature, history, journalism, and social studies classes. *Subjects*: Martí, José, 1853–1895; Revolutionaries; Authors—Cuban; Spanish Language Materials—Bilingual.

Gleiter, Jan. *Miguel Hidalgo y Costilla*. Austin, TX: Steck-Vaughn Company, 1991. Raintree Hispanic Stories Series. English and Spanish. Hardcover $15.33 (ISBN 0–8172–2905–1); paper $3.75 (ISBN 0–8114–6757–0). Fry Reading Level 5+. Interest Level Grade 5–Adult.

Covers Mexico's ongoing turbulent internal struggle for freedom and equality in politics and religion. Biography of the Mexican priest who fought for and led his Indian followers to revolt against the Spaniards. One of several known as the Father of Mexican Revolution. Shows his life from his middle-class youth through his school years and times as a priest, a revolutionary, a soldier, and a prisoner until he was shot for his beliefs. Teaches perseverance, compassion, and pride. Text in English and Spanish. Half text, half color illustrations. For history and social studies units. *Subjects*: Hidalgo y Costilla, Miguel, 1753–1811; Revolutionaries; Mexico—History—War of Independence, 1810–1821; Spanish Language Materials—Bilingual.

Gleiter, Jan. *Simón Bolívar.* Austin, TX: Steck-Vaughn Company, 1991. Raintree Hispanic Stories Series. English and Spanish. Hardcover $15.33 (ISBN 0–8172–2902–7); paper $3.75 (ISBN 0–8114–6751–1). Fry Reading Level 5+. Interest Level Grade 5–Adult.

About one of the best known of the South American liberators (Bolivia was named after him). His victories over Spain won freedom for Bolivia, Colombia, Ecuador, Peru, and Venezuela. Traces his life from his childhood with rich parents in Venezuela, where his tutor taught him the precepts of Rousseau, particularly as they applied to survival and equality. Shows both sides of Bolivar's ambition to free the land from Spain: his desire for personal glory and his desire for freedom. Lets the reader know that Bolivar was not a hero to all and that his revolutions were steeped in blood and hardship. Half text, half color illustrations. Text in English and Spanish. For units about South America, history, and social studies. *Subjects*: Bolívar, Simón, 1783–1830; Revolutionaries; Spanish Language Materials—Bilingual.

Goss, Linda, and Clay Goss. *It's Kwanzaa Time.* New York: Putnam, 1995. Hardcover $19.95 (ISBN 0–399–22505). Fry Reading Level 4. Interest Level Grade 4–Adult.

Collection of stories, activities, and information about Kwanzaa, the African American holiday. Excellent to use to promote understanding. Contains good activities and illustrates the emotions and feelings that are a part of the celebration. Use for units about African Americans, ethnic diversity, holidays, and customs, social studies, and literature. *Subjects*: Holidays—African American; Celebrations.

Harrison, Supenn. *Cooking the Thai Way.* Minneapolis, MN: Lerner Publications Company, 1986. Easy Menu Ethnic Cookbook Series. Hardcover $14.95 (ISBN 0–8225–0917–2). Fry Reading Level 5+. Interest Level Grade 5–Adult.

Introduction to the cooking of Thailand, with information on Thai history, geography, and customs. Discusses the holiday feasts as well as typical Thai meals. Includes recipes for staples, noodles, salads, soups and curries, stir fries, and fried dishes as well as grilled and steamed dishes and desserts. Explains how to make satay, wrap egg rolls, and what types of special ingredients will be needed. Index, metric conversion chart. Many colorful illustrations, as well as black and white. For units on social studies, foods, ethnic diversity, home economics, and popular culture. *Subjects*: Cookery—Thai; Thailand—Social Life and Customs.

Hughes, Helga. *Cooking the Irish Way*. Minneapolis, MN: Lerner Publications, 1996. Easy Menu Ethnic Cookbook Series. Hardcover $14.95 (ISBN 0–8225–0931–8). Fry Reading Level 4+. Interest Level Grade 4–Adult.

Briefly discusses Ireland and the people. Tells what cooking utensils are needed, explains cooking terms, and notes special ingredients used. Typical menus for breakfast, lunch, afternoon tea, and dinner are included. Recipes presented include soda bread, Dublin coddle, Irish stew, tea, chicken and leek pie, brussels sprouts, colcannon, champ, boxty bread, and corned beef and cabbage. Praties, or potatoes, are a staple. All Irish terms are explained. Map of Ireland showing crops and foodstuffs available. Useful index, metric conversion chart. Foods are well presented in color photographs. For home economics, life skills, and social studies classes. *Subjects*: Cookery—Irish: Ireland—Social Life and Customs.

Katz, William Loren. Exploration to the War of 1812, 1492–1814. Austin, TX: Steck-Vaughn Company, 1993. History of Multicultural America Series. Hardcover $21.28 (ISBN 0–8114–6275–7); paper $5.95 (ISBN 0–8114–2912–1). Fry Reading Level 6+. Interest Level Grade 6–Adult.

Discusses various ethnic groups during the discovery of America through the War of 1812. Notes which ethnic groups may have had a hand in the discovery of America, including the makeup of Columbus's expeditions. Discusses the Native Americans and their treatment, the clash of the divergent cultures from the European nations, the arrival of the Africans, and religious differences. Many tribes of Indians are discussed, as are different religious settlements. Some thumbnail sketches of important people and events included. Well indexed, useful bibliography. Black and white illustrations. There are seven other books in this series. For units in history, ethnic diversity, and social sciences. *Subjects*: United States—History—Colonial Period, United States—History—Revolution, Minorities—History.

Katz, William Loren. *World War II to the New Frontier, 1940–1963*. Austin, TX: Steck-Vaughn Company, 1993. History of Multicultural America Series. Hardcover $21.28 (ISBN 0–8114–6280–3); paper $5.95 (ISBN 0–8114–2917–2). Fry Reading Level 5+. Interest Level Grade 6–Adult.

Women and minorities figure heavily in this look at multiculturalism from 1940 through the 1960s. Covers World War II racial problems through the March on Washington with Martin Luther King, Jr. The treatment of Japanese

Americans, the intolerance of things German, political persecutions, and changes in immigration are traced. Problems of equality in the armed forces are shown, as well as the problems both women and returning soldiers faced in postwar America. Puerto Ricans and other Hispanics became a force to reckon with as did Native Americans. Covers the Civil Rights movement and school desegregation. Well indexed useful bibliography for both students and teacher. Black and white photographs. For units in modern history, ethnic diversity, and social studies. There are seven more books in this series by Katz, and all are useful. I particularly recommend *The Great Society to the Reagan Era* (ISBN 0–8114–6282–X) and *Minorities Today* (ISBN 0–8114–6281–1). *Subjects*: United States—History—20th Century; Minorities—History.

Kennedy, James H. *Contemporary's Celebrate with Us*. Chicago: Contemporary Books, 1995. Hardcover $15.24 (ISBN 0–8092–3413–0). Fry Reading Level 4+. Interest Level Grade 4–Adult.

A workbook-type text that is a beginning ESL reader dealing with holidays and festivals. Coverage is mainly of United States holidays, but some ethnic celebrations are included. Discusses the holidays of historical significance such as Labor Day, Veterans' Day, Memorial Day, Martin Luther King, Jr., Day, Presidents' Day, and Independence Day, as well as traditional holidays such as Mother's Day, Father's Day, and Valentine's Day. Religious and seasonal festivals covered include Chinese New Year, the Cherry Blossom Festival, and Carnival and Mardi Gras. Exercises and answers. Black and white illustrations. For reading classes and units on ethnic diversity and social studies. *Subjects*: Holidays; Festivals.

Larsen, Ronald J. *The Puerto Ricans in America*. Minneapolis, MN: Lerner Publications Company, 1989. In America Series. Hardcover $15.95 (ISBN 0–8225–0238–0); paper $9.95 (ISBN 0–8225–1036–7). Fry Reading Level 6+. Interest Level Grade 6–Adult.

Gives a brief history of Puerto Rico, the Puerto Rican immigration to the mainland area, and the individual contributions of Puerto Ricans to American culture and way of life. Discusses barrios, discrimination, prejudice, and the need not to lose identity. Features many sports, entertainment, and political personalities, including Roberto Clemente, Geraldo Rivera, Rita Moreno, and Raul Julia. Black and white photographs. Index. For units in history, social studies, popular culture, cultural diversity, and cultural literacy. *Subject*: Puerto Ricans in the United States.

Leathers, Noel L. *The Japanese in America*. Minneapolis, MN: Lerner Publications, 1991. In America Series. Hardcover $15.95 (ISBN 0–8225–0241–0); paper $7.95 (ISBN 0–8225–1042–1). Fry Reading Level 6. Interest Level Grade 6–Adult.

Examines the life of Japanese immigrants to the United States and their contributions to the professions and the quality of life. Covers their persecution and relocation during World War II; discrimination against them through-out American history; and the life of the Japanese in Hawaii. Brief biographical sketches of Japanese Americans who have contributed to American life. Well illustrated, useful index, bibliography. Use for units on immigration, discrimination, biography, social history, and careers. *Subject*: Japanese in the United States.

Margulies, Stuart. *Readings in Cultural Literacy: Topics across the Curriculum.* New York: Educational Design, 1989. Paper $7.50 (ISBN 0–87694–320–2). Fry Reading Level 5. Interest Level Grade 5–Adult.

A collection of readings on many subjects. The commonality is that the topics are things everyone should know something about. Discusses subjects that appear in papers and magazines and on TV. Knowing about these subjects will help people better understand everyday language, jokes, speeches, and events in this country. There are eleven units of study in the book, covering literature, social studies, biography, science, arts, and the Bible. Literature contains proverbs and sayings, monsters, American authors, children's stories, and Shakespeare. Social studies look at world religions, Indian civilizations in the Americas, the Holocaust, war, segregation, and governments. Biography includes women, criminals, famous people and their sayings, and ethnic heroes. Science includes evolution, explorers, life science, psychology, and astronomy and astrology. Art, music, and architecture are covered. Workbook format. Pronunciation and definition given for difficult words. Helpful for all students. *Subject*: Cultural Literacy.

Marston, Elsa. *The Lebanese in America.* Minneapolis: Lerner Publications, 1987. In America Series. Hardcover $7.95 (ISBN 0–8225–0234–8); paper $15.95 (ISBN 0–8225–1032–4). Fry Reading Level 6+. Interest Level Grade 5–Adult.

Discusses and surveys Lebanese immigrants who came to the United States and their contributions to American life and culture. Looks at the history of Lebanon; modern Lebanon and why people left the country; Lebanese women who emigrated; and Lebanese who became prominent in medicine, public service, government, academia, arts and entertainment, sports, and business. Some people included are Dr. Michael DeBakey, heart surgeon; Philip Habib, diplomat; Ralph Nader, public service; William Blatty, author; Danny Thomas, comedian and actor, and Doug Flutie, football. Black and white photographs. Index. For units in history, social studies, popular culture, and cultural literacy. Can be used to help promote awareness of cultural diversity. *Subject*: Lebanese Americans.

*My Native Land.* New York: Literacy Volunteers of New York City, 1992. New Writers Voices Series. Paper $3.95 (0–929631–65–X). Fry Reading Level 3–4. Interest Level Grade 5–Adult.

Anthology of brief essays written by learners at the Literacy Volunteers of New York City's classes. Countries of origin include Mexico, Poland, Cuba, Haiti, Puerto Rico, West Indies, Russia, El Salvador, Palestine, and China. Subjects include trips, childhood, gifts, emotions, seasons, travel, relationships, events, and hurricanes. Very short and easy to read. Can be used to teach reading and writing. *Subjects*: Personal Narratives; English as a Second Language.

Nabwire, Niie. *Cooking the African Way.* Minneapolis, MN: Lerner Publications Company, 1988. Easy Menu Ethnic Cookbook Series. Hardcover $14.95 (ISBN 0–8225–0919–9); paper $7.95 (ISBN 0–8224–9564–8). Fry Reading Level 5. Interest Level Grades 5–Adult.

Introduction to the cookery of East and West Africa, with information on the land and the peoples of the areas. Map showing countries included as well as the foodstuffs they produce and use. Some countries from West Africa included are Liberia, Ghana, and Nigeria; some included from East Africa are Ethiopia and Kenya. Describes utensils and ingredients needed, as well as terms used in the instructions and recipes. Provides menus from each region. Recipes for fufu, chapatis, samusas, meat on a stick, plantain, steamed fish, jollof rice, and meat curry. Color photos. For cooking classes and social studies units. Can be used in homes. *Subjects*: Cookery—African; Africa—Social Life and Customs.

Nguyen, Chi. *Cooking the Vietnamese Way.* Minneapolis, MN: Lerner Publications Company, 1985. Easy Menu Ethnic Cookbooks Series. Hardcover $7.95 (ISBN 0–8225–0914–8). Fry Reading Level 5. Interest Level Grade 5–Adult.

Introduction to the cooking and cuisine of Vietnam, with information on the land, history, and the holiday feasts and foods of the country. Includes a typical Vietnamese menu as well as recipes for staples, salads, soups, and stir fries. Recipes for braised and steamed dishes include chicken and tofu. Metric conversion table, index. Color photographs. For units on geography, ethnic diversity, foods, popular culture, and social studies. Can be used at home. *Subjects*: Cookery—Vietnamese; Vietnam—Social Life and Customs.

Parnwell, E. C. *The New Oxford Picture Dictionary.* New York: Oxford University Press. Paper $15.95 Fry Reading Level 4 +. Interest Level Grade 4–Adult.
*The New English Picture Dictionary.* 1991. English/Cambodian. (ISBN 0–19–434349–6).
*The New Oxford Picture Dictionary.* 1989. English/Japanese. (ISBN 0–19–43456–1).
*The New Oxford Picture Dictionary.* 1989. English/Korean. (ISBN 0–19–434360–X).
*The New Oxford Picture Dictionary.* 1989. English/Spanish. (ISBN 0–19–434355–3).
*The New Oxford Picture Dictionary.* 1989. English/Vietnamese. (ISBN 0–19–434358–8).

All of these dictionaries have the same easy-to-use format and can be used at nearly any age and ability level. These all use the same colored illustrations on the same pages. The pictures are appropriate for the words defined, and the portion of the picture that is the definition is well marked and matches a number elsewhere on the page. A different color ink has been used to indicate a language other than English. Indexes in English and the language represented. *Subjects*: Picture Dictionaries—English; English as a Second Language; Cambodian Language Materials—Bilingual; Japanese Language Materials—Bilingual; Korean Language Materials—Bilingual; Spanish Language Materials—Bilingual; Vietnamese Language Materials—Bilingual.

Patrick, Diane. *Family Celebrations.* New York: Silver Moon, 1993. Hardcover $11.95 (ISBN 88188–904–1). Fry Reading Level 6. Interest Level Grade 6–Adult.

Families everywhere have special celebrations that are not built around national and religious holidays. Tells how families celebrate birthdays, marriages, deaths, and other family events. Shows how traditions begin and how to create them. Encourages respect for traditions of all peoples. *Subject*: Celebrations.

Patterson, Wayne, and Hyung-Chan Kim. *The Koreans in America.* Minneapolis, MN: Lerner Publications Company, 1992. In America Series. Hardcover $15.95 (ISBN 0–8225–0248–8); paper $7.95 (ISBN 0–8225–1045–6). Fry Reading Level 6+. Interest Level Grade 5–Adult.

Surveys the immigration of Koreans to the United States from 1903 until the early 1990s. Discusses their contributions to American life and culture; the relationship of Korea with Japan, and China and the problems of population; and the Korean War. Features personalities who contributed in government and public affairs, business, community service, literature, art, music, and entertainment and arts. Black and white photographs. Index. For units in history, geography, popular culture, cultural diversity, and social studies. *Subjects*: Korean Americans; Korean Americans—History.

Pinchot, Jane. *The Mexicans in America*. Minneapolis: MN: Lerner Publications Company, 1989. In America Series. Hardcover $15.95 (ISBN 0–8225–0222–4); paper $7.95 (ISBN 0–8225–1016–2). Fry Reading Level 6+. Interest Level Grade 6–Adult.

Brief history of the Mexicans in the United States. Discusses their life in the American Southwest before the states were formed and the American government acquired their land and how they went from being the native people to being alien residents. Relates their contributions to America's culture and way of life. Discusses discrimination, prejudice, and poverty. Relates personal accomplishments in art, government, community service, literature, sports, and entertainment. Some famous names included are Katherine Ortega, Henry Cisneros, Federico Pena, Jim Plunkett, Lee Trevino, Joan Baez, and James Edward Olmos. Black and white photographs. Index. For units on self-esteem, social studies, history, popular culture, and cultural diversity. *Subject*: Mexican Americans.

Reneaux, J. J. *Haunted Bayou and Other Cajun Tales*. Little Rock, AR: August House, 1994. American Storytelling Series. Hardcover $19.95 (ISBN 0–87483–384–1); paper $9.95 (ISBN 0–87483–342–6). Fry Reading Level 5+. Interest Level Grade 5–Adult.

A collection of ghost tales from the swamps of Louisiana that contains classic Cajun tales, traditional stories, and contemporary original stories. Themes include truth versus illusion, temptation, and good and evil. Humorous as well as terrifying characters people the tales. Swamp spirits and bogeymen, real, and imagined, will delight all ages of readers. To read aloud or read to one's self. Black and white illustrations. Extensive glossary to explain the many colloquial words. For classes in reading, social sciences, local color, and literature. *Subjects*: Ghosts; Ghost Stories; Myths and Legends—Louisiana; Storytelling.

Rutledge, Paul. *The Vietnamese in America*. Minneapolis, MN: Lerner Publications Company, 1987. In America Series. Hardcover $15.95 (ISBN 0–8225–1235–6); paper $7.95 (ISBN 0–8225–1033–2). Fry Reading Level 6 +. Interest Level Grade 6–Adult.

Surveys Vietnamese immigration to the United States. Discusses the contributions made by these people to American life and culture. Talks about the refugees, the "boat people," and their scattering to many locations in America. Mentions some notable Vietnamese Americans and pinpoints states with the most new residents from Southeast Asia. Black and white photographs. Index. For units in history, geography, popular culture, cultural diversity, and cultural literacy. *Subject*: Vietnamese Americans.

Saeteurn, Meuy Yaan. *Pieces of Life from Laos to America.* Oakland, CA: Second Start
Adult Literacy Program, Oakland Public Library, 1996. Paper $3.95 Fry Reading Level 4 +.
Interest Level Grade 6–Adult.

Written by a refugee who experienced childhood in war-torn Laos. She
eventually escaped to Thailand and then came to the United States and finally
settled in California. Written in English, though her native language is Mien,
a Laotian dialect. Descriptions of life in Laos include differences in customs
of courtship and medical options and addiction to opium. Tells of her work to
learn to speak, read, and write English. Inspirational biography of a determined woman. For social studies and history classes. *Subjects*: Autobiography;
Laos; Thailand; English as a Second Language.

Silverman, Robin Landew. *A Bosnian Family.* Minneapolis, MN: Lerner Publications
Company, 1997. Journey between Two Worlds Series. Hardcover $16.95
(ISBN 0–8225–3494–5); paper $8.95 (ISBN 0–8225–9754–3). Fry Reading Level 6 +.
Interest Level Grade 6–Adult.

Describes in detail the events that led to the war in the former Yugoslavia
and the efforts of the Dusper family to escape from Bosnia and make a new
life in Grand Forks, North Dakota. The Duspers are a family of mixed heritage, and this makes their life harder. Forceful look at a current event. Describes Muslim life. Uses a technique somewhat like a docudrama to tell the
story of this displaced family. Color and black and white photographs. Pronunciation guide, bibliography, index. Also includes a folktale from the Dusper's culture. For units on current events, geography, history, politics, social
studies, ethnic diversity, and popular culture. Other books in this series are
available for Armenian, Eritrean, Guatemalan, Haitian, Hmong, Kurdish, Li-
berian, Mien, Nicaraguan, Russian Jewish, Sudanese, and Tibetan families. All
useful with ESL students and their families. *Subjects*: Bosnian Americans;
Refugees.

Sumption, Christine. *Carlos Finlay.* Austin, TX: Steck-Vaughn Company, 1991. Raintree
Hispanic Stories Series. English and Spanish. Hardcover $12.95 (ISBN 0–8172–3378–4);
paper $3.75 (ISBN 0–8114–6755–4). Fry Reading Level 5+. Interest Level Grade 5–Adult.

Examines the life of the Cuban-born physician who developed the theory
that yellow fever is transmitted to people by mosquitoes but was not recog-
nized internationally or scientifically for this work until 1954. Finlay's father
was Scottish and his mother French, but love of their adopted country caused
them to take Spanish names and give them to their children. Carlos was born
a Cuban citizen. Tells of his studies abroad, his return to Cuba, his exile
because of revolution, his many articles about yellow fever and his determined
study of the disease and its causes, his disclosure in 1881 at medical confer-
ences in Havana and Washington, D.C., of his theory about the tie between

the disease and the mosquitoes and its rebuff by scientists. When Walter Reed and others sought a cause for the disease, Finlay's theory was finally studied. Tells how Finlay was slighted in the report and all credit given to Reed for the momentous discovery of cause and contagion. *Subjects*: Finlay, Carlos Juan, 1833–1915; Physicians; Spanish Language Materials—Bilingual.

Thompson, Kathleen. *Sor Juana Ines de la Cruz.* Austin, TX: Steck-Vaughn Company, 1991. Raintree Hispanic American Stories. English and Spanish. Hardcover $12.95 (ISBN 0–8172–3377–6); $3.75 paper (ISBN 0–8114–6752–X). Fry Reading Level 5+. Interest Level Grade 5–Adult.

Examines the life of a seventeenth-century Mexican woman who was a poet, won a place in the court of the New Spain viceroy, and eventually became a nun. Explains her childhood desire to learn as much as she could, her ability to read and write at an early age, her strange beliefs about appearance, and her love of her grandfather's library. Tells how her writing of poetry was encouraged in the viceroy's court. Explains how a young woman who was poor had little chance of a good marriage and how the church might offer the best future. Tells how one of the most brilliant poets in the Spanish language was courted then stifled by church politics. *Subjects*: Juana Ines de la Cruz, Sor, 1651?–1695; Authors—Mexican; Nuns—Mexico—Biography; Spanish Language Materials—Bilingual.

Torrence, Jackie. *The Importance of Pot Liquor.* Little Rock, AK: August House, 1994. American Storytelling Series. Hardcover $12.00 (ISBN 0–87483–338–8). Fry Reading Level 5. Interest Level Grade 5–Adult.

Pot liquor is the by-product of simmered meats and vegetables and the "pot liquor" presented here are tales simmered out of the author's family life, as well as twelve traditional stories shared by her family. The stories can serve as a catalyst for getting students to relate their own stories and tell the traditional tales of their native lands. Black and white pictures of the author and her family. For classes in popular culture, social studies, local history, local color, and literature. *Subjects*: Afro-Americans—North Carolina—Biography; Afro-Americans—Social Life and Customs.

Tunnell, Michael O., and George W. Chilcoat. *The Children of Topaz: The Story of a Japanese-American Internment Camp.* New York: Holiday House, 1996. Hardcover $16.95 (ISBN 0–8234–1239–3). Fry Reading Level 6 +. Interest Level Grade 6–Adult.

Day-to-day account of life in a Japanese American internment camp during World War II. This book documents life for a teacher, Lillian "Anne" Yamauchi Hori, and her 1943 third-grade students in the camp at Topaz, Utah. The daily diary kept by students has words and drawings from twenty entries. The authors have expanded on life in the camp and added archival photographs to place the diary in historical context. Actual diary entries are included. Bibliography, reference sources. For social studies, history, and ethnic awareness. *Subjects*: Japanese Americans—Evacuation and Relocation, 1942–1945; World War—1939–1945—Children; Central Utah Relocation Center.

*Vegetarian Cooking around the World.* Minneapolis, MN: Lerner Publications Company, 1992. Easy Menu Ethnic Cookbook Series. Hardcover $14.95 (ISBN 0–8225–0927–X). Fry Reading Level 5. Interest Level Grade 5–Adult.

Collection of meatless recipes from around the world. Talks about vegetarianism and its forms throughout the world. Explains that attitudes about foods stem from cultures and what is readily available. Tells why religion, ethics, health concerns, and ecology affect our ideas about eating. Explains how to plan an appropriate vegetarian menu. Tells what utensils will be needed, defines cooking terms, and notes special ingredients used. International menus are provided, with both English and ethnic name and pronunciation. Recipes for hot chocolate, unleavened whole bread, rice pancakes, fruit muesli, lentil soup, rice and peas, and jonny cakes. Color photographs. Conversion and equivalency charts. Use for units in health, life skills, home economics, food, religion, ethnic diversity, and customs and lifestyle. *Subjects*: Vegetarian Cookery; Cookery—International.

Winchester, Faith. *African-American Holidays.* Mankato, MN: Capstone Press, Bridgestone Books, 1996. Read and Discover Ethnic Holidays Series. Hardcover $13.25 (ISBN 1–56065–456–2). Fry Reading Level 3 +. Interest Level Grade 5–Adult.

Discusses special times of years that African Americans celebrate, with predominantly color photographs vividly illustrating the text. Holidays include the birthdays of Martin Luther King, Jr., Marcus Garvey, and Malcolm X. Harrambee, Juneteenth, Junkanoo, and Kwanzaa are described. A hands-on section gives a recipe for a special dough to make sculptures during Harambee, a time for focusing on art. Fast facts, words to know, pronunciation guide, address of Internet sites and national organizations, brief bibliography. For social studies, communications classes, and multicultural units. *Subjects*: Holidays; Afro-Americans—Social Life and Customs.

Winchester, Faith. *Asian Holidays.* Mankato, MN: Capstone Press, Bridgestone Books, 1996. Read and Discover Ethnic Holidays Series. Hardcover $13.25 (ISBN 1–56065–458–9). Fry Reading Level 3 +. Interest Level Grade 5–Adult.

Brief facts about the Asian continent. Explains differences in solar and lunar calendars, discusses Asian customs, and illustrates Chinese New Year, Ch'ing Ming (celebrating the beginning of spring and is the Chinese Memorial Day),

Japanese New Year, Buddha's Birthday, Doll Festival, Boys' Festival, and Harvest Moon Festival. Includes a hands-on project for the Chinese New Year. Low reading level. Lists more books to read, includes addresses and Internet sites, defines unfamiliar words. For social studies classes and multicultural units. *Subjects*: Holidays, Asia; Asia—Social Life and Customs.

Winchester, Faith. *Hispanic Holidays*. Mankato, MN: Capstone Press, Bridgestone Books, 1996. Read and Discover Ethnic Holidays Series. Hardcover $13.25 (ISBN 1–56065–457–0). Fry Reading Level 3+. Interest Level Grade 5–Adult.

Colorful photographs of Hispanics in traditional holiday costume illustrate the easy-to-read text. Approximately one page of illustration for one page of text. Briefly lists demographics for Hispanics in the United States. Holidays or fiestas presented include Cinco de Mayo, Corpus Christi, Saint John's Day, Day of the Dead, Posados, Three Kings' Day, Our Lady of Guadalupe, and the traditional Easter season. Has a hands-on project for students to make confetti eggs for the Easter celebration. Brief pronunciation guide and words to know, list of resource books, addresses of note and Internet sites. Use for units on holidays, customs, religion, and Latin America. *Subjects*: Holidays, Latin America; Holidays, Hispanic; Hispanic Americans—Social Life and Customs.

Winchester, Faith. *Muslim Holidays*. Mankato, MN: Capstone Press, Bridgestone Books, 1996. Read and Discover Ethnic Holidays Series. Hardcover $13.25 (ISBN 1–56065–459–7). Fry Reading Level 3+. Interest Level Grade 5–Adult.

Gives brief facts about Islam (the religion) and Muslims (the people who follow Islam). Holidays or celebrations covered are Murharram, Ashura, Mohammad's Birthday, Ramadan, Eid-ul-Fitr, Ide Ahha, Hajj, and other holy days. Discusses prayers, feasts, fasts, and observing the holidays, with one page of illustration illuminating each page of text. Hands-on project for making a bookmark for use with the Koran, the most holy book for Muslims. Helps explain cultural and religious backgrounds and differences. Words to know, brief punctuation guide, list of more books to read, useful addresses and sites on the Internet. Low reading level. For multicultural units and social studies. *Subjects*: Fasts and Feasts—Islam; Holidays—Islamic Countries; Islam—Customs and Practices; Muslims—Social Life and Customs.

Winter, Frank H. *The Filipinos in America*. Minneapolis, MN: Lerner Publications Company, 1988. In America Series. Hardcover $15.95 (ISBN 0–8225–0237–2); paper $8.95 (ISBN 0–8225–1035–9). Fry Reading Level 6+. Interest Level Grade 6–Adult.

Surveys Filipino immigration to the United States and the relationship the United States has had with the Philippines. Examines the history and the people of the Philippines, including the pre-Hispanic times, the revolution, World War II, and independence. Discusses early and modern immigration and personal contributions made to American life and culture by these immigrants, among them Jose Areugo, Barbara Luna, Tai Babilonia, and Roman Gabriel. For units in history, geography, popular culture, cultural diversity, cultural literacy, and social studies. *Subject*: Filipino Americans.

You, Ling. *Cooking the Chinese Way*. Minneapolis, MN: Lerner Publications Company, 1982. Easy Menu Ethnic Cookbooks Series. Hardcover $14.95 (ISBN 0–8225–0902–4). Fry Reading Level 5. Interest Level Grade 5–Adult.

The basics of Chinese cooking, including what utensils and special ingredients will be needed. Discusses the land and people of China and the diverse cooking of the regions. Graphics show how to eat with chopsticks. Shows how a Chinese table is set, as well as a typical Chinese menu. Recipes for egg flower soup, fried rice, Chinese cabbage, and almond cookies. Tells how to prepare tea and rice. Recipe names in Chinese and English. Black and white illustrations and color photographs. For units on social studies, geography, popular culture, ethnic diversity, and home economics. Can use at home also. *Subjects*: Cookery—Chinese; China—Social Life and Customs.

## FICTION

Anaya, Rudolfo A. *Selected from Bless Me, Ultima*. Syracuse, NY: Signal Hill, 1989. Writers' Voices Series. Paper $3.50 (ISBN 1–929631–06–4). Fry Reading Level 5+. Interest Level Grade 7–Adult.

About a young Chicano boy and his family. Ultima, an old woman who is a *curandera* (healer), comes to live with them and changes their lives; hence, it looks at two-intergenerational relationships as well as family living. The author writes about Chicano life in New Mexico particularly. This book contains an adapted selection from the novel, as well as a discussion of the different lifestyles of the Chicano ranchers and farmers. Spanish-English glossary, study guides. Paperback format make it attractive to readers. For units in popular culture, ethnic diversity, geography, and regional culture; for classes in literature; and for recreational reading. *Subjects*: Healers—Fiction; Chicanos—Fiction.

Keller, Rosanne. *Fighting Back*. Syracuse, NY: New Readers Press, 1990. Paper $3.50 (ISBN 0–88336–985–0). Fry Reading Level 3–4. Interest Level Grade 5–Adult.

Tells of the troubles a Korean youth has adjusting to a high school in the United States. Describes the differences in schools and attitudes here and there and covers the troubles with belonging and identifying and the bullying and name calling that can occur. Looks at tae kwon do. Shows that differences can be worked out and strengths are found in many places. Black and white illustrations. For classes in reading, life skills, popular culture, ethnic diversity, social studies and social problems, and sports. *Subjects*: Immigrants—Korean—Fiction; High Schools—Fiction.

Keller, Rosanne. *Honorable Grandfather*. Syracuse, NY: New Readers Press, 1990. Paper $3.50 (ISBN 0–88336–993–1). Fry Reading Level 4. Interest Level Grade 5–Adult.

Deals with the feelings generated when older immigrants come to this country to live with relatives and the problems that the differences in lifestyles and mores can cause for the families. Deals with honor, respect and the treatment of older people. Discusses life in Taiwan and customs there in the past and now. Covers different sports and recreations. Black and white line drawings. For units on intergenerational problems, popular culture, family problems, social life and customs, ethnic diversity, psychology, and for reading classes and recreational reading. *Subjects*: Immigrants—Taiwanese—Fiction; United States—Social Life and Customs—Fiction; Aged—Fiction.

Keller, Rosanne. *The Race*. Syracuse, NY: New Readers Press, 1990. Paper $3.50 (ISBN 0–88336–995–8). Fry Reading Level 4+. Interest Level Grade 5–Adult.

Black and white illustrations enhance this easy-to-read story dealing with Alberto, an immigrant from Colombia who speaks little English. Discusses the difficulties of survival in the workplace as well as socially with few English skills and how he relaxes by running. Tackles discrimination and the treatment of language impairment. Shows how Alberto uses his running skills to better his life and prove he can be the same as his fellow workers. Also teaches that each side has to tackle the differences that separate them. Upbeat story that rewards perseverance. Use for units on ethnic diversity, immigrants, life and social skills, and workplace etiquette. *Subjects*: Immigrants—Colombian—Fiction; Immigrants—South American—Fiction; Races (Running)—Fiction; Employment—Fiction.

Keller, Rosanne. *Talk Like a Cowboy*. Syracuse, NY: New Readers Press, 1990. Paper $3.50 (ISBN 0–88336–996–6). Fry Reading Level 4+. Interest Level Grade 5–Adult.

Story of a Polish immigrant whose family trained horses in Poland and who came to Texas because of the horses. Language is a real barrier to his employment. A moving story that includes humor of the struggle of the hired hand to work his way up to horse trainer. Touts work, study, and perseverance. Appeals to animal lovers. Characters are appealing. Black and white line drawings enhance the well-written story. For classes in reading, biology, popular culture, life skills, and ethnic diversity. *Subjects*: Immigrants—Polish—Fiction; Ranches—Fiction; Texas—Fiction; Horses—Fiction.

Kudlinski, Kathleen V. *Shannon: A Chinatown Adventure, San Francisco, 1880.* New York: Simon & Schuster, 1996. Girlhood Journeys Series. Hardcover $13.00 (ISBN 0–689–81138–1). Fry Reading Level 4–6. Interest Level Grade 4–10.

Fictional account of a young girl who comes with her mother and younger brothers from Ireland to join her father in San Francisco. Explains why the family left Ireland to find religious freedom. Through the eyes of Shannon O'Brien, San Francisco of the 1880s comes alive, as does Chinatown, one of the places she visits with her doctor father. The intrepid Shannon and her friend Betsy unite to help a young Chinese orphan girl who had been sold into slavery and brought to this country from Hong Kong. Features sibling conflict, lost children, animals, and adventure in the historical setting of the bustling and growing city. Cultural conflicts. Good for extra credit reading. More appealing to girls. Features an afterword explanation of historical events covered in the book by the author, whose great-grandmother emigrated from Ireland to this country in 1880. Color and black and white illustration by Bill Farnsworth. Use for units in history, ethnic diversity, immigration, and Irish Americans as well as for recreational reading. *Subjects*: Emigration and Immigration—Fiction; Irish Americans—Fiction; San Francisco (Calif.)—Fiction.

Lee, Marie. *If It Hadn't Been for Yoon Jun.* Boston: Houghton Mifflin, 1993. Hardcover $13.95 (ISBN 0–395–62941). Fry Reading Level 6. Interest Level Grade 6–12.

Adopted as a baby and with a Korean heritage, Alice is happy to be the all-American seventh grader as a cheerleader and with a boy interested in her. Parental pressure to befriend a new Korean student at school is not what she wants. Shows how the friendship with Yoon Jun grows and how her interest in her own heritage is awakened. For units in social studies, popular culture, family and adoption, and ethnic diversity and for recreational reading. *Subject*: Korean Americans—Fiction.

McKissack, Patricia, and Fredrick McKissack. *Christmas in the Big House, Christmas in the Quarters.* New York: Scholastic, 1994. Hardcover $15.95 (ISBN 0–590–43027–0). Fry Reading Level 5+. Interest Level Grade 5–Adult.

A Coretta Scott King Award winner as well as PLA/ALLS Top Title selection for 1994. The illustrations are exceptional in this coffee table–size rendition of both sides of Christmas in the days of slavery in Virginia in 1859. Gives an alternating view of a holiday as seen from very different perspectives: the traditions, foods, and customs at the big house contrast with the amount of time allocated to those in slave quarters after work and service for their own feast and celebration. Excellent for units on history, cultural diversity, and African American history. *Subject*: Holidays—Christmas—Fiction.

Prowse, Philip. *Death of a Soldier*. New York: Educational Design, 1992. Heinemann Guided Readers Series. Paper $5.00 (ISBN 0–435–27167–9). Fry Reading Level 3–4. Interest Level Grade 5–Adult.

Beginner-level story in this guided reader series about a soldier in the war between Catholics and Protestants in Northern Ireland. Shows map of England and Ireland. Gives the background of the religious differences between England and Ireland. The soldier was a youth without a job who joined the army and was sent to Belfast, where soldiers were not welcome, after training. Tells of the patrols when even the children attacked them and the patrol when David was shot to death. Moving description of the deception practiced by the killers and the use of innocent and not-so-innocent civilians. No clues are offered as to whether a Catholic or Protestant sympathizer killed David. Told in a factual, terse fashion with color comic-strip-like illustrations fleshing out the story. Use for units dealing with history, current events, geography, conflict, as well as Ireland and England. *Subject*: Ireland—History—Fiction.

Reiff, Tana. *Hopes and Dreams II Series*. Belmont, CA: Fearon/Quercus, 1993. Paper $4.80 each. Fry Reading Level 3. Interest Level Grade 5–Adult.
   *Fair Fields*. (ISBN 0–8224–3808–9).
   *Here and There*. (ISBN 0–224–3807–0).
   *Making Heaven*. (ISBN 0–8224–3801–1).
   *Many Miles*. (ISBN 0–8224–3804–6).
   *Never So Good*. (ISBN 0–8224–3806–2).
   *Next Life*. (ISBN 0–8224–3802–X).
   *Sent Away*. (ISBN 0–8224–3800–3).
   *Ties to the Past*. (ISBN 0–8224–3803–8).
   *Two Hearts*. (ISBN 0–8224–3805–4).
   *Who Is My Neighbor?* (ISBN 0–8224–3809–7).

An easy-to-read series providing glimpses into the lives of people coming to live in America from all over the world. Ethnic groups represented are Filipinos, Puerto Ricans, Polish, Greeks, Salvadorans, Koreans, Arabs, Indians, Jamaicans, and Japanese. Use for units on ethnic diversity, immigration, geography, social studies, as well as for recreational reading. Attractive format with plenty of white space. The look of a regular paperback makes them more desirable for young people. *Subject*: Immigrants—Fiction.

Reiff, Tana. *The Magic Paper*. Belmont, CA: Fearon Education, 1989. Pacemaker Hopes and Dreams Series. The Mexicans. Paper $3.59 (ISBN 0–8224–3686–8). Fry Reading Level 2–4. Interest Level Grade 5–Adult.

Very easy reading. Tells of the struggle of Mexicans trying to get visas to get into the United States to visit and work and how they sometimes use false papers and pay bribes to be allowed to cross the border. Discusses working conditions and the troubles of people for whom language is a barrier. Tells the story of Lupe and Benito and their struggle to better themselves in Los Angeles and the 1982 law that helped solve their problems. Questions for discussion about ethics and decision making. Use for teaching reading as well as for units in social studies, history, immigration, ethics, and decision making. *Subjects*: Immigrants—Fiction; Immigrants—Mexican—Fiction.

Reiff, Tana. *Nobody Knows*. Belmont, CA: Fearon Education, 1989. Pacemaker Hopes and Dreams Series. The Africans. Paper $3.59 (ISBN 0–8224–3683). Fry Reading Level 2–4. Interest Level Grade 5–Adult.

Fictional story of how a black family coped in the North and South during World War II. Use for teaching reading as well as for units in social studies, history, segregation, United States history, geography, and civil rights. Also use for units on African Americans as well as World War II. Very easy reading in mass market size paperback for new learners. Discusses segregation in the South during World War I and the beginning of the migration north for many blacks. Tells how this was a new way to be segregated. Includes some fictional and early civil rights protests in the South. *Subjects*: United States History—20th century—Fiction; Afro-Americans—Fiction.

Tan, Amy. *Selected from the Joy Luck Club*. New York: Literacy Volunteers of New York City, 1992. Writers Voices Series. Hardcover (ISBN 0–929631–51–X). Fry Reading Level 4+. Interest Level Grade 7–Adult.

An easy-to-read selection from the popular novel about a Chinese American family in California. This selection is about what happens when one woman dies and her daughter is asked to take her place at the mah jong table. June is also asked to go to China and settle her mother's past so she can face her own. Contains a short biography of the Chinese American author, brief history of modern China, and explanation of the game of mah jong, material to discuss, and other useful features. Mass market paperback format makes it attractive to readers. For literature, popular culture, cultural diversity, cultural literacy, and learning to read. *Subject*: Chinese Americans—Fiction.

Tarner, Margaret. *Weep Not, Child*. New York: Educational Design, 1992. Heinemann Guided Readers Series. Paper $5.00 (ISBN 0–435–27267–5). Fry Reading Level 8. Interest Level Grade 5–Adult.

A retelling of an original story by Ngugi Wa Thiong'o, set in Kenya in the 1950s. Tells of the war and strife in the country that pits black against white, white against white, and black against black. Lots of characters in the story, which has love, adventure, and history. Black and white block prints make bold and graphic illustrations of the tragic story. Lists subjects to discuss and understand and provides explanations for uncommon terms. A graphic retelling of a painful and tragic era in African and Kenyan history. For advanced readers. Use for units on African or Kenyan history, well as for recreational reading. *Subjects*: Africa—Fiction; Kenya—Fiction.

# 6

# History and Geography

History and geography are an appropriate link because both involve exploration and the study of lands and countries. This section includes geographical books as well as books with political or historical content about the United States and many other countries. Some biographies of historical figures are included.

## NONFICTION

*Amazing Century: Book Three 1945–1960*. Chicago: Contemporary Books, 1992. Amazing Century Series. Paper $5.58 (ISBN 0–8092–4017–3). Fry Reading Level 4. Interest Level Grade 5–Adult.

Covers the biggest news stories of the period: the cold war, beginnings of rock and roll, the Beat Generation, teens of the times, the Nuremberg war trials, school desegregation, medical successes and inventions, the birth of the National Basketball Association, the Olympics, as well as much more. People included are Jackie Robinson, Joe McCarthy, Harry Truman, and Dwight Eisenhower. Very readable. Workbook format with a magazine layout. Maps, index. For classes in history, social studies, and civil rights and for background reading to increase cultural literacy. Other volumes in this series are recommended. *Subjects*: United States—Civilization—20th Century; Civilization—Modern—20th Century.

Anderson, Dale. *Battles That Changed the Modern World*. Austin, TX: Raintree/Steck-Vaughn, 1994. 20 Event Series. Hardcover $15.96 (ISBN 0–8114–4928–9). Fry Reading Level 5–6. Interest Level Grade 5–Adult.

Oversize book containing maps, charts, photographs, and illustrations that ably present battles ranging from Waterloo to Desert Storm. Includes Gettysburg, Guernica, and Normandy, as well as naval battles. Graphically illustrates how and why battles were won or lost. Index. For units on American or world history, specific eras of history, geography, psychology, social science, political science, and emigration. *Subject*: Battles.

Asikinack, Bill. *Exploration into North America.* Parsippany, NJ: New Discovery Books, 1995. Hardcover $15.95 (ISBN 0–02–718086–7); paper $9.95 (ISBN 0–382–39228–0). Fry Reading Level 4+. Interest Level Grade 4–Adult.

Discusses exploration, cultures, and history of North America from earliest times to the present. American cultures as well as the explorers who mapped and settled the interior of the country. Oversize format provides lot of white space for easy reading and space for many color and black and white photographs, illustrations, and maps. Useful time chart, a glossary, index. Excellent for social studies, history classes, and units on Native Americans as well as a background builder for cultural literacy. *Subject*: North America—History.

Blue, Rose, and Corinne J. Naden. *Who's That in the White House Series.* Austin, TX: Raintree/Steck-Vaughn, 1998. Hardcover $27.83. Fry Reading Level 6+. Interest Level Grade 7–Adult.

Six-volume set that is well illustrated with cartoons, drawings, paintings, and photographs. Includes names of some of the most important people of the era. Gives physical descriptions of each president, as well as his political history. Explores personal lives and achievements. Map, index, glossary, time lines for each president. For units in American history, world history, political science, popular culture, popular history, segregation, discrimination, immigration and emigration, wars and conflicts, current events, money crises, the United Nations, conservation, consumerism, muckraking, literature, civil rights, racial riots, political protest, and geography. *Subjects*: Presidents— United States—Biography; United States—Politics and Government.

*The Expansion Years: 1857 to 1901.* Hardcover $15.95; paper $9.95 (ISBN 0–8172–4302–X).

Informative look at the ten presidents serving from 1857 to 1901: Lincoln, Johnson, Grant, Buchanan, Hayes, Garfield, Arthur, Benjamin Harrison, and McKinley.

*The Formative Years: 1829–1847.* (ISBN 0–8172–4301–1).

The eight presidents are Jackson, Van Buren, William Henry Harrison, Tyler, Polk, Taylor, Fillmore, and Pierce.

*The Founding Years: 1789–1829.* (ISBN 0-8172-4300-3).

The first six presidents of the United States are covered: Washington, John Adams, Jefferson, Madison, Monroe, and John Quincy Adams.

*The Modern Years: 1969–2001.* (ISBN 0-8172-4304-4).

Highlights the presidencies of Nixon, Ford, Carter, Reagan, Bush, and Clinton.

*The Progressive Years: 1901–1933.* (ISBN 0-8172-4303-8).

Covers the terms of Theodore Roosevelt, Taft, Wilson, Harding, Coolidge, and Herbert Hoover.

*The Turbulent Years: 1933–1969.* (ISBN 0-8172-4304-6).

Covers the years of Franklin Roosevelt, Truman, Eisenhower, Kennedy, and Lyndon Johnson. Ranges from public works to public strife, from atomic war to the cold war, and from peace protests to the Peace Corps.

Bowen, Andy Russell. *The Back of Beyond: A Story about Lewis and Clark.* Minneapolis, MN: Carolrhoda Books, 1997. Creative Minds Series. Hardcover $14.95 (ISBN 1-5705-010-2); paper $5.95 (ISBN 1-5705-224-5). Fry Reading Level 5. Interest Level Grade 5–12.

Black and white block illustrations accent this story of the explorations of Meriwether Lewis and William Clark and their intrepid Corps of Discovery. Covers the two years the expedition spent journeying from St. Louis to the Pacific Ocean as they trekked through parts of the Louisiana Purchase that had hitherto been unexplored by Americans. Fairly easy to read. For units on geography, exploration, American West, nature, history, and going into an unknown way of life. *Subjects:* Lewis and Clark Expedition; Explorers.

Buettner, Dan. *Africatrek: A Journey by Bicycle Through Africa.* Minneapolis, MN: Lerner Publications, 1997. Hardcover $17.97 (ISBN 1-8225-2951-3). Fry Reading Level 8. Interest Level Grade 7–Adult.

Oversize book makes an attractive package for the color photographs that highlight the author's 11,855-mile bicycle trek across Africa, from northern Africa to the south and covering fourteen of the fifty-two countries of Africa. Modern adventure with maps. Covers customs, descriptions of the land, and people of the areas visited, as well as the multicultural team that made the trek. From deserts to rain forests. Pronunciation guide, glossary, index. For units in geography, travel, cultural diversity, history, bicycling, and African popular culture. *Subject*: Africa—Description and Travel.


Capstone Press Geography Department. Minneapolis, MN: Capstone Press. One Nation Series.

All of the Capstone Press state books listed below are recommended for classroom use, as are the ones not listed. Each gives an overview of the history, geography, people, and living conditions in that state. Each includes a time line, glossary, Internet sites, addresses, index, and brief bibliographies. All are very easy to read, have striking color photographs and illustrations, and include two pages of quick facts about the states that cover location, size in miles and kilometers, capital, the date admitted to the union, as well the state nickname, state bird, state flower, state tree, and state song. Each book presents in a very brief manner that which is special to each state. For classes and units on history, social studies, and geography and for fun and informative reading.


Capstone Geography Department. *Arizona*. Mankato, MN: Capstone Press, 1996. One Nation Series. Hardcover $18.40 (ISBN 1–56065–440–6). Fry Reading Level 3+. Interest Level Grade 3–Adult.

*Subject*: Arizona.


Capstone Press Geography Department. *California*. Rev. ed. Mankato, MN: Capstone Press, 1996. One Nation Series. Hardcover $18.40 (ISBN 1–856065–354–X). Fry Reading Level 3+. Interest Level Grade 3–Adult.

*Subject*: California.


Capstone Press Geography Department. *Colorado*. Rev. ed. Mankato, MN: Capstone Press, 1996. One Nation Series. Hardcover $18.40 (ISBN 1–56065–356–6). Fry Reading Level 3+. Interest Level Grade 3–Adult.

*Subject*: Colorado.


Capstone Press Geography Department. *Florida*. Rev. ed. Mankato, MN: Capstone Press, 1996. One Nation Series. Hardcover $18.40 (ISBN 1–56065–357–4). Fry Reading Level 3+. Interest Level Grade 3–Adult.

*Subject*: Florida.

Capstone Press Geography Department. *Illinois.* Rev. ed. Mankato, MN: Capstone Press, 1996. One Nation Series. Hardcover (ISBN 1–56065–353–1). Fry Reading Level 3+. Interest Level Grade 3–Adult.

*Subject*: Illinois.

Capstone Press Geography Department. *Louisiana.* Mankato, MN: Capstone Press, 1996. One Nation Series. Hardcover (ISBN 1–56065–442–2). Fry Reading Level 3+. Interest Level Grade 3–Adult.

*Subject*: Louisiana.

Capstone Press Geography Department. *Massachusetts.* Mankato, MN: Capstone Press, 1996. One Nation Series. Hardcover (ISBN 1–56065–437–6). Fry Reading Level 3+. Interest Level Grade 3–Adult.

*Subject*: Massachusetts.

Capstone Press Geography Department. *Michigan.* Mankato, MN: Capstone Press, 1996. One Nation Series. Hardcover (ISBN 1–56065–436–8). Fry Reading Level 3+. Interest Level Grade 3–Adult.

*Subject*: Michigan.

Capstone Press Geography Department. *Nebraska.* Mankato, MN: Capstone Press, 1996. One Nation Series. Hardcover (ISBN 1–56065–443–0). Fry Reading Level 3+. Interest Level Grade 3–Adult.

*Subject*: Nebraska.

Capstone Press Geography Department. *New York.* Rev. ed. Mankato, MN: Capstone Press, 1996. One Nation Series. Hardcover (ISBN 1–56065–352–3). Fry Reading Level 3+. Interest Level Grade 3–Adult.

*Subject*: New York (State).

Capstone Press Geography Department. *Ohio.* Mankato, MN: Capstone Press, 1996. One Nation Series. Hardcover (ISBN 1–56065–439–2). Fry Reading Level 3+. Interest Level Grade 3–Adult.

*Subject*: Ohio.

Capstone Press Geography Department. *Pennsylvania.* Mankato, MN: Capstone Press, 1996. One Nation Series. Hardcover (ISBN 1–56065–438–4). Fry Reading Level 3+. Interest Level Grade 3–Adult.

*Subject*: Pennsylvania.

Capstone Press Geography Department. *Texas.* Rev. ed. Mankato, MN: Capstone Press, 1996. One Nation Series. Hardcover (ISBN 1–56065–355–8). Fry Reading Level 3+. Interest Level Grade 3–Adult.

*Subject*: Texas.

Capstone Press Geography Department. *Washington.* Mankato, MN: Capstone Press, 1996. One Nation Series. Hardcover (ISBN 1–56065–441–4). Fry Reading Level 3+. Interest Level Grade 3–Adult.

*Subject*: Washington (State).

Cleveland, Will, and Mark Alvarez. *Yo, Millard Fillmore! (And All Those Presidents You Don't Know).* New York: Millbrook Press, 1997. Paper $6.95 (ISBN 0–7613–0236–6). Fry Reading Level 5+. Interest Level Grade 6–Adult.

Fun facts about each president with cartoons and comic book captions to make the learning of the presidents of the United States easier. Chronological order. For reading, history, politics, and government units. *Subject*: Presidents—United States.

Cleveland, Will, and Mark Alvarez. *Yo! Sacramento! (And All Those Other State Capitals You Don't Know).* New York: Millbrook Press, 1997. Paper $6.95 (ISBN 0–7613–1237–9). Fry Reading Level 5+. Interest Level Grade 5–Adult.

Mnemonic captions and crazy cartoons enhance a fun and informative look at the learning of America's state capitals, facts about geography, events in history, landmarks of the areas, and famous people of the eras and areas. For units in state government, reading, American geography, history, and popular culture. *Subject*: Geography—United States.

Cone, Patrick. *Grand Canyon.* Minneapolis, MN: Carolrhoda Books, 1994. Nature in Action Series. Hardcover $18.95 (ISBN 0–82714–628–0). Fry Reading Level 5. Interest Level Grade 5–Adult.

The Grand Canyon is handsomely presented through the use of color photographs and an informative text. Covers the history of the canyon, its geography, its geology, its ecology and human impact on it, and its future. Can be used to advantage in conjunction with the Rawlins book, *Grand Canyon*, published by Raintree/Steck-Vaughn (see p. 105). For units on history, travel, geography, and the environment. *Subjects*: Grand Canyon; Grand Canyon—Ecology.

Conrad, Pam. *Our House: The Story of Levittown*. New York: Scholastic, 1995. Hardcover $14.95 (ISBN 0–0590–47370–0). Fry Reading Level 4. Interest Level Grade 7–Adult.

Easy-to-read account of the first Levittown created in the mid-1940s and the effect that these developments had on family life. Chronicles the suburban life and bedroom communities in this country. Shows the effect on the people and the cities themselves when commuting became a way of life. For units on sociology, family living, and popular culture. *Subjects*: Levittown; United States—Social Life and Customs.

Cox, Reg, and Neil Morris. *The Seven Wonders of the Ancient World*. Parsippany, NJ: Silver Burdett Press, 1996. Seven Wonders Series. Hardcover $14.95 (ISBN 0–382–39266–3); paper $7.95 (ISBN 0–382–3967–1). Fry Reading Level 4+. Interest Level Grade 3–Adult.

Looks at the phenomenal architectural achievements of the ancients: the Great Pyramid at Giza, the Hanging Gardens of Babylon, the Colossus at Rhodes, the Parthenon, the Mausoleum at Halicarnassus, the Temple of Artemis at Ephesus, the Statue of Zeus at Olympia, and the Pharos at Alexandria. Contains materials about the times and the people involved in their building. Good material for history and geography units and teaches the history of other cultures as well as scientific discovery. *Subject*: Seven Wonders of the World.

Cox, Reg, and Neil Morris. *The Seven Wonders of the Historic World*. Parsippany, NJ: Silver Burdett Press, 1996. Seven Wonders Series. Hardcover $14.95 (ISBN 0–382–39269–8); paper $7.95 (ISBN 0–382–39270–1). Fry Reading Level 4+. Interest Level Grade 3–Adult.

The Middle Ages is the time frame for these seven wonders: the Krak des Chevaliers in Syria, the Alhambra citadel in Spain, an Aztec city (Tenochtitlán), the Cave of Ten Thousand Buddhas, Great Zimbabwe, Angkor Wat, and the Salisbury Cathedral. The wonders were chosen from the thousand years of history from about 500 A.D. until about 1500, when modern times are said to begin. Oversize format. Color maps, illustrations, and photographs. Glossary, brief index. Easy to read. For geography, history, travel, science, and cultural literacy. *Subjects*: Seven Wonders of the World; Curiosities and Wonders; Middle Ages.

Cox, Reg, and Neil Morris. *The Seven Wonders of the Modern World.* Parsippany, NJ:
Silver Burdett Press, 1996. Seven Wonders Series. Hardcover $14.95
(ISBN 0–382-39271–X); paper $7.95 (ISBN 0–382-3972–8). Fry Reading Level 4. Interest
Level Grade 3–Adult.

Features seven engineering feats that pushed the boundaries of information
and technology forward: the opera house in Sydney, Australia; the Aswan High
Dam; the Channel Tunnel, the Kansai Airport; the Concorde; the Sears Tower;
and the Kennedy Space Center. These seven were chosen by the authors and
editors to represent outstanding examples of human achievement. Covers
problems created by these achievements as well as benefits. Easy to read.
Oversize format. Colorful illustrations and photographs. Glossary, index, diagrams. Fine for classes and units in science, exploration, mathematics, history,
current events, and geography. *Subjects*: Engineering; Seven Wonders of the
World; Architecture.

Cox, Reg, and Neil Morris. *The Seven Wonders of the Natural World.* Parsippany, NJ:
Silver Burdett Press, 1996. Seven Wonders Series. Hardcover $14.95 (ISBN 382–3927–6);
paper $7.95 (ISBN 0–382-39274–4). Fry Reading Level 4. Interest Level Grade 3–Adult.

The natural wonders and spectacles that were chosen for this book are
nature's extremes: the Grand Canyon, the Great Barrier Reef, Mount Everest,
the Sahara Desert, Angel Falls, Sarawak Chamber, and Mauna Loa—all the
largest of their kind. Studying this material is an excellent way to learn about
the planet and provides a sense of place. Oversize format. Colorful illustration,
diagrams, maps, and photographs. Glossary, index. For science, geography,
history, and fun reading. *Subjects*: Landforms; Earth Science; Natural Mon-
uments: Seven Wonders of the World.

Darian-Smith, Kate. *Exploration into Australia.* Parsippany, NJ: New Discovery Books,
1996(95). Exploration into . . . Series. Hardcover $14.95 (ISBN 0–02-718088–3);
paper $7.95 (ISBN 0–382-39227–3). Fry Reading Level 4. Interest Level Grade 4–Adult.

The story of Australia studied from the earliest times to the present, covering at least 50,000 years of very diverse Aboriginal societies. Covers exploration by Asian and European travelers. Excellent historical maps, legends
and myths of the country, indigenous animals, travel, and rock art are included. Penal colonies, importation of cheap labor, and native uprisings are
discussed in this well-done book about the opening of the Australian continent
to trade and settlement. A thorough look at the land down under. Time chart,
glossary, brief index. Oversize format provides lots of white space for easy
reading and accommodates many color illustrations and photographs. For history, geography, social studies, ethnic studies, and general information classes.
*Subjects*: Australia; Australia—History.

Denenberg, Barry. *Voices from Vietnam*. New York: Scholastic, 1995. Hardcover $13.95 (ISBN 0590-44267-5). Fry Reading Level 6. Interest Level Grade 7-Adult.

A collection of first-person accounts, arranged in chronological order, of the longest war in this century: the conflict in Vietnam. Covers the many countries involved. Detailed time line, well indexed, inclusive bibliography. For classes with Vietnamese students as well as other students; units in world history, ethnic diversity, and social studies. *Subject*: Vietnam—History.

Dunnahoo, Terry. *Boston's Freedom Trail*. New York: Macmillan, 1994. Places in American History Series. Hardcover $14.95 (ISBN 0-97518-623-8). Fry Reading Level 3-5. Interest Level Grade 5-Adult.

Easy-to-read material gives good background information on the historical places and events that occurred in Boston. Illustrations enhance the text. Well indexed for easy use. For units on the beginning and fighting of the Revolutionary War in America, popular culture, and the city of Boston. Also a good travel guide. *Subjects*: Boston—History—Revolutionary War; United States—History—Revolution.

Dunnahoo, Terry. *Sacramento, California*. Parsippany, NJ: Dillon Press, 1997. Places in American History Series. Hardcover $26.74 (ISBN 0-382-39333-3); paper $14.95 (ISBN 0-382-39334-1). Fry Reading Level 4. Interest Level Grade 4-Adult.

A guidebook for tourists that also provides a great way to look at America's and California's past. Includes a visit to old Sacramento, a historical district in the capital of California. Time line, some visitor information, well indexed. Easy-to-read format with good use of white space. Color and black and white illustrations and photographs and maps. Good representations of life in an earlier time. Great for use in or near Sacramento. Fun and informational reading. Excellent for geography, history, social studies, and ethnic units. *Subject*: Sacramento (Calif.)—History.

Dyer, Robert L. *Jesse James and the Civil War in Missouri*. Columbia, MO: University of Missouri Press, 1994. Missouri Heritage Series. Paper $5.95 (ISBN 0-8262-0972-6). Fry Reading Level 8. Interest Level Grade 7-Adult.

A different look at the infamous western outlaw, Jesse James, with regional appeal, and at one of the areas hit by the Civil War. Missouri was one of the border states that had conflicts of philosophy in its own territory. Looks at the Missouri Compromise, politics, and wartime gangs. For more advanced readers. Has the flavor of a western. For units on the American West, the American Civil War, and American popular culture. *Subjects*: James, Jesse; United States—History—Civil War; Crime and Criminals—United States.

Echo-Hawk, Roger C., and Walter R. Echo-Hawk. *Battlefields and Burial Grounds: The Indian Struggle to Protect Ancestral Graves in the United States.* Minneapolis, MN: Lerner Publications Company, 1994. Hardcover $19.95 (ISBN 0–8225–2663–8). Fry Reading Level 5. Interest Level Grade 5–Adult.

An excellent description of the ongoing struggle for Native Americans to rebury their ancestral human remains and grave offerings in sacred tribal grounds. Concentrates on the efforts of the Pawnee Indians to reclaim their dead. Describes the problems of recovery from institutions and museums to facilitate this work. Describes burial and mortuary customs; examines the morality and ethics of the problem, as well as the legal aspects. Well-thought-out and-presented thesis. Photographs of human remains. Color and black and white photographs. Well indexed, chapter notes. Use for units on Native American death and burial rites and customs, religion, social studies, ethics, and history. For advanced readers. *Subjects*: Indians of North America—Social Life and Customs; Indians of North America—Mortuary Customs; Indians of North America—Legal Status, Laws, etc.; Archaeology—Moral and Ethical Aspects; Human Remains (Archaeology)—United States—Law and Legislation.

Fisher, Leonard Everett. *Tracks Across America: The Story of the American Railroad 1825–1900.* New York: Holiday House, 1992. Hardcover $17.95 (ISBN 0–8234–0945–7). Fry Reading Level 5+. Interest Level Grade 5–Adult.

Oversize book that takes an in-depth look at the early history of rail transportation in America. Text can be read all at once or broken up into pieces for assignments in specific times or specific places. Covers rail travel in the eastern United States, as used in Civil War, and as used in the expansion westward; the people who were imported to work on the railroads; the adventures and unsettling conditions the first travelers had to endure; and infamous train robberies. Excellent photographs and drawings. For units on history, exploration, American history, popular culture, and treatment of immigrants. *Subjects*: Railroads—United States; Railroads—History; Transportation—History—United States.

Freedman, Russell. *An Indian Winter.* New York: Holiday House, 1992. Hardcover $21.95 (ISBN 0–832409–30–9). Fry Reading Level 6–8+. Interest Level Grade 5–Adult.

Beautiful and accurate drawings and illustrations by Karl Bodmer enhance the telling of the history of the Native Americans, the People of the First Man. Much of the text is from the writing of the explorer Prince Maximilian, who chronicled the life of Native Americans as he saw it in the nineteenth century. The dress, culture, artifacts, and scenery of the area are vividly presented. Will cause readers to stretch their capabilities, but the illustrations add to the interpretation. Appeals to students and adults. For classes on American history, cultural diversity, art, literature, religion, and ethnic diversity. *Subjects*: Indians of North America—History; Indians of North America—Social Life and Customs; Explorers.

Geography Department of Lerner Publications. *Russia*. Minneapolis, MN: Lerner Publications, 1992. Then and Now Series. Hardcover $15.95 (ISBN 0–822528–05–3). Fry Reading Level 5+. Interest Level Grade 5–Adult.

Looks at the popular culture of Russia before and after the breakup of the Soviet Union. Fairly inclusive glossary. Runs the gamut, with illustrations of the jeweled and golden decorations from the times of Peter the Great to the prolific and golden arches of McDonalds. Excellent and profuse color and black and white illustrations. For multicultural classes and units on geography or travel, history, and popular culture. *Subjects*: Soviet Union; Russia.

Hills, Ken. *The 1940s*. Austin, TX: Steck-Vaughn, 1992. Take Ten Years Series. Hardcover $15.95 (ISBN 0–8114–3044–4). Fry Reading Level 6+. Interest Level Grade 7–Adult.

Newspaper-like format makes this an easy-to-use source. Thumbnail-type look at the 1940s provides a very simplistic view of world events, as well as those in the United States. Covers popular cultural events too. Brevity is a plus in an era of factoids and capsule reviews as well as for completeness of coverage of events of the era. Well illustrated. Excellent for units on American or world history, popular culture, and social science. *Subjects*: United States—History—1940–1950; World War—1939–1945.

Holmes, Burnham. *Nefertiti: The Mystery Queen*. Austin, TX: Steck-Vaughn, 1992. Hardcover $26.24 (ISBN 0–8172–1056); paper $14.94 (ISBN 0–8114–0863). Fry Reading Level 3+. Interest Level Grade 5–Adult.

Brief biography of the famous and mysterious Egyptian queen that concentrates on the period in her life when her husband, Amenhotep IV, was trying to change the system of gods and worship in ancient Egypt. Short chapter about the discovery of the tomb of Nefertiti in 1912. The story is then re-created as though Nefertiti were telling it. Tells of her life and the importance of death in their lives. Black and white and color illustrations and photographs show historical artifacts. For units in ancient history, social studies, and customs and for recreational reading. *Subjects*: Nefertiti, Queen of Egypt, 14th Century B.C.; Queens; Egypt—History—To 332 B.C.

Krensky, Stephen. *Striking It Rich: The Story of the California Gold Rush*. New York: Simon & Schuster, 1996. Ready-to-Read Series. Hardcover $14.00 (ISBN 0–689–80804–6); paper (ISBN 0–689–80803–8). Fry Reading Level 2. Interest Level Grade 2–Adult.

An easy-to-read book about the discovery of gold in California and the impact it had there and in the rest of the country. Picture book–type illustrations and maps of the fields and the area. One map shows the really difficult task of getting to the gold fields. For today's students who travel the world in an airplane, understanding the length of the journey and the length of time it took as well as the perils involved can be a surprise. Tells about the journeys; includes some amusing stories about miners and material about Levi Strauss, famous for his blue jeans. For lower grade levels and lower reading levels for units on history, geography, social studies, and customs. *Subjects*: California—Gold Discoveries; California—History—1846–1850.

Kuklin, Susan. *Irrepressible Spirit: Conversations with Human Rights Activists*. New York: G. P. Putnam's Sons. Hardcover $18.95 (ISBN 0–399–22762–8); paper $9.95 (ISBN 0–399–23045–9). Fry Reading Level 6. Interest Level Grade 6–Adult.

Relates the personal experiences of men and women who have encountered human rights abuses. Tells of the cases that human rights workers have been involved in and explains the organization, Human Rights Watch. Talks about political dissidents in China, massacres in Rwanda, ethnic cleansing in Bosnia and Croatia, and street murders in Brazil. A serious book with chapter notes, a bibliography, lots of biographies, and good indexing. For better readers and more mature students. For units on ethnic groups, human and civil rights, history, politics, government, and social studies. *Subjects*: Human Rights; Human Rights Watch (Organization); Human Rights Workers.

Lavender, Davis. *Snowbound: The Tragic Story of the Donner Party*. New York: Holiday House, 1996. Hardcover $16.95 (ISBN 0–8234–1231–8). Fry Reading Level 4+. Interest Level Grade 4–Adult.

The story of the tragedy that overtook the Donner party on the way to the West. This book relates the ordeal of this group as they traveled from Illinois to California in 1846. Describes the trek of the naive Donners across the country; their implicit faith in the less-than-truthful guidebook they were using; and the hardships, the weather, the feuding, and the gruesome winter spent snowed in on the eastern edge of the Sierras. Oversized format provides lots of white space for easy reading. Maps, illustrations, and some photographs are all black and white. For history, geography, travel and adventure, personal narrative, and social studies. *Subjects*: Donner Party; California—History—1846–1850.

Lemke, Nancy. *Missions of the Southern Coast: San Diego de Alcala, San Luis de Feancia, San Juan Capistrano*. Minneapolis, MN: Lerner Publications Company, 1996. California Missions Series. Hardcover $14.96 (ISBN 0–8225–1925–9). Fry Reading Level 4. Interest Level Grade 4–Adult.

A history of the missions along the southern coast of California. Briefly describes the life of the Indians affected by the missions, the impact of the

Spaniards on the Indians' culture, and how the missions influenced the development and growth of California. Full color and black and white photographs and illustrations. Index, glossary, time line, charts and diagrams, pronunciation guide, author information. Particularly useful in California schools, but very helpful for world history, American history, religion, geography, social studies, and ethnic studies. *Subject*: Indians of North America—Missions—California.

Lourie, Peter. *In the Path of Lewis and Clark: Traveling the Missouri River.* Parsippany, NJ: Silver Burdett Press, 1997. Hardcover $19.95 (ISBN 0–382–39307–4); paper (ISBN 0–382–39308–2). Fry Reading Level 5. Reading Level Grade 5–Adult.

Describes Lourie's trip up the Missouri by canoe and motorboat as the traveling companion of William Least-Heat-Moon in his trek across America by water in 1995. He compares it to the trek of Lewis and Clark in American history. Journal format. Color and black and white photographs and illustrations. Lourie interweaves his tale with that of Lewis and Clark. This is a wild and dangerous river that changes course constantly as it crosses seven states. Discusses the Indians still in the vicinity and looks at the landscape through his and historical eyes. Oversized format with an easy-to-use layout, good index. For units on travel, Indians, explorations, American history. geography, and the opening of the West. Also as an example of journal writing in classes to help ESL students express themselves in English. *Subjects*: Missouri River—Description and Travel; Lewis and Clark Expedition (1804–1806).

MacMillan, Diane. *Missions of the Los Angeles Area: San Gabriel Archangel, San Fernando Rey de Espana, San Buenaventura.* Minneapolis, MN: Lerner Publications Company, 1996. California Missions Series. Hardcover $14.96 (ISBN 0–8225–1927–5). Fry Reading Level 4. Interest Level Grade 4–8.

Describes the mission buildings constructed in the early history of California. Balanced treatment of the impact of the indigenous people and their culture by the Spanish missionaries. Attractive material presented with both black and white and color photographs and illustrations. Maps, charts, diagrams, chronology, index, glossary, pronunciation guide. Excellent for use in California schools as well as elsewhere. For regional history, religious history, travel, geography, and American history. *Subjects*: Spanish Missions—Buildings (Calif.); Indians of North America—Missions—California.

Mason, Paul, ed. *Atlas of Threatened Cultures.* Austin, TX: Raintree/Steck-Vaughn, 1997. Atlas of . . . Series. Hardcover $32.83 (ISBN 0–8172–4155–6). Fry Reading Level 6+. Interest Level Grade 6–Adult.

Easy-to-use-book with information about 1,000 different peoples around the world. Highlights people from many different environments and provides detailed case studies of twenty-nine groups. "People pages" tell about different groups and their ways of life and how they are threatened with destruction (maps show where people live and are located). "Continent pages" discuss general situations and common problems facing the peoples, and the maps explain locations of different groups on continents. Excellent color illustrations and maps. List of organizations, books for further reading by level and location, useful web sites, index. For units on anthropology, cultures, popular cultures, environment, geography, history, and cultural diversity. *Subjects*: Atlases; Cultural Diffusion; Population—Maps.

Meyer, Miriam Weiss. *The Blind Guards of Easter Island.* Austin, TX: Steck-Vaughn, 1992. Hardcover $24.26 (ISBN 0–8172–1048–2); paper $14.94 (ISBN 0–8114–6853–4). Fry Reading Level 3+. Interest Level Grade 5–Adult.

Brief discussion of the human-appearing rock structures on Easter Island, with speculation on how and why they got there. Discusses the remarkable lack of interest the original discoverers of the statues and of Easter Island had in the people who lived there in 1722. Covers Captain Cook's later visit to the islands and his finding many statues overturned. Discusses the legends and the mysteries proposed and suggested as possible solutions throughout history. Covers the modern exploration by Thor Heyerdahl. Asks as many questions as it answers. Maps. Color and black and white photographs and illustrations. For units on critical thinking, geography and travel, history, social studies, and anthropology and also fine for recreational reading. *Subjects*: Easter Island—Antiquities; Man, Prehistoric—Easter Island—History.

Murphy, Jim. *The Great Fire.* New York: Scholastic, 1995. Hardcover $16.95 (ISBN 0–590–61547267–4). Fry Reading Level 5+. Interest Level Grade 5–Adult.

Exciting and well-done narrative of the great Chicago fire of 1871 gives readers a feeling of "you are there" by using first-person accounts of the conflagration as told by actual survivors. Photographs and illustrations. Maps, bibliography, index. People who enjoy disaster movies will like this. For units on American history, regional studies, disasters, popular culture, and safety. *Subjects*: Great Chicago Fire—1871; Chicago (Illinois)—History.

O'Mahoney, Kieran. *The Dictionary of Geographical Literacy: The Complete Geography Reference.* Seattle: EduCare Press, 1993. Hardcover $19.95 (ISBN 0–944936–08–2). Fry Reading Level 5+. Interest Level Grade 5–Adult.

Contains most of the essential vocabulary and core knowledge in brief form to understand geography, with over 2,000 concepts, ideas, and places described and explained. A book that can be used by both teacher and pupil. Excellent for increasing the awareness of all students as to where things are in the world and what they mean. Many illustrations and graphics in color and black and white. Easy-to-read format. A cultural literacy book for geography of the world. For science, history, and geography classes as well as in classes to learn to spell these names. *Subjects*: Geography; Place Names; Dictionaries—Geography.

Rawlins, Carol. *Grand Canyon*. Austin, TX: Raintree/Steck-Vaughn, 1994. Wonders of the World Series. Hardcover $16.98 (ISBN 0–8114–6364–8). Fry Reading Level 5. Interest Level Grade 5–Adult.

Contains a wealth of information about the Grand Canyon. Covers history, geology, and geography. Excellent glossary to explain unfamiliar technical terms and extensive listing of other materials about this subject, including videos. Complements the book on the same subject by Patrick Cone and published by Carolrhoda Books. For units in geography, history, geology, and ecology. *Subjects*: Grand Canyon; Grand Canyon—History.

Reeves, Nicholas. *Into the Mummy's Tomb*. New York: Scholastic, 1995. Time-Quest Series. Hardcover $16.95 (ISBN 0–590456–52–7). Fry Reading Level 6+. Interest Level Grade 5–Adult.

Oversize book with spectacular illustrations and photographs in color and black and white. This is a book that will stretch the reader's capabilities. Discusses religions of Ancient Egypt and the Egyptians' burial rites and customs, together with their significance in regard to preparing and outfitting the tombs of the people for their life in the next world. The book covers the lifestyle and social history of these inhabitants in antiquity and presents some of the historical myths and legends that have grown up around the pyramids and mummies. Book can be used as a whole for a unit on Egypt or in separate chapters for units on burial customs, religion, art, architecture, and social studies, as well as ancient history. *Subjects*: Burial Customs; Mummies.

Reiff, Stephanie Ann. *Secrets of Tut's Tomb and the Pyramids*. Austin, TX: Steck-Vaughn, 1992. Hardcover $14.95 (ISBN 0–8172–1051–2); paper $4.95 (ISBN 0–8114–0864–X). Fry Reading Level 3+. Interest Level Grade 5–Adult.

Tells of the building of the Egyptian pyramids and discusses the strange legends and stories associated with these structures. Talks about the possibilities of the pyramids' possessing the powers often attributed to them. Covers the first pyramids, the Great Pyramid of Cheops, and the search for the famed tomb of Tut. Black and white and color photographs. Trade paper size is attractive for readers. For units in history, social studies, popular culture, ancient history, and Egypt and for recreational reading. *Subjects*: Pyramids; Tutankhamen, King of Egypt—Tomb; Egypt—Antiquities.

Rubel, David. *Scholastic Encyclopedia of the Presidents and Their Times*. New York: Scholastic, 1994. Reference Series. Hardcover $16.95 (ISBN 0–590–49366–3). Fry Reading Level 8+. Interest Level Grade 7–Adult.

Fairly complete look at each president, with maps, political cartoons, informational reading, and references on the presidential campaigns. Contains election results from 1788 to 1992. Well illustrated and well indexed. For advanced readers. Best used as a reference source but has a lot of interesting and fun reading. Fine reference source for classes in history and political science and for units on biography, popular culture, and social studies. *Subjects*: Presidents—United States; United States—History.

Steen, Sandra, and Susan Steen. *Historic St. Augustine*. Parsippany, NJ: Dillon Press, 1997. Places in American History Series. Hardcover $14.95 (ISBN 0–382–39332–5); paper $5.95 (ISBN 0–382–39331–7). Fry Reading Level 4. Interest Level Grade 4–Adult.

Looks at the oldest continuously inhabited European settlement in the United States from its earliest days to the present. Discusses Spanish explorers of the sixteenth century and their relationship with the Native Americans; the need for and the uses of the Castillo de San Marcos; colonial St. Augustine; the ethnic transformation of St. Augustine from Spanish to British to Spanish to American; and the generals who fought in Florida and the Indians who bravely fought for their homeland. Easy to read and look at and has black and white and color photographs and illustrations. Can be used as a guidebook. Maps, good index. For units on ethnic groups, Native Americans, American history, travel, Spanish exploration, regional history, and American and Native American heroes. *Subject*: Saint Augustine (Fla.)—History.

Sterling, Dorothy. *Freedom Train: The Story of Harriet Tubman*. New York: Scholastic. Paper $3.99 (ISBN 0–590–43628–7). Fry Reading Level 5. Interest Level Grade 6–Adult.

Tells the story of the woman who constantly risked her life to help other slaves escape via the Underground Railroad in the American Civil War era. A well-written classic. For units in American history and politics, the Underground Railroad, slavery, popular history, geography, black history, and biography. *Subjects*: Slavery; Underground Railroad.

Stevens, Leonard A. *The Case of Roe v. Wade*. New York: G. P. Putnam's Sons, 1996. Hardcover $16.95 (ISBN 0–399–22812–8). Fry Reading Level 7. Interest Level Grade 9–Adult.

Discusses the people and events that led to the decision by the U.S. Supreme Court that legalized abortion. Provides an overview on the history of women's rights and freedom of choice in this country and discusses the problems caused by the decision. The book may be helpful to new immigrants in helping them to understand American mores. A controversial subject. For older readers. Bibliography, some glossaries, amendments to the Constitution, index. Good for classes in social studies, health, women's studies, and civics. *Subjects*: Wade, Henry—Trials, Litigation, etc.; Abortion—Law and Legislation—United States.

Thomas, Paul. *Campaigners*. Austin, TX: Raintree/Steck-Vaughn, 1998. Rebels with a Cause Series. Hardcover $24.97 (ISBN 0–8172–4657–6). Fry Reading Level 6+. Interest Level Grade 7–Adult.

Looks at historic world figures who have campaigned for political, social, environmental, and economic reform: Thomas Paine, Elizabeth Fry, Gandhi, Marcus Garvey, Jacques Cousteau, and others. Easy to read. Color and black and white illustrations and photographs. Index, glossary. Wide coverage. Use for units in political science, the environment, history, economics, social reform, and civil rights. *Subject*: Reformers.

Thomas, Paul. *Outlaws*. Austin, TX: Raintree/Steck-Vaughn, 1998. Rebels with a Cause Series. Hardcover $24.97 (ISBN 0–8172–4658–4). Fry Reading Level 6+. Interest Level Grade 7–Adult.

International and historical flavor to this well-illustrated collection of people who lived outside the law: criminals, gangsters, as well as rebels with legitimate causes who were forced to live outside accepted society. Looks at William Tell, Blackbeard the Pirate, Robin Hood, Jesse James, Ned Kelly, Bonnie and Clyde, and others. Does not glamorize the lifestyles. Easy to use and read. Glossary, index. For units in history, crime and criminals, popular culture, geography, freedom fighters, rebellions, and evildoers. *Subject*: Robbers and Outlaws.

Thomas, Paul. *Revolutionaries*. Austin, TX: Raintree/Steck-Vaughn, 1998. Rebels with a Cause Series. Hardcover $24.97 (ISBN 0–8172–4656–8). Fry Reading Level 6+. Interest Level Grade 7–Adult.

Includes revolutionaries from the United States, Haiti, South America, Russia, Mexico, Ireland, and China. People included are Samuel Adams, Toussaint L'Ouverture, Simón Bolívar, Emma Goldman, Lenin, Zapata, and Michael Collins—all rebels who tried to reform their society. Index, glossary. Photographs and illustrations in easy-to-use format. For units in history, reform, politics and government, culture, revolutions, and heroes. *Subject*: Revolutionaries.

Thomas, Paul. *Undercover Agents*. Austin, TX: Raintree/Steck-Vaughn, 1998. Rebels with a Cause Series. Hardcover $24.97 (ISBN 0-8172-4659-2). Fry Reading Level 6+. Interest Level Grade 7-Adult.

Ten historic undercover agents covered: Guy Fawkes, Daniel Defoe, Raoul Wallenberg, Benedict Arnold, Mata Hari, Tito, and others. Some of the countries represented are England, the United States, Yugoslavia, Germany, Russia, and Sweden. Well written and easy to use, with good illustrations. Index, glossary. For units in world history, American history, spies, wars, secret agents, and psychology. *Subject*: Spies.

Trumble, Kelly. *Cat Mummies*. New York: Clarion Books, 1996. Hardcover $15.95 (ISBN 0-395-68707-1). Fry Reading Level 4+. Interest Level Grade 4-Adult.

Fascinating book with color illustrations about the cat mummies of ancient Egypt. Discusses religions and funeral practices of the Egyptians and looks at everyday life in ancient Egypt. Chapter on the history and development of the domestic cat. List of animals and gods they symbolized, brief chronology of ancient Egyptian history, list of museums in the United States where mummies may be viewed, good bibliography, chapter notes with study information. For classes in history, religion, and popular culture and for units on myths and legends and geography. *Subjects*: Mummies—Egypt; Cats—Religious Aspects; Cats—Egypt; Egypt—Religion; Egypt—Antiquities.

Vaillancourt, Beverly. *Our United States Geography: Our Regions and People*. Maywood, NJ: Peoples Publishing Group, 1994. Our United States Geography Series. Hardcover $11.51 (ISBN 1-56256-119-7). Fry Reading Level 5. Interest Level Grade 5-Adult.

Covers the fifty states, plus Puerto Rico, the Virgin Islands, Guam, Samoa, the Midway Islands, and Micronesia. Contains a map with political divisions, topography, environment, and the migration and settlement of the United States. A workbook-type book in black and white with blue headers for easy delineation of areas. Broken down into geographical regions and not arranged alphabetically. Each sectional division is shown and briefly described. Each state or territory is given three pages of explanation plus highlighted facts, pictures, illustrations, and questions. Presents little-known as well as commonly known information. Although some words and concepts are explained in the text, there is also a glossary plus an alphabetical index. Excellent for classes in history and geography and units on travel and reading. *Subjects*: United States—Geography; United States—States.

White, Tekla. *Missions of the San Francisco Bay Area: Santa Clara de Asis, San Jose de Guadalupe, San Francisco de Asis, San Rafael Archangel, San Francisco Solano.* Minneapolis, MN: Lerner Publications Company, 1996. California Missions Series. Hardcover $14.96 (ISBN 0–8225–1926–7). Fry Reading Level 4. Interest Level Grade 4–8.

A reexamination of the regional early history of California that discusses the establishment of the missions, and describes the buildings and the mission life. Shows their impact on the local culture at the time and their influences on the development of California. Formatted for easy reading, with full-color and black and white photographs and illustrations, as well as maps, charts, and diagrams. Chronology, table of contents, pronunciation guide, glossary. For regional histories, history of religions in North America, explorations, geography, social studies, and American history. *Subjects*: Spanish Mission Buildings—California; Missions—California; Miwok Indians—Missions—California; Indians of North America—Missions—California.

Whitman, Sylvia. *This Is Your Land.* Minneapolis, MN: Lerner Publications, 1994. People's History Series. Hardcover $18.95 (ISBN 0–8225–1729–9). Fry Reading Level 8+. Interest Level Grade 8–Adult.

Looks at the land and history of the United States through an ecological approach. Shows what it was like from the time of the Louisiana Purchase in 1803 and what has changed since then. For advanced readers. For regional studies and units on history, travel, and geography. *Subjects*: United States—History; United States—Geography.

Wilcox, Charlotte. *Mummies and Their Mysteries.* Minneapolis, MN: Carolrhoda Books. 1993. Carolrhoda Photo Book Series. Hardcover $17.21 (ISBN 0–87614–767–8). Fry Reading Level 7. Interest Level Grade 7–Adult.

Not just Egyptian-style mummies are examined but preserved people from all over the world. Helps explain the burial customs of many races and religions and includes the presentation of a doll-like mummy found in Greenland. Can be used in conjunction with the Scholastic Publication by Nicholas Reeves on mummies (see p. 105). Well illustrated with color and black and white photographs and illustrations. For courses in cultures, history, burial customs, and social studies. *Subjects*: Mummies; Burial Customs.

Young, Robert. *Real Patriots of the American Revolution.* Parsippany, NJ: Dillon Press, 1996. Both Sides Series. Hardcover $14.95 (ISBN 0–87518–612–2); paper $5.95 (ISBN 0–0362–39171–3). Fry Reading Level 4. Interest Level Grade 4–Adult.

A balanced look at who were the true patriots during the American Revolution. Discusses those who fought for freedom and those who remained loyal to the crown. Covers the surrender at Yorktown and what led up to it and the struggle for control of the American continent by several countries. A debate format lets students see both sides of the story and provides a forum for making up their own minds. Black and white illustrations and maps. Time lines, bibliography. For history, critical thinking, and social studies. *Subjects*: United States History—Revolution, Revolutionaries—United States—History—18th Century; American Loyalists.

Young, Robert. *The Transcontinental Railroad: America at Its Best?* Parsippany, NJ: Dillon Press, 1996. Both Sides Series. Hardcover $14.95 (ISBN 0–87518–611–4); paper $5.95 (ISBN 0–382–39172–1). Fry Reading Level 4. Interest Level Grade 4–Adult.

Easy-reading material that covers both sides of the building of this railroad, finished in 1869. Debate format that uses the various viewpoints of the historians as well as the political leaders of the time. Presents a few challenges for the readers to any preconceived concept about the railroad. Tries to determine if the building of the railroad was the United States at its best or sheer greed, racism, and unfairness. The dichotomy is well explored. Time line, glossary, index. For ethnic studies, history, critical thinking, social studies and geography, and transportation. *Subjects*: Pacific Railroads; Railroads—History.

## FICTION

Fleischman, Paul. *Bull Run.* New York: Harper, 1994. Paper $4.95 (ISBN 0–06–440588–5). Fry Reading Level 6+. Interest Level Grade 5–10.

Award-winning story of the first big battle of the Civil War. Sixteen participants tell their view of events. Seen from the viewpoints of North and South, black and white, and male and female. Excellent for units in American history, psychology, war, geography, and literature. *Subject*: Civil War—Fiction.

Garden, Nancy. *Dove and Sword: A Novel of Joan of Arc.* New York: Scholastic. Paper $4.99 (ISBN 0–590–92949–8). Fry Reading Level 7+. Interest Level Grade 7–Adult.

Tale of the famous French girl whose voices told her to join the fight to crown the dauphin the king of France. Shows how her faith drove her actions and relates how her best friend questions her sanity but follows her into the quest. For units in literature, comparative religions, French history, psychology, and friendship. *Subject*: Joan d'Arc—Fiction.

Hunt, Irene. *Across Five Aprils.* New York: Berkley, 1996. Paper $4.95 (ISBN 0–425–10241–6). Fry Reading Level 5+. Interest Level Grade 7–12.

The story of a boy's coming of age during the turbulence of the Civil War. Adventurous, bloody, violent, full of love, hate, and tears, as well as faith and loyalty, it teaches about compassion and features well-developed characters. For classes in literature and history and for units in psychology, conflict resolution, and character study. *Subject*: Civil War—Fiction.

Kenna, Gail Wilson. *Along the Gold Rush Trail.* Syracuse, NY: Signal Hill, 1990. Sundown Books. Paper $3.95 (ISBN 0–88336–203–1). Fry Reading Level 4. Interest Level Grade 5–Adult.

Chronicles a young man's trek from Vermont to California in the 1848 gold rush and his bouts with danger and loneliness. Shows the beauty that he sees along the way. The story of a young man's rites of passage in the historical past. Use for units on American westward expansion, history, the Gold Rush, and for personal development. *Subject*: California Gold Rush—1849—Fiction.

McKissack, Patricia. *Run Away Home.* New York: Scholastic, 1997. Hardcover $14.95 (ISBN 0–590–4675–4). Fry Reading Level 3+. Interest Level Grade 4–10.

Inspired by the author's search into her own history. An African American family living in Alabama takes in a runaway Apache teenager in the late 1800s. The main character is a twelve-year-old girl whose mother is part Seminole and whose father is a former slave. Slavery may have ended, but greed, distrust, and hatred of people and things different have not. Looks at the plight of minorities after the Civil War. For younger readers. For units in history, geography, psychology, popular history, slavery, discrimination, prejudice, and genealogy. *Subjects*: Afro-Americans—Fiction; Expansion Years—Fiction.

Myers, Walter Dean. *Glory Field.* New York: Scholastic, 1994. Paper $4.99 (ISBN 0–590–45898–1). Fry Reading Level 7+. Interest Level Grades 7–12.

Chronicles 250 years in the life of an African American family, beginning with the capture and removal from Africa and ending in modern America. Shows the mental and psychological scars that can keep a people down for generations; teaches pride, determination, love, and perseverance; and provides a sense of place and the symbols that signify family. For units in history, family, personal histories, and literature and for recreational reading. *Subjects*: Families—Fiction; African American History—Fiction.

Stadelhofen, Marcie Miller. *The Freedom Side.* Syracuse, NY: Signal Hill, 1990. Sundown Books. Paper $3.95 (ISBN 0–88336–204–X). Fry Reading Level 4. Interest Level Grade 5–Adult.

Tells of the struggle of a black slave named Becky to make it to Canada and freedom. Explores trust between the races and the courage and intelligence needed to make a successful run for freedom. Also has a love theme.

Use for units on family, civil rights, history, and slavery, as well as bravery. *Subjects*: Slavery—Fiction; Underground Railroad—Fiction.

Stadelhofen, Marcie Miller. *Last Chance for Freedom.* Syracuse, NY: Signal Hill, 1990. Paper $3.95 (ISBN 0–88336–206–6). Fry Reading Level 4. Interest Level Grade 5–Adult.

The sequel to *The Freedom Side*, telling of the desire of the slave Gregory to escape to Canada and join the woman he loves, Becky. Gregory's flight north on the Underground Railroad also gives him the option to fight for the freedom of all slaves. Explores decisions on freedom and honor and love. *Subjects*: Slavery—Fiction; Underground Railroad—Fiction.

Wright, Betty Ren. *Red Badge of Courage.* Austin, TX: Steck-Vaughn, 1991. Short Classics Series. Hardcover $11.54 (ISBN 0–8172–1670–7); Paper $5.95 (ISBN 0–8114–6837–2). Fry Reading Level 3+. Interest Level Grade 6–Adult.

An adaptation of the classic by Stephen Crane about a young man's service to the Union side in the American Civil War. The story relates his passage from youth to manhood and his struggle to understand the reality of war. As pertinent for modern times as at the time it was written. Trade paper edition is attractive for use. Color illustrations by Charles Shaw. Brief glossary. For units in American history, peace studies, psychology, and literature, and for recreational reading. *Subjects*: United States—History—Civil War—Fiction.

# 7

# Nature and Science

This chapter includes but is not limited to the biology of humans and other animals, the study of plants, physical sciences, earth sciences, and environmental science. The books listed have subjects that are representative of as many nations as possible. This chapter contains no fiction. Fiction featuring nature and science can be found in chapters 1 ("Adventure, Mystery, and Suspense") and 4 ("Folktales, Myths, Poetry, and Classics").

Bassano, Sharron, and Mary Ann Christison. *Earth and Physical Science: Contents and Learning Strategies*. Reading, MA: Addison-Wesley. Star Science through Active Reading Series. Paper $10.80 (ISBN 0–8013–1348–6); $12.48 teacher's edition (ISBN 0–8013–0986–7). Fry Reading Level 4+. Interest Level Grade 6–Adult.

Program developed for ESL students that covers meteorology, topography, astronomy, oceanography, chemistry, and physics. Includes cooperative experiments, extensive vocabulary activities and glossaries, and strategies to learn science. Workbook format. Use for units in general science, weather, space, and for science experiments. *Subjects*: Earth Science; Physical Science.

Bassano, Sharron, and Mary Ann Christison. *Life Sciences: Content and Learning Strategies*. Reading, MA: Addison-Wesley. Star Science through Active Reading Series. Paper $10.80 (0–8013–0347–8); teacher's edition $12.48 (ISBN 0–8013–0985–9). Fry Reading Level 4+. Interest Level Grade 6–12.

Especially designed program for ESL students that covers botany, zoology, human anatomy, human physiology and human ecology. Provides extensive vocabulary activities and glossaries and has lots of learning strategies for understanding science. Helps students to work cooperatively to learn through scientific thinking processes and do scientific experiments. Use for teaching beginning ESL students in reading and science. *Subject*: Life Science.

Blau, Melinda. *Killer Bees*. Austin, TX: Steck-Vaughn, 1992. Hardcover $14.94 (ISBN 0–8172–1055–5); paper $5.95 (ISBN 0–8114–6857–7). Fry Reading Level 4+. Interest Level Grade 5–Adult.

Story of the special strain of bees developed by the Brazilian government to increase honey production. Discusses their fierce combative and belligerent attitude; the fear and panic these bees created in South America when people were killed by their stings; their spread into the countryside; and measures taken to keep them from coming into the United States. Black and white and color photographs and illustrations. For classes in science, biology, and ecology and the environment. *Subject*: Brazilian Honey Bee.

Buell, Janet. *Bog Bodies*. New York: Twenty-First Century Books, 1997. Time Traveler Series. Hardcover $19.98 (ISBN 0–8050–5615–7). Fry Reading Level 5+. Interest Level Grade 5–Adult.

Describes the finding of the Lindow Man, a Celtic man preserved in an English bog. Discusses methods of identifying and dating ancient finds; Celtic culture and daily life; and how technical advances help us to learn more about the past. Color and black and white photographs and illustrations. Glossary, bibliography. For units in science, technology, history, social studies, and cultures of other lands and the past. *Subjects*: Anthropology; Mummies; Celtic Culture; Forensic Methods.

Buel, Janet. *Ice Maiden of the Andes*. New York: Twenty-First Century Books, 1997. Time Travelers Series. Hardcover $16.98 (ISBN 0–8050–5185–6). Fry Reading Level 5+. Interest Level Grade 5–Adult.

The frozen and well-preserved body of a young Inca girl was recently found in the Andes Mountains in Peru. This book discusses the modern forensic method that made it possible to study her body and date it. From this and other frozen mummies located in these mountains, scientists can acquire information on the life of the Incas. Arranged for easy reading. Color and black and white photographs and illustrations. Glossary, index, further readings section. For classes in science, technology, geography, and social studies. *Subjects*: Anthropology; Mummies: Forensic Methods; Incas.

Burckhardt, Ann L. *Apples*. Mankato, MN: Bridgestone Books, 1996. Early Science Readers Series. Hardcover $14.59 (ISBN 1–56065–448–1). Fry Reading Level 3+. Interest Level Grade 3–Adult.

Very simple text introducing apples: how many kind of apples there are, where and how they grow, and a simplistic history and overview. Shows how to make an apple pomander. For readers at a very low skill level in English. Easy-to-read large print, lots of white space, and very colorful and attractive illustrations. Glossary, brief bibliography. Good for science and life skill units. *Subjects*: Apples; Nature Craft.

Burckhardt, Ann L. *Corn*. Mankato, MN: Bridgestone Books, 1996. Early Science Readers Series. Hardcover $14.59 (ISBN 1–56065–450–3). Fry Reading Level 3+. Interest Level Grade 3–Adult.

Very easy-to-read, colorful book introducing corn: the different types of corn, how and where corn grows and how it is used, and a simple history. In the hands-on section are directions for making a corn husk wreath. Lot of white space in this book that has as much illustration as text. Glossary, a brief list of books for further reading. For units on food, plants, and crafts. *Subjects*: Corn; Nature Craft.

Burckhardt, Ann L. *Potatoes*. Mankato, MN: Bridgestone Books, 1996. Early Science Readers Series. Hardcover $14.59 (ISBN 1–56065–451–1). Fry Reading Level 3+. Interest Level Grade 3–Adult.

An introduction to potatoes: what they are, where they came from, what types there are, where they are grown, and how we use them. Tells how to use a potato to make a hand stamper. Mentions Irish potato crop failure. Simple text profusely illustrated with color photographs. Large print and good use of white space to make these easy to use for low-level readers. Explanatory words, bibliography. For units on food, special studies, and art. *Subjects*: Potatoes; Nature Craft.

Burckhardt, Ann L. *Pumpkins*. Mankato, MN: Bridgestone Books, 1996. Early Science Readers Series. Hardcover $14.59 (ISBN 1–56065–449–X). Fry Reading Level 3+. Interest Level Grade 3–Adult.

Discusses the use and growing of pumpkins in the United States. Explains how to make pumpkin tambourines. Very simple text with lots of color illustrations. Mentions Japanese belief that pumpkin is a good luck food. Glossary, list of more books to read. For units on food, plants, and music. *Subjects*: Pumpkins; Nature Craft.

Coleman, Penny. *Corpses, Coffins and Crypts: A History of Burial*. New York: Henry Holt, 1997. Hardcover $16.95 (ISBN 0–80505066–3). Fry Reading Level 5. Interest Level Grade 7–12.

Funeral sciences both past and present are covered in this easy-to-follow book that will interest readers from all cultures. Covers death and burial across time and across cultures. Lots of historical and anthropological research. Well illustrated. For units on death, customs and traditions, history, social studies, and cultural diversity. *Subjects*: Death and Dying.

Cone, Patrick. *Wildfire*. Minneapolis, MN: Carolrhoda Books, 1997. Nature in Action Series. Hardcover $14.96 (ISBN 0–87614–936–0); paper $5.95 (ISBN 1–57505–017–7). Fry Reading Level 4+. Interest Level Grade 4–Adult.

Describes uncontrolled fires—wildfires—and explains how they burn grasslands and forests all over the world. Explains how and where these fires start and when they are harmful and when they are important to a healthy ecosystem. Explains how fires are fought and how they can be prevented. Attractively formatted book makes judicial use of illustration to highlight the text. Diagrams included. Glossary, index, author biography on jacket. For units in science and social studies and for extra credit. *Subjects*: Wildfires; Forest Fires; Fires.

Dahl, Michael. *Inclined Planes*. Mankato, MN: Bridgestone Books, 1996. Early Reader Science Series. Hardcover $14.59 (ISBN 1–56065–447–3). Fry Reading Level 3+. Interest Level Grade 3–Adult.

A simple book about simple machines, for low-level learners. This well-illustrated book has minimal text and explains what an inclined plane is and how it can be used to make life and work easier. Includes a simple science experiment. Boldface words explained, list of more books on the subject. For units in physics and science. *Subjects*: Simple Machines; Inclined Planes.

Dahl, Michael. *Levers*. Mankato, MN: Bridgestone Books, 1996. Early Reader Science Series. Hardcover $14.59 (ISBN 1–56065–444–9). Fry Reading Level 3+. Interest Level Grade 3–Adult.

Explains some of the nature of work and how it can be made easier. Includes a science experiment that shows how to make a lever. Profusely illustrated to help explain the principle of the lever. Very easy-to-read text with a lot of white space and large print, for low-level learners. Boldface words defined, list of suggested readings. For units on science, automotive shop, and physics. *Subjects*: Simple Machines; Levers.

Dahl, Michael. *Pulleys*. Mankato, MN: Bridgestone Books, 1996. Early Reader Science Series. Hardcover $14.59 (ISBN 1–56065–445–7). Fry Reading Level 3+. Interest Level Grade 3–Adult.

A very simple text, surrounded by white space and amply illustrated with color photographs, that defines machines and explains pulleys. Includes a science experiment that shows how to make a block and tackle pulley system.

Boldface words defined, list of suggested readings. For low-level readers. For units in physics, science, and automotive shop. *Subjects*: Simple Machines; Pulleys.

Dahl, Michael. *Wheels and Axles*. Mankato, MN: Bridgestone Books, 1996. Early Reader Science Series. Hardcover $14.59 (ISBN 1–56065–446–5). Fry Reading Level 3+. Interest Level Grade 3–Adult.

Defines machines, explains wheels, axles, and gears and their use in work and play; and explains clockwise and counterclockwise. Shows how to make a wheel. Very simple text with many useful illustrations. For low-level readers. For units in physics, science, and automotive shop. *Subjects*: Simple Machines; Wheels; Axles.

Dudley, Karen. *Bald Eagles*. Austin, TX: Raintree/Steck-Vaughn, 1998. Untamed World Series. Hardcover $26.40 (ISBN 0–8172–4571–5). Fry Reading Level 6+. Interest Level Grade 6–Adult.

Provides a unique combination of science, legend, environment, and literature in covering the social life, habitat, food, rivalry, and current status of this eagle. Presents opposing views on issues of conservation. Easy to read. Good mix of photographs and illustrations, mainly in color. Uses sidebars to highlight facts. Lists twenty interesting facts about the subject. Index, glossary, bibliography. Excellent for units dealing with conservation, the environment, birds, biology, and popular customs and beliefs. *Subjects*: Bald Eagles; Eagles.

Dudley, Karen. *Giant Pandas*. Austin, TX: Raintree/Steck-Vaughn, 1998. Untamed World Series. Hardcover $26.40 (ISBN 0–8172–4566–9). Fry Reading Level 6+. Interest Level Grade 5–Adult.

Food, life cycle, habitat, social life, and endangerment of this native of China are covered. Includes folklore, literature, and fascinating facts. The sidebar and box arrangement for interesting highlights make this book easy to read and use. Judicious mix of photographs and illustrations enhances explanations of the panda's features, such as its markings and size and adaptations it has made for its survival. Bibliography, glossary, index. For units on geography, animals, endangered species, and popular culture and beliefs. *Subjects*: Giant Pandas; Pandas.

Dudley, Karen. *Wolves*. Austin, TX: Raintree/Steck-Vaughn, 1998. Untamed World Series. Hardcover $26.40 (ISBN 0–8172–4561–8). Fry Reading Level 6+. Interest Level Grade 5–Adult.

Looks at the lives of wolves as pack creatures. Investigates their food habits, life cycles, physical characteristics, and habitats and discusses their family and social order, environmental status, and the literature, folklore, and controversy surrounding them. Excellent mix of illustration and photographs in color. List of facts, glossary, suggested further reading, index. For units on life sciences, animals, territories, environment, prejudice, and popular culture. *Subject*: Wolves.

Fornari, Giuliano. *Inside the Body*. New York: DK Publishing, 1996. Lift-the-Flap-Book. Hardcover $16.95 (ISBN 0–7894–0999–2). Fry Reading Level 4+. Interest Level Grade 4– Adult.

This oversize book has only a few pages but is spectacularly illustrated and diagrammed to reveal the working of the inner body of a human being when the over sixty flaps are folded up. Opens downward like a hanging calendar. Color. Brief and succinct explanations and definition of scientific terms. Excellent illustrations and diagrams that are easy to comprehend. For classes in science, biology, and health as well as science experiments. Unusual and useful. *Subjects*: Human Anatomy; Human Body; Biology; Health.

Fortman, Janis L. *Creatures of Mystery*. Austin, TX: Steck-Vaughn, 1992. Hardcover $14.94 (ISBN 0–8172–1063–6); paper $5.95 (ISBN 0–8114–6855–0). Fry Reading Level 4+. Interest Level Grade 5–Adult.

An easy-to-read and simple-to-understand book that details the curious behavior of several animals, including salmon, lemmings, whales, caribou, and plants that eat insects. Tells of the instincts that drive them to mate and also to death. Color and black and white illustrations and photographs. For science, biology, and reading; classes to study animal and human behavior; and for recreational reading. *Subjects*: Zoology—Miscellanies; Animal Migration; Insectivorous Plants; Animals—Miscellanies.

Fradin, David Brindell. *Searching for Alien Life: Is Anyone Out There?* New York: Twenty-First Century Books, 1997. Hardcover $16.98 (ISBN 0–8050–4573–2). Fry Reading Level 5+. Interest Level Grade 7–Adult.

Discusses several of the projects across the world (and out of it) that have tried to locate signs of extraterrestrial life. Explains probes to other planets and outer space. Color and black and white photographs and illustrations, text. Index, bibliography. For units in science, physics, astronomy, space, and technology. *Subject*: Outer Space.

Gottlieb Joan S. *Plant Life*. Austin, TX: Steck-Vaughn, 1996. Wonders of Science Series. Hardcover $14.94 (ISBN 0–8114–7489–5). Fry Reading Level 4+. Interest Level Grade 5– Adult.

A workbook of use to students studying all kinds of plant life. Black and white drawings, photographs, and illustrations to make plant recognition easier. Can be useful for home situations to know and grow plants. Pertinent questions and answers for learners. Excellent for biology and botany classes, as well as geography and learning to read. *Subjects*: Plants; Botany; Gardening.

Jarrow, Gail, and Paul Sherman. *Naked Mole-Rats*. Minneapolis, MN: Carolrhoda Books. Nature Watch Series. Hardcover $14.96 (ISBN 0–87614–995–6). Fry Reading Level 2–4. Interest Level Grade 4–Adult.

Interesting book about some weird creatures. East African creature who lives under hard soil is strange looking, and some of the color photographs could be considered repulsive. For students who are interested in animals. Well-presented text and full-color photographs explain the text. Glossary, index, author information. For units on biology, geography, animals, and nature. Could also be used for special reports. *Subjects*: Naked Mole Rat; Rodents.

Johnson, Sylvia A. *Ferrets*. Minneapolis, MN: Carolrhoda Books, 1997. Nature Watch Series. Hardcover $14.95 (ISBN 1–57505–014–5). Fry Reading Level 6. Interest Level Grade 6–Adult.

Colorful illustrations (as well as black and white) help readers learn about the lifestyle and the family tree of this little animal known all over the world and is easily recognizable by students from many lands. Helpful for those with ferrets as pets. Describes their use as a working animal. Easy to read. Author information. For units on pets, animals, and popular culture and customs. *Subjects*: Ferrets; Ferrets as Pets.

Levine, Marie. *Great White Sharks*. Austin, TX: Raintree/Steck-Vaughn, 1998. Untamed World Series. Hardcover $24.60 (ISBN 0–8172–4569–3). Fry Reading Level 5+. Interest Level Grade 5–Adult.

Examines the life and habitat of the great white shark as well as its place in the environment and conservation actions. Covers the legends, literature, and folklore that surround them and includes opposing viewpoints about the sharks, as well as twenty interesting facts about them. Good mix of color photographs plus diagrams. Glossary, index, list of further reading. This is a good series about animals of the world. For units in environment, marine biology, adventure, biology, zoology, and popular culture and beliefs. *Subjects*: White Sharks; Sharks; Endangered Species.

Lewington, Anne. *Atlas of the Rain Forest*. Austin, TX: Raintree/Steck-Vaughn, 1997. Atlas of . . . Series. Hardcover $32.83 (ISBN 0–9172–4756–4). Fry Reading Level 6+. Interest Level Grade 5–Adult.

A thematically arranged atlas that is profusely illustrated for easy understanding. Covers endangered plants and animals and indexes them for easy availability. Detailed maps and oversized for better use of illustrations. Explains how to use the book and describes the rain forests of the world—in North America, South America, Africa, mainland Asia, Southeast Asia, and Australasia—and the endangered species of plants and animals. Some plants included are the western red cedar, the chewing gum tree, the Brazil nut tree, the African oil palm, and bamboo; some animals included are the spotted owl, the jaguar, the mountain gorilla, the sloth bear, birdwing butterflies, and tree kangaroos. Glossary, bibliography, multimedia suggestions, addresses for information. For units on the environment, endangered species, ecology, geography, animals, plants, and how to use maps. *Subjects*: Rain Forests—Maps; Rain Forest Ecology—Maps.

Lisker, Tom. *Terror in the Tropics: The Army Ants*. Austin, TX: Steck-Vaughan, 1992. Hardcover $11.97 (ISBN 0–81172–1060–1); paper $9.27 (ISBN 0–8114–6866–6), Fry Reading Level 4+. Interest Level Grade 4–Adult.

Introduction to army ants and their habits and habitats. Discusses the social aspect of ant lives and their effect on humans. Covers the myths and legends that surround these and other ants and discusses their bodily makeup and their uses in history and medicine. Drawings, cartoons, and photographs in both color and black and white. For units in biology, science, ecology, environment, geography, and sociology. *Subjects*: Army Ants; Ants.

Mara, W. P. *Anoles*. Mankato, MN: Capstone Press, 1996. Lizards Series. Hardcover $18.40 (ISBN 1–56065–425–2). Fry Reading Level 4. Interest Level Grade 4–Adult.

Describes the physical characteristics, habitat, and behavior of the anole lizard, with two pages of fast facts. Briefly explains the scientific classification system and shows which countries have anoles. Discusses conservation. Color photographs, illustrations, and diagrams. Maps, glossary, index, Internet sites, bibliography. For units on science, conservation, nature, animals, geography, and biology. Also good as special credit for students who like lizards. *Subjects*: Anoles; Lizards.

Mara, W. P. *Chameleons*. Mankato, MN: Capstone Press, 1996. Lizards Series. Hardcover $18.40 (ISBN 1–56065–399–X). Fry Reading Level 4. Interest Level Grade 4–Adult.

Two pages of fast facts on chameleons for information highlights, with a map showing where true chameleons live and a diagram explaining the animal kingdom. Discusses the physical characteristics of these lizards, their daily life, and how they reproduce, and the beautiful photographs illustrate their ability to change colors. Discusses how students can aid in their conservation. Glossary, index, bibliography, Internet sites. For classes in biology and geography and units on animals and conservation. Extra credit material for students interested in lizards. Can tie in with native lands. *Subjects*: Chameleons; Lizards.

Mara, W. P. *Geckos*. Mankato, MN: Capstone Press, 1996. Lizards Series. Hardcover $18.40 (ISBN 1–56065–427–9). Fry Reading Level 4. Interest Level Grade 4–Adult.

Discusses one of the world's most widespread lizards. Two pages of fast facts as well as brilliant color photographs, maps, and diagrams. Discusses the physical characteristics of this lizard, as well as its habits and its way of life, and offers suggestions for their conservation. For intermediate readers. Glossary, bibliography, index, Internet sites. Excellent for use in biology, geography, and classes and units on conservation. Helpful for students who like lizards and want something extra to read. Represent several countries. *Subjects*: Geckos; Lizards.

Mara, W. P. *Iguanas*. Mankato, MN: Capstone Press, 1996. Lizards Series. Hardcover $18.40 (ISBN 1–56065–426–0). Fry Reading Level 4. Interest Level Grade 4–Adult.

Describes kinds of iguanas, where they live, their physical characteristics, their daily life, and what they eat. Tells where iguanas can be seen and how students can help conserve them. As many pages of illustrations as of text. For intermediate readers who are interested in animals or may have a lizard as a pet. Color photographs illustrate the text. Diagrams and maps explain it. Two pages of fast facts about iguanas. Index, glossary, bibliography, Internet sites. For classes in biology and geography and for units on conservation and exotic pets. *Subjects*: Iguanas; Lizards.

Martin, James. *Great White Sharks: The Ocean's Most Deadly Killers*. Minneapolis, MN: Capstone Press, 1995. Animals and the Environment Series. Hardcover $19.00 (ISBN 1–56065–241–1). Fry Reading Level 4+. Interest Level Grade 4–Adult.

These deadly killers of the ocean are covered in equal amounts of text and illustration. Color photographs add life to the printed word, and a range map shows where they live. Brief shark facts included. Discusses the lifestyle of the shark, their ancient relatives, and what they hunt and eat. Tells how they live and how they relate to people. Talks about their future. For intermediate readers. Glossary, suggested readings, useful addresses. For units on sharks, predators, and conservation. Good for special reports. International interest. *Subjects*: White Sharks; Sharks.

Martin, James. *Komodo Dragons: Giant Lizards of Indonesia*. Minneapolis, MN: Capstone Press, 1995. Animals and the Environment Series. Hardcover $19.00 (ISBN 1–56065–238–1). Fry Reading Level 4+. Interest Grade Level 4–Adult.

Colorful photographs provide visual amplification of the text in this book that tells about the largest lizard living today. Map of range of dragon provided, as well as fast facts. Known as the dragon with bad breath because of its feeding habits and also because of the bacteria in its mouth. These dangerous dragons have been known to attack their own kind and an occasional human. Provides a history of the animal and talks about its endangered status. Index, glossary, bibliography. For units in biology, zoology, conservation, and geography. *Subjects*: Komodo Dragons; Lizards.

Martin, James. *Lemurs and Other Animals of the Madagascar Rain Forest.* Minneapolis, MN: Capstone Press, 1995. Animals and the Environment Series. Hardcover $19.00 (ISBN 1–56065–237–3). Fry Reading Level 4+. Interest Level Grade 4–Adult.

Describes primates, the island of Madagascar, early animals of the island and those there now, some of the plants, and the endangered rain forest. Contains brief facts page as well as a range map. Excellent color photographs make up as much of the book as the text. Full of interesting information, including some useful for multicultural units. Glossary, suggested readings, useful addresses, index. For classes in biology, geography, and science and for units dealing with conserving ecosystems and endangered species. *Subjects*: Lemurs; Rain Forest Animals; Zoology—Madagascar.

Martin, James. *Poisonous Lizards: Gila Monsters and Mexican Beaded Lizards.* Minneapolis, MN: Capstone Press, 1995. Animals and the Environment Series. Hardcover $19.00 (ISBN 1–56065–240–3). Fry Reading Level 4+. Interest Level Grade 4–Adult.

Features Gila monsters and Mexican beaded lizards. Has a listing of brief facts and a range map and discusses the physical habitat and characteristics of these lizards and their ancestry. Color photographs well illustrate the text and make up about half of the book. Includes tall tales and legends of the Gila monster, points out how the life of a poisonous lizard differs from the nonpoisonous, and discusses the future of these endangered animals. Glossary, index, useful addresses. For intermediate readers. For classes in biology and geography and for units on social studies and conservation. Good for special reports. *Subjects*: Gila Monster; Mexican Beaded Lizard.

Martin, James. *Spitting Cobras of Africa.* Minneapolis, MN: Capstone Press, 1995. Animals in the Environment Series. Hardcover $19.00 (ISBN 1–56065–239–X). Fry Reading Level 4+. Interest Level Grade 4–Adult.

Discusses the physical characteristics and living arrangements of this highly poisonous snake, its enemies (both human and animal), and its endangered species classification and methods being used to protect it. Makes good use of highlighted information. Half color photography, half text. For intermediate readers. There is a range map and a collection of brief facts. Glossary, index, bibliography. For units on animals, reptiles, Africa, biology, geography, and conservation. *Subjects*: Cobras: Poisonous Snakes; Snakes.

McMillan, Bruce. *The Weather Sky.* New York: Farrar Straus Giroux, 1991. Hardcover $16.95 (ISBN 0–374–38261–1). Fry Reading Level 5. Interest Level Grade 5–Adult.

Shows how to interpret weather maps and to recognize what the sky has to say about weather. Understandable and easy to read. Good photographs, illustrations, and graphics. Very good to use with the Internet weather sites and the television weather channels for learning. For units in science, weather, and reading. *Subject*: Weather.

Nielsen, Nancy J. *Killer Whales: The Orcas of the Pacific Ocean.* Minneapolis, MN: Capstone Press, 1995. Animals and the Environment Series. Hardcover $19.00 (ISBN 1–56065–236–5). Fry Reading Level 4+. Interest Level Grade 4–Adult.

Orcas, or killer whales, are beautifully illustrated here with color photographs. There is a range map and a page of quick facts. Explains what and how much they eat, their physical characteristics, their speed and how they breathe, their lives, how they communicate, their place in the environment, and their lives in captivity. Glossary, bibliography, index. Lists places where killer whales may be seen, as well as useful addresses. For units in biology, zoology, endangered species, oceanography, and conservation. Usually a popular subject. *Subjects*: Killer Whale; Killer Whale—Behavior; Whales.

Platt, Stephen. *Stephen Biesty's Incredible Explosions.* New York: DK Publishing, 1996. Hardcover $19.95 (ISBN 0–7894–1024–9). Fry Reading Level 4+. Interest Level Grade 3–Adult.

A picture book that takes a humorous look at twelve places, past and present, from a different point of view. Places and things are taken apart in the picture so that the parts are visible and explainable. We get a detailed and explanatory look at a fire, a steam tractor, a windmill, Venice, a cross-section of a city, a tower bridge, a space station, the Antarctic base, a human body, an airport, a movie studio, and the Grand Canyon. A neat way to learn what things are. Layers and strata and words to explain. Oversized. Index. Use for classes in reading, life skills, art, and drawing, as well as for recreational reading. *Subject*: Construction.

Sayre, April Pulley. *Exploring Earth's Biomes.* New York: Twenty-First Century Books. Hardcover $197.96 (set), $15.98 (per volume) (ISBN 0–8050–3710–1). Fry Reading Level 5+. Interest Level Grade 5–Adult.

A twelve-book series on ecology that is easy to read and comprehend yet of interest to older students. Topics covered are coral reefs, desert, grassland, lake and pond, ocean, river, and stream, seashore, taiga, temperate deciduous forests, tropical rain forests, tundra, and wetland. Contains science projects. Each book has a What You Can Do to Help section. Photographs and diagrams help explain the text. Glossaries, indexes, bibliographies. Helpful for reports and term papers. For in units on nature, ecology, geography, environment, biology, and botany. *Subject*: Ecology.

Souza, D. M. *Hurricanes*. Minneapolis, MN: Carolrhoda Books, 1996. Nature in Action Series. Hardcover $14.96 (ISBN 0–87614–861–5); paper $7.95 (ISBN 0–87614–955–7). Fry Reading Level 4+. Interest Level Grade 4–Adult.

Hurricanes and their devastation are graphically illustrated in color in this up-to-date book. Covers how and why a hurricane develops and what it can do, the damage these storms can cause, and ways to predict and survive them. Contains some fascinating facts. Metric conversion chart, index, glossary. For use in hurricane areas, particularly for people who have no experience with this type of storm. For units on weather, climate, geography, nature, and science. *Subject*: Hurricanes.

Staiger, Ralph C. *Thomas Harriot, Science Pioneer*. New York: Clarion Books, 1997. Hardcover $18.00 (ISBN 0–395–67296–1). Fry Reading Level 5. Interest Level Grade 5–Adult.

An interesting study of the Renaissance scholar who made many contributions to mathematics, astronomy, and botany. Harriot was an explorer who also studied alchemy and Jupiter. Illustrated with archival prints and maps. For units on science, nature, writing, botany, and mathematics. *Subject*: Harriot, Thomas.

Stewart, Gail. *The Appaloosa Horse*. Minneapolis, MN: Capstone Press, 1995. Learning about Horses Series. Hardcover $18.40 (ISBN 1–56065–243–8). Fry Reading Level 4. Interest Level Grade 4–Adult.

Two pages of quick facts introduce this book about these striking and distinctive horses. Discusses their history and arrival in America, their linkage with the Nez Percé Indians, and how this link nearly caused their extinction. Half illustration, half text. Color photographs. Index, glossary, useful addresses, suggested reading. For horse-loving students. Also a good way to introduce this American horse to students from other countries. For units on American history, geography, Native Americans, social studies, and animals. *Subjects*: Appaloosa Horse; Horses.

Stewart, Gail. *The Arabian Horse*. Minneapolis, MN: Capstone Press, 1995. Learning about Horses Series. Hardcover $18.40 (ISBN 1–56065–244–6). Fry Reading Level 4. Interest Level Grade 4–Adult.

Two pages of quick facts set the stage for a well-illustrated book about a horse that is at home in Poland, Saudi Arabia, Egypt, Canada, England, and many other countries, as well as the United States. Describes the legend of the beginning of the Arabian line with Mohammed and other history of this oldest horse breed. Identifies the physical parts of the horse and the life and activities involved in training these horses. Discusses their value and uses. Useful addresses, glossary, bibliography, index. For units on geography, animals, social studies, and multicultural studies and for elective reading. *Subjects*: Arabian Horse; Horses.

Stewart, Gail. *The Quarter Horse*. Minneapolis, MN: Capstone Press, 1995. Learning about Horses Series. Hardcover $18.40 (ISBN 1–56065–242–X). Fry Reading Level 4. Interest Level Grade 4–Adult.

Traces the history of this "do-it-all horse," which originated in North America. Looks at its beginnings and development and shows it as a work horse and a great competitor. Half color photographs, half text. Useful glossary, index, suggested reading, addresses for more information. For classes on contemporary life, social studies, and American history and units on animals. For horse lovers and for recreational reading. *Subjects*: Quarter Horse; Horses.

Stewart, Gail. *The Thoroughbred Horse: Born to Run*. Minneapolis, MN: Capstone Press, 1995. Learning about Horses Series. Hardcover $18.40 (ISBN 1–56065–245–4). Fry Reading Level 4. Interest Level Grade 4–Adult.

The horse that is billed as the fastest creature on earth is represented through pictures, words, and diagrams, as well as two pages of quick facts. Covers the history and development of the thoroughbred and its uses and popularity today. Discusses its racing history throughout the world. Bibliography, glossary, index, useful addresses. Can be used for recreational reading, and animal and horse lovers enjoy it. For social studies, lifestyles, geography, and animal units. *Subjects*: Thoroughbred Horse; Horses.

Streissguth, Tom. *Tractors*. Minneapolis, MN: Capstone Press, 1995. Cruisin' Series. Hardcover $13.80 (ISBN 1–56065–254–3). Fry Reading Level 4. Interest Level Grade 4–Adult.

Colorful photographs depict tractors of all types, sizes, colors, and ages. Describes the history of tractors and the use of both steam and gasoline to power them; early and modern manufacturers; and the constant experimentation to build better tractors, even driverless ones. Glossary is helpful, but there are many words and concepts here to work on. Bibliography, index, addresses. For units on machines in physics, American farm life, inventors, and social studies. *Subjects*: Farm Tractors; Tractors.

Watt, E. Melanie. *The Black Rhinoceros*. Austin, TX: Raintree/Steck-Vaughn. 1998. Untamed World Series. Hardcover $26.40 (ISBN 0–8172–4572–3). Fry Reading Level 5+. Interest Level Grade 5–Adult.

The attractive format using sidebars for highlighting pertinent information aids the readability of this book on one of the world's endangered species. Reports on the black rhino's life span, classification, prey, place in the food chain, lifestyle, and how they communicate. An animal that is known to several cultures for different reasons. Discusses myths and legends surrounding them, as well as medical powers attributed to their horns. Quick and fascinating facts, glossary, index, bibliography. For units in geography, endangered species, animals, popular culture, and beliefs. *Subjects*: Black Rhinoceroses; Rhinoceroses; Endangered Species.

Welsbacher, Anne. *Tiger Sharks*. Minneapolis, MN: Capstone Press, 1995. Animals and the Environment Series. Hardcover $18.40 (ISBN 1–56065–269–1). Fry Reading Level 4. Interest Level Grade 4–Adult.

Action color photos show the second largest of the three most dangerous sharks, as well as a scarred victim of a white shark. Discusses tiger shark's appetites, life, and characteristics and includes tales of attacks and shark murders. Index, useful glossary, suggested readings. For readers who like adventure, sea stories, or stories of danger. For recreational reading and units on zoology, oceanology, geography, and animals. *Subjects*: Tiger Shark; Sharks.

Welsbacher, Anne. *Whale Sharks*. Minneapolis, MN: Capstone Press, 1995. Animals and the Environment Series. Hardcover $18.40 (ISBN 1–56065–271–3). Fry Reading Level 4. Interest Level Grade 4–Adult.

A look at the biggest fish in the oceans. Explains how the big fish has tiny teeth and eats by sucking and sieving. Talks about the sharks' travels, lack of fear of humans, and some legends associated with them, including being a Japanese god of good fortune. The range map tells where this largest of the sharks will travel in its lifetime. Index, brief author information, glossary. Profusely illustrated with color action photographs. For classes on zoology, animals, oceanography, geography, and social studies. Excellent for recreational reading. *Subjects*: Whale Shark; Sharks.

Wilcox, Charlotte. *The German Shepherd*. Mankato, MN: Capstone Press, 1996. Learning about Dogs Series. Hardcover $18.40 (ISBN 1–56065–398–1). Fry Reading Level 4. Interest Level Grade 4–Adult.

Introduces readers to this popular, intelligent, and fearless dog: its history and development, its many working uses (seeing eye dog, law enforcement animal), and how to care for the dog and keep it for a pet. Excellent color photographs and diagram of the anatomy of a dog are included. Action photos in black and white. Glossary, index, useful addresses, two pages of quick facts. For units on law enforcement, disabilities, working animals, animals, social studies, and history. Excellent for recreational reading and for pet lovers. *Subject*: German Shepherd Dogs.

Wilcox, Charlotte. *The Golden Retriever*. Mankato, MN: Capstone Press, 1996. Learning about Dogs Series. Hardcover $18.40 (ISBN 1–56065–397–3). Fry Reading Level 4. Interest Level Grade 4–Adult.

Often considered the perfect dog because of its temperament, its work habits, and its looks, the golden retriever is well displayed in this profusely illustrated book. Covers the history and development of this friendly dog and its uses today, including working with disabled people. Two pages of quick facts. Action photos in black and white and color. Index, glossary, Internet sites and addresses, bibliography. For units on hunting, geography, animals, pets, and disabilities. Can be used for recreational reading for dog owners. *Subjects*: Golden Retrievers.

Wilcox, Charlotte. *The Labrador Retriever*. Mankato, MN: Capstone Press, 1996. Learning about Dogs Series. Hardcover $18.40 (ISBN 1–56065–396–5). Fry Reading Level 4. Interest Level Grade 4–Adult.

An introduction to the breed that is considered America's most popular dog: its place of origin, its history and development, its uses as both pet and working dog (for hunting, law enforcement, and as a guide dog). Facts for reference as well as a list of dog terms. The pictures depict all aspects of the dog's life and use. Index, good glossary, suggested readings, useful addresses. For units on hunting, pets, working animals, geography, and disabilities. Excellent for recreational reading for pet lovers. *Subject*: Labrador Retriever.

Wilcox, Charlotte. *The Rottweiler*. Mankato, MN: Capstone Press, 1996. Learning about Dogs Series. Hardcover $18.40 (ISBN 1–56065–395–7). Fry Reading Level 4. Interest Level Grade 4–Adult.

The origin in Germany and history of this large and intelligent dog. Discusses its development and some of the myths and misconceptions that surround it. Facts about dogs in general and rottweilers in particular presented in abbreviated form. Explains that rottweilers are very protective dogs and need to be around humans. Shows their uses as working dogs in law enforcement, herding, guarding, and pulling carts and sleds. Color photographs. Glossary, index, addresses of useful organizations. For units on law enforcement, working dogs, geography, psychology, and animals. Good for recreational reading for animal lovers. *Subject*: Rottweiler Dog.

# 8

# Sports

This chapter encompasses many world sports and their adaptations and has entries on both sports and athletes. It also includes materials on recreational activities, motor sports, and martial arts, plus biographies of famous athletes. Although these books have been selected particularly to appeal to young people, they are also suitable for adult ESL use.

## NONFICTION

Billings, Melissa Stone, and Henry Billings. *Winners: Olympic Games*. Austin, TX: Steck-Vaughn, 1993. Winners Series. Hardcover $21.74 (ISBN 0–8114–4787–4). Fry Reading Level 3+. Interest Level Grade 5–Adult.

Workbook-style book contains brief biographies of Olympic gold medal winners (in swimming, track, skating, skiing, and gymnastics) from the United States, and other countries including France, Australia, and Kenya. Countries are not stressed as much as character and the people. Teaches perseverance and the ability to overcome disabilities and other difficulties. Easy-to-read, simple stories. Questions, words to learn. About equally divided between sexes. For sports, units on life skills and self-esteem and for teaching reading. *Subjects*: Olympics; Sports; Biography.

Boga, Steve. *On Their Own: Adventure Athletes in Solo Sports*. Books 1, 2, and 3. Novato, CA: High Noon Books, 1992. Paper $11.00 (set) (ISBN 0–87879–928–1). Fry Reading Level 3. Interest Level Grade 5–Adult.

Three-volume set covering fifteen athletes who do single-person competition shows adolescents and adults that people can do things alone. Greg

LeMond represents the internationally popular sport of bicycle racing; Eric Heiden, Olympic gold medalist, represents speed skating. Other solo sports represented are hang gliding, mountain climbing, cross-country skiing, triathlon, motorcycle racing, rock climbing, running, ski racing, surfing, and canoeing. Short profiles illustrated by black and white action photographs. For personal development classes, work on self-esteem and personal achievement, and supplementary reading. *Subjects*: Athletes—United States—Biography; Determination (Personality Trait).

Cebulash, Mel. *Bases Loaded.* Syracuse, NY: New Readers Press, 1993. Paper $4.25 (ISBN 0–88336–742–4); tape $12.00 (ISBN 0–88336–899–4). Fry Reading Level 3–5. Interest Level Grade 5–Adult.

Cebulash, Mel. *Fast Break.* Syracuse, NY: New Readers Press, 1993. Paper $4.25 (ISBN 0–88336–744–0); tape $12.00 (ISBN 0–88336–928–1). Fry Reading Level 3–5. Interest Level Grade 5–Adult.

Cebulash, Mel. *Lights Out.* Syracuse NY: New Readers Press, 1993. Paper $4.25 (ISBN 0–88336–741–6); tape $12.00 (ISBN 0–88336–898–6). Fry Reading Level 3–5. Interest Level Grade 5–Adult.

Cebulash, Mel. *3rd and Goal.* Syracuse, NY: New Readers Press, 1993. Paper $4.25 (ISBN 0–88336–743–2); tape $12.00 (ISBN 0–88336–900–1). Fry Reading Level 3–5. Interest Level Grade 5–Adult.

Four-book set that can be read alone or used as a read-along with the tapes. Crisply written and easy to read and comprehend. Representative sports stars and heroes from the all eras of American sports. Basketball includes Michael Jordan; baseball includes Babe Ruth; Joe Montana is included in football and Jack Dempsey in boxing. Helpful read-along tapes are word by word for the entire book. Sportscaster and former coach Dick Vitale reads basketball; sportscaster and former New York Giant football star Frank Gifford reads football; sportscaster and former baseball great Phil Rizzuto reads baseball; and ring expert and sportscaster Sean O'Grady reads boxing. Black and white and color photographs. Index, glossary. Excellent for beginning students, particularly if the tapes are used. Appeals to all sports fans. Supplementary reading. *Subjects*: Athletes—United States—Biography; Baseball—United States; Basketball—United States; Boxing—United States; Football—United States.

Chandler, Gil. *Roller Coasters.* Minneapolis, MN: Capstone Press, 1995. Cruisin' Series. Hardcover $18.40 (ISBN 1–56065–221–7). Fry Reading Level 3–4. Interest Level Grade 4–Adult.

Very easy-to-read book about roller coasters and the recreational thrills they provide. Describes the sensations they provide, discusses their history and how they are constructed, explains the differences between those constructed of wood and those constructed of steel, refers to specific roller coasters in the United States and Canada, and identifies which amusement parks have them. Half of text, half color photographs. Glossary, a brief bibliography, addresses of organizations. Use for units in popular culture. *Subject*: Roller Coasters.

Dippold, Joel. *Troy Aikman: Quick Draw Quarterback*. Minneapolis, MN: Lerner, 1994. Sports Achievers Biographies Series. Paper $5.95 (ISBN 0–8225–9663–6); hardcover $17.59 (ISBN 0–8225–2880–0). Fry Reading Level 8+. Interest Level Grade 7–Adult.

A biography of high-profile and internationally known franchise player Troy Aikman. Highlights his college and professional careers and his love for country western music. Geared to the advanced readers. For supplementary reading, primarily male football fans. *Subjects*: Aikman, Troy—Biography; Athletes—Football—Biography.

Freman, David. *Negro Baseball Leagues*. Morristown, NJ: Silver Burdett Press, 1994. American Events Series. Hardcover $14.95 (ISBN 0–02–734595–7). Fry Reading Level 8+. Interest Level Grade 7–Adult.

History of the Negro baseball leagues in America. Shows the hustle and tussle of the barnstorming black players of the early leagues. Covers the budding league formed in 1887, the formation of the Negro National League in 1920, and the end of the leagues in 1960. Emphasizes the frustration and perseverance that preceded the breaking of the color barrier in professional baseball with Jackie Robinson in 1946. Looks at Satchel Paige, Rube Foster, and Charlie Grant. Plentiful black and white photographs of people and teams. More appropriate for advanced readers, although can be used to stretch an interested student's ability to read. For supplementary reading and for classes in American history or social studies. Appeals primarily to men and boys. *Subjects*: Negro Leagues—History; Baseball—United States; Afro-American Baseball Players.

Gillespie, Loran. *Mustangs*. Mankato, MN: Capstone Press, 1996. High Performance Series. Hardcover $18.40 (ISBN 1–56–65–392–2). Fry Reading Level 3–4. Interest Level Grade 4–Adult.

An overview of the history of the classic Ford car, the Mustang. Introduced at the New York World's Fair on April 17, 1964, the pony car, as it became known, was a success. Book briefly covers the Ford Motor Company, Lee Iacocca, and marketing of the Mustang. Talks about all the generations of the Mustang. Plentiful color photographs. Glossary, brief bibliography, addresses. Can be used for reluctant readers. Use for units in social studies, popular culture, American history, business, and transportation. Car enthusiasts will enjoy this. *Subject*: Mustang Automobiles—History.

Goldstein, Margaret J., and Jennifer Larson. *Jackie Joyner Kersee: Superwoman.* Minneapolis, MN: Lerner, 1994. Sports Achiever Biographies Series. Paper $4.95 (ISBN 0-8225-9653-9); hardcover $13.50 (ISBN0-8225-0524-X). Fry Reading Level 8+. Interest Level Grade 7–Adult.

A role model for young women, Jackie Joyner Kersee has shown it is possible to overcome illness and other obstacles in life to become a champion. The biography shows her as a person and shows that not all athletes are one-sided people. Spells out the work and determination required to succeed in any endeavor. Basic appeal is to girls and women. Color and black and white photographs. Career statistics, index. For supplementary reading, to teach self-esteem, for social studies classes, and to provide role models. *Subjects*: Afro-American Women in Sports—Biography; Sports—Track and Field—Biography.

Green, Michael (Michael R.) *Jaguars.* Mankato, MN: Capstone Press, 1996. High Performance Series. Hardcover $18.40 (ISBN 1-56-65-393-0). Fry Reading Level 3–4. Interest Level Grade 4–Adult.

The high-performance and stylish automotive Jaguar is covered in this easy-to-read book. The English partnership that built them went from motorcycle sidecars to the internationally acclaimed and expensive Jaguar. Overview of the history of the car and the people who were the force behind it covers current and historical vehicles (with pictures), the racing side of the business, some of the famous cars built, and the famous and infamous people who owned them. For car and racing buffs. Glossary without pronunciation, brief bibliography, addresses. Use for units on lifestyle or popular culture. *Subject*: Jaguar Automobile.

Green, Michael (Michael R.) *Lamborghinis.* Minneapolis, MN: Capstone Press, 1996. High Performance Series. Hardcover $8.40 (ISBN 1-56065-393-1). Fry Reading Level 3+. Interest Level Grade 4–Adult.

This unique supercar from Italy is well covered in easy text and pertinent photos, mainly in color. Explains that these cars are handmade, look totally different from regular cars, and are built for speed and handling, not for comfort. Talks about the company that produces these cars and the family behind it all. Provides a history of the car and discusses and illustrates the models. Glossary, brief selection of further reading, addresses. Car buffs will like. Use for units on lifestyle or popular culture. *Subject*: Lamborghini Automobile.

Gronvall, Kal. *Corvettes.* Mankato, MN: Capstone Press, 1996. High Performance Series. Hardcover $18.40 (ISBN 1-56065-391-4). Fry Reading Level 3–4. Interest Level Grade 4–Adult.

The classic American "Vette," a popular sports car since 1953 and perhaps the best-known American one, is well explained and illustrated in this easy-to-read overview. Made by the Chevrolet division of General Motors, it has spawned car clubs across the world. Discusses the people who have been involved in its production, as well as the history and changes in this fiberglass car. Glossary of car terms, brief list of further reading, useful addresses. Explains a bit of Americana. For social studies, supplemental reading, and car enthusiasts. *Subject*: Corvette Automobile.

Gutman, Bill. *Bicycling*. Minneapolis, MN: Capstone Press, 1995. Action Sports Series. Hardcover $18.40 (ISBN 1–56065–264–0). Fry Reading Level 3–4. Interest Level Grade 4–Adult.

An easy-to-read book relating the history and development of bicycles. Covers biking sports and the types of bicycles needed and available for them. Discusses the beginning of the sport, possibly in France, and its development in Scotland and then the United States. Color photographs to illustrate the bicycle and its parts. Addresses of organizations and publications, glossary, bibliography. International in scope. Useful background for cyclists. Use for units on sports, fitness, lifestyle, or transportation. *Subjects*: Bicycles and Bicycling; Cycling.

Gutman, Bill. *Karate*. Minneapolis, MN: Capstone Press, 1995. Action Sports Series. Hardcover $10.01 (ISBN 1–56065–250–0). Fry Reading Level 3+. Interest Level Grade 4–Adult.

A how-to book of karate. Explains that karate is a sport, science, a means of self-defense, and a way to stay in good physical shape. Includes a brief history of karate and a list of countries in which it has historical roots. Explains that Japan and China are only a few of the countries that practice some form of martial arts. Tells how to get started in karate and discusses some of the basic moves. Postures and movements are explained as well as illustrated. Half vivid color photographs, half text. Bold-print words in the text are explained in the glossary, and other words or expressions are defined throughout the text. Appeals to readers of all ages. Useful with reluctant readers and helpful for several cultures. Use for sports, fitness, self-defense, cultural diversity, popular culture, and recreational reading. *Subject*: Karate.

Gutman, Bill. *Kung Fu*. Minneapolis, MN: Capstone Press, 1995. Action Sports Series. Hardcover $18.40 (ISBN 1–56065–267–5). Fry Reading Level 3+. Interest Level Grade 4–Adult.

Very easy-to-read and -comprehend book explaining kung fu and its various systems. Explains and illustrates profusely the many styles. Refers to the late and popular Bruce Lee and the methods and the Wing Chun style he used and popularized. Some other styles mentioned and shown are the Monkey Style, the Praying Mantis Style, the White Crane Style, and the Drunken Man style. Illustrates the preparations needed to be effective. List of several books for further reading, addresses of two pertinent magazines. Pertinent to several cultures. Use for units on sports, fitness, cultural diversity, self-defense, and popular culture. *Subject*: Kung Fu.

Gutman, Bill. *Roller Hockey*. Minneapolis MN: Capstone Press, 1995. Action Sports Series. Hardcover $10.01 (ISBN 1–56065–250–0). Fry Reading Level 4–6. Interest Level Grade 5–Adult.

Bright and colorful photographs complement the text in this short book about roller hockey, which has attracted international appeal, with followings in the United States, Canada, and Japan. Covers rules for both professional and amateur roller hockey, equipment needs, playing surfaces, vocabulary, and playing positions. Readers learn what skills are necessary to play roller hockey beyond basic in-line skating. Photographs do a fine job of illustrating rules, plays, and skills necessary. An easy-to-read book with an inviting format. Brief index, glossary, addresses for sports organizations. Mainly of interest to boys. Use for units on sports, fitness, and popular culture. *Subject*: Roller Hockey.

Gutman, Bill. *Sumo Wrestling*. Minneapolis, MN: Capstone Press, 1995. Action Sports Series. Hardcover $18.40 (ISBN 1–56–65–273–X). Fry Reading Level 3+. Interest Level Grade 4–Adult.

An easy-reading book about the ancient Japanese art and sport of sumo. Covers the rules, the preparation, and the techniques that the wrestler must know and use and explains the difference between fat and bulk in the bodies of the wrestlers. Half text, half color photographs. Glossary, bibliography, addresses. For classes in social studies and physical fitness. *Subject*: Sumo Wrestling.

Gutman, Bill. *Tae Kwon Do*. Minneapolis, MN: Capstone Press, 1995. Action Sports Series. Hardcover $18.40 (ISBN 1–56–65–266–7). Fry Reading Level 4. Interest Level Grade 5–Adult.

Describes the kicking and striking techniques of this martial art, originally a Korean art and now a worldwide sport practiced by young and old alike and both sexes. Describes the preparations involved, the clothing usually worn during the sessions, and the kicks and punching and blocking movements. Color photographs. Explains the competitions. Glossary, further readings, addresses. Easy to read. Multicultural. Use for units on sports, fitness, health, and popular culture. *Subject*: Tae Kwon Do.

Hamner, Trudy J. *All American—Girls Professional Baseball League*. Morristown, NJ: Silver Burdett, 1994. American Events Series. Hardcover $14.95 (ISBN 0–02–742595–5). Fry Reading Level 8+. Interest Level Grade 7–Adult.

History of women's professional baseball that started during the 1940s while men were serving in World War II. Depicted here with statistics, sports memories, and profuse black and white photographs. Many teams in this league, started by the owner of the Chicago Cubs, were located in small midwestern cities. Tells how the women, then usually called girls, were taught how to dress, use makeup, behave, and were always well chaperoned on road trips. Describes their heyday and their fade from the scene when the major leagues got into full swing after the war. Index. Appeals to sports fans as well as to girls and women. For classes in American history, social studies, and women's history. *Subjects*: Sports—Baseball; Women in Baseball; Women in Sports.

Hintz, Martin. *Monster Truck Drag Racing*. Mankato, MN: Capstone Press, 1996. Drag Racing Series. Hardcover $18.40 (ISBN 1–56065–390–6). Fry Reading Level 3+. Interest Level Grade 5–Adult.

An easy-to-read book about monster truck drag races and the vehicles. Includes a history of the sport. Explains techniques and rules of the races and how the vehicles are made. Spectacular color action photographs and a color diagram of the parts of the vehicle. Describes car crushing event. Glossary, Internet sites, bibliography, index. Use for units on sports, hobbies, popular culture, trucks, transportation, and for recreational reading. *Subjects*: Truck Racing; Monster Trucks; Drag Racing.

Hintz, Martin. *Motorcycle Drag Racing*. Mankato, MN: Capstone Press, 1996. Drag Racing Series. Hardcover $18.40 (ISBN 1–56065–387–6). Fry Reading Level 3+. Interest Level Grade 5–Adult.

Easy-to-read book about motorcycle drag racing. Explains the history of the sport from its beginning in the 1930s. Since motorcycles are international in use, this should have wide appeal. Describes the tracks, the races, the rules, and the associations. Explains the equipment used and the training needed. Color illustrations. Bibliography, glossary, organizations. Use for units on sports, hobbies, transportation, or popular culture. *Subjects*: Motorcycle Racing; Drag Racing.

Hintz, Martin. *Top Fuel Drag Racing*. Mankato, MN: Capstone Press, 1996. Drag Racing Series. Hardcover $18.00 (ISBN 1–56065–389–2). Fry Reading Level 4. Interest Level Grade 4–Adult.

Easy-to-read history and description of the sport of top fuel drag racing and the cars. Shows the development of the sport from the California street dragsters to today's funny cars, which are illustrated and defined. Discusses sport safety, rules, equipment, and the famous racers, such as "Big Daddy" Garlits, Prudhomme, and Shirley Muldowney. Appeals to car buffs and race fans. Provides a look at American nostalgia and trivia. Shows women in a nontraditional sport. Black and white and color illustrations. Glossary, bibliography, addresses. Use for units in sports, racing, hobbies, and popular culture. *Subject*: Drag Racing.

Jensen, Julie. *Beginning Mountain Biking.* Adapted from Andy King's *Fundamental Mountain Biking.* Minneapolis, MN: Lerner Publications Company, 1996. Beginning Sports Series. Hardcover $14.95 (ISBN 0–8225–3509). Fry Reading Level 3–5. Interest Level Grade 5–Adult.

Features full-color action photos and easy-to-follow instructions for mountain biking. Provides a history of the sport and the bikes, explains the skills and techniques needed and used, discusses the competitions and some of trick riding uses, and refers to the people instrumental in the development of these bikes—Joe Breeze, Charlie Kelley, and the pioneering John Finley Scott. Illustrates where and how to ride, repairs to make, how to maneuver. Explains the necessity of practice for competitions and tells how to train. Good glossary. For those who like the outdoors. Use for units on sports, world cultures, fitness and health, and for recreational reading. *Subjects*: All Terrain Cycling.

Jensen, Julie. *Beginning Soccer.* Adapted from Lori Coleman's *Fundamental Soccer.* Minneapolis, MN: Lerner Publications Group, 1995. Beginning Sports Series. Hardcover $21.50 (ISBN 0–8225–3501). Fry Reading Level 4–4+. Interest Level Grade 5–Adult.

About this game that has universal appeal and is the most widely played sport outside the United States. Readable how-to book that is clear and understandable, with primary appeal to sports buffs, both men and women. Good graphics to illustrate the techniques and methods explained in the text. For physical education classes and for informational reading for students who wish to brush up their own skills. *Subject*: Soccer.

Jensen, Julie. *Beginning Softball*: Adapted from Kristin Wolden Nitz's *Fundamental Softball.* Minneapolis, MN: Lerner Publications, 1997. Beginning Sports Series. Hardcover $15.95 (ISBN 0–8225–3510–6). Fry Reading Level 5+. Interest Level Grade 5–Adult.

Color photographs and diagrams enhance the oversize and easy-to-use look at how to play softball. For both sexes, but girls are most often in the illustrations. Includes rules and history of the game and techniques for playing (fielding and throwing, pitching, hitting, and running). Index, bibliography, softball glossary. Will help students of other cultures understand this sport that is part of many community amateur athletic leagues. For sports instructors and physical education teachers, as well as for units in cultural diversity and popular culture and for recreational use. *Subject*: Softball.

Johnston, Scott D. *The Original Monster Truck: Bigfoot.* Minneapolis, MN: Capstone Press, 1994. Cruisin' Series. Hardcover $10.01 (ISBN 1–56065–200–4). Fry Reading Level 3+. Interest Level Grade 5–Adult.

Car crunching and car jumping are vividly illustrated in this short, informative book. Explores the history of monster trucks and the work and cost that go into preparing them for races and shows. Brilliantly colored photographs complement the very basic text. Brief index, glossary, addresses for national monster truck organizations. This publisher can often provide colorful posters illustrating some of its books. For reluctant readers interested in automotive sports, vocational and career schools, for popular culture classes, and supplementary reading. *Subjects*: Monster Trucks; Truck Racing; Trucks.

Kavanaugh, Jack. *Barry Sanders: Rocket Running Back.* Minneapolis, MN: Lerner, 1994. Sports Achievers Biographies Series. Paper $4.95 (ISBN 0–8225–9635–0); hardcover $13.50 (ISBN 0–8225–9635–0). Fry Reading Level 8+. Interest Level Grade 5–Adult.

Portrayal of college football hero Barry Sanders who went on to become a superstar with the Detroit Lions. The profile of Sanders as an exemplary person on and off the field provides a breath of fresh air in the often-scandal-ridden world of sports. Inspiring biography of a contemporary football star with a team player attitude can provide a role model for youth. Color and black and white illustrations and photographs. Index, statistics, and personal records. For motivational reading, social studies classes, and supplementary reading. Appeals especially to boys and men. *Subjects*: Afro-American Men in Sports; Sports—Football.

Kelly, Emery J. *Paper Airplanes: Models to Build and Fly.* Minneapolis, MN: Lerner Publications, 1997. Hardcover $17.95 (ISBN 0–8225–2401–5). Fry Reading Level 7+. Interest Level Grade 5–Adult.

Shows twelve different models to create, including the flying wing, the flying pancake, the stealth wing, and the always popular dragonfly. Includes aerodynamic principles and flying techniques along with instructions. Oversized book, well illustrated with diagrams and photographs. Fun for all students and teachers. Glossary. For units in science, mathematics, physics, and art. A fun book to have available. *Subject*: Paper Airplanes.

Lund, Bill. *Kayaking*. Mankato, MN: Capstone Press, 1996. Extreme Sports Series. Hardcover $18.40 (ISBN 1–56065–328–7). Fry Reading Level 4. Interest Level Grade 5–Adult.

Looks at the history of kayaking, describes historical and modern kayaks, and delineates the different types of kayaking and the equipment necessary to do it. Explains methods of kayaking, the degrees of difficulty in courses and river, the necessity of fitness to participate, and the competitions. Easier to read than to do. Photographs fully illustrate methods, materials, and techniques. Teaches perseverance. For supplemental reading. *Subject*: Kayaking.

Lund, Bill. *Weight Lifting*. Mankato, MN: Capstone Press, 1996. Extreme Sports Series. Hardcover $18.40 (ISBN 1–65065–431–7). Fry Reading Level 4. Interest Level Grade 5–Adult.

Describes the history of the sport, the equipment used and needed, and the contemporary practice of weight lifting. Talks about muscles and how they should be developed. Explains different types of weight lifting used for strength training and specific sports, as well as safety precautions. Illustrations in color and black and white make the text more understandable. Easy to read. Since weight conditioning and body building are popular, this book is excellent for interested young men and women. Suggestions for further reading, glossary use for units in physical education, health and fitness and for recreational reading. *Subject*: Weight Lifting.

Lund, Bill. *Rock Climbing*. Mankato, MN: Capstone Press, 1996. Extreme Sports Series. Hardcover $18.40 (ISBN 1–56065–429–5). Fry Reading Level 4. Interest Level Grade 6–Adult.

Rock climbing is not for everyone, but many will like to read about this extreme and fairly dangerous sport that officially began as a sport in 1760 when a prize was offered for climbing a mountain in Switzerland. Most climbers are amateur sportsmen, and it is a worldwide sport. The book covers techniques used in climbing, places to climb, various types of climbs, famous climbs, and famous places to climb. Illustrations show techniques and label the equipment needed. Glossary, bibliography, Internet sites. Easy reading. For students who like to read about adventure or plan to be outdoors. *Subject*: Rock Climbing.

Lund, Bill. *Triathlon*. Mankato, MN: Capstone Press, 1996. Extreme Sports Series. Hardcover $18.40 (ISBN 1–56065–430–9). Fry Reading Level 4. Interest Level Grade 7–Adult.

Tells how to be competitive in more than one sport. Easy to read; half text, half illustration. It is a young sport and at present involves swimming, biking and running. Describes the kind of triathlons practiced and who participates. Talks about the personalities of these athletes and the fact that many all-around athletes are triathletes because they do more than one sport. Brief glossary, suggested biographies, useful addresses for adults and youth, and Internet sites. Provides a balanced look at a young sport. Use for units in sports, fitness and health, physical education, and for recreational reading. *Subject*: Triathlon.

Morgan, Terri, and Schmuel Thaler. *Chris Mullins: Sure Shot*. Minneapolis, MN: Lerner, 1994. Sports Achievers Biographies Series. Hardcover $10.15 (ISBN 0–8225–2887–7). Fry Reading Level 4–8+. Interest Level Grade 5–Adult.

Behind-the-scenes look at the troubled life of basketball star Chris Mullins. Profiles his basketball career in college and professional play. Showing how fame and fortune often take their toll, this biography chronicles Mullins's fight with alcoholism and his ability to conquer his demons. Color and black and white photographs. Many basketball statistics included. Mullins's struggle highlights the ability to achieve in spite of oneself. For supplemental reading, to build esteem, or for problem solving. For advanced and intermediate readers. Appeals to basketball fans of both genders. *Subjects*: Mullins, Chris; Alcoholism; Sports—Basketball—Biography.

Morgan, Terri. *Junior Seau: High Voltage Linebacker*. Minneapolis, MN: Lerner Publications Company, 1996. Sports Achievers Biographies Series. Hardcover $14.96 (ISBN 0–8225–2896–7); paper $5.95 (ISBN 0–8225–974602). Fry Reading Level 4. Interest Level Grade 4–Adult.

Story of one of the best and best-known defensive football players in the National Football League. Born in California to parents who had emigrated from American Samoa, Seau spent his childhood in a closely knit family that values honor. Covers life in an immigrant family, high school and college football, and Seau's work as a professional athlete. It talks of his dedication to bettering the lives of youth and about the Junior Seau Foundation, which works to fight juvenile delinquency. Teaches honesty, integrity, and determination. Profusely illustrated with color photographs. Seau's statistics, good index. For sports enthusiasts. *Subjects*: Seau, Junior; Samoan Americans—Biography; San Diego Chargers.

Naden, Corinne J., and Rose Blue. *Heroes Don't Just Happen: Biographies of Overcoming Bias and Building Character*. Maywood, NJ: Peoples Publishing Group, 1996. Hardcover $5.00 (ISBN 1–56256–425–0). Fry Reading Level 4+. Interest Level Grade 5–Adult.

Profiles five sports heroes of the past and present who represent five different sports: Arthur Ashe from tennis, Roberto Clemente from baseball, Emmitt Smith from football, Florence Griffeth Joyner from track, and Kristi

Yamaguchi from figure skating. These African Americans, Japanese, and a native of Puerto Rico overcame racial bias and discrimination and strengthened their characters in the process. Black and white photos. Book can be used in sections. Career highlights for each person, vocabulary list. Use for units on biography, sports, women in sports, role models and heroes, discrimination, perseverance, and for recreational reading. *Subjects*: Sport—Biography.

Pernu, Dennis. *Hot Rods*. Minneapolis, MN: Capstone Press, 1995. Cruisin' Series. Hardcover $13.35 (ISBN 1–56065–253–5). Fry Reading Level 3+. Interest Level Grade 4–Adult.

Easy-to-read book that covers one of the icons of America's love affairs with cars: the hot rod. Defines what makes up a hot rod, refers to their history, and describes customizing, the engines, the paint jobs, and all the things that go into a hot rod. Great color pictures. For history, social studies, and shop. Glossary, bibliography, useful addresses. *Subjects*: Hot Rods; Automobiles.

Savage, Jeff. *Andre Agassi: Reaching the Top—Again*. Minneapolis, MN: Lerner Publications, 1997. Sports Achievers Biographies Series. Hardcover $14.95 (ISBN 0–8225–2894–0); paper $5.95 (ISBN 0–8225–9750–0). Fry Reading Level 7+. Interest Level Grade 5–Adult.

Chronicles Agassi's rise to the top as a cocky teenage star and, as he matures, his determination to get back to top form again. Thumbnail biography and a look at tennis. Color and black and white photographs. Career outline, index, glossary of tennis terms. For units in popular culture, sports, famous people, biographies, problem solving, and psychology. *Subjects*: Agassi, Andre, 1970–; Tennis Players; Tennis.

Savage, Jeff. *Demolition Derby*. Parsipanny, NJ: Crestwood House, 1997 Action Events Series. Hardcover $14.95 (ISBN 0–89686–891–5); paper $4.90 (ISBN 0–382–394292–9). Fry Reading Level 4+. Interest Level Grade 4–5–Adult.

Explains an American automotive sport that may appear strange to nonnatives. Covers the history of the demolition derby and derby competition, as well as the types of vehicles used. Explains the events, the tactics used, and why some cars are better for this sport than others. Also discusses figure 8 racing. Colorful format that resembles a magazine in layout and has facts separated in boxes, with bullets for emphasis. Good photographs. Glossary, index. For teaching a bit of Americana, particular southern and midwestern. *Subjects*: Demolition Derbies; Automobile Racing.

Savage, Jeff. *Drag Racing*. Parsipanny, NJ: Crestwood House, 1997. Action Events Series. Hardcover $14.95 (ISBN 0–89686–890–7); paper $4.98 (ISBN 0–382–39293–0). Fry Reading Level 4+. Interest Level Grade 4–Adult.

Covers the great race drivers and the great races in the history of drag racing. Explains how the cars and tracks are constructed, the equipment needed, and the rules and regulations to keep the sport safe. Covers all types of this motorsport, including the nationals and junior nationals. Format is like a magazine and very colorful. Brief facts in boxes and with bullets are eye catching. Pictures of the racers and their cars. Use for units in sports, popular culture, transportation, and for recreational reading. Index. *Subject*: Drag Racing.

Savage, Jeff. *Monster Trucks*. Parsipanny, NJ: Crestwood House, 1997. Action Events Series. Hardcover $14.95 (ISBN 0–89686–899–3); paper $4.98 (ISBN 0–382–39295–7). Fry Reading Level 4+. Interest Level Grade 5–Adult.

Action-packed photographs are included in this colorful history of monster truck racing in America. Looks at the sport's major personalities, events, and types of trucks. Magazine-like format with information in boxes and with bullets for emphasis. A fun read. Glossary, index. Use for units on popular culture, sports, transportation, and for recreational reading. *Subjects*: Monster Trucks; Truck Racing.

Savage, Jeff. *Mud Racing*. Parsipanny, NJ: Silver Burdett Press, 1997. Action Events Series. Hardcover $14.95 (ISBN 0–89686–888–5); paper $4.98 (ISBN 0–382–39297–3). Fry Reading Level 4+. Interest Level Grade 5–Adult.

An introduction to this young American automotive sport. Discusses the object of the sport, the rules and the dangers, the races, their locations, and the types of vehicles used. Tom Martin, known as the Father of Mud Racing, and other personalities are covered. Action photographs are abundant. In a colorful and readable format with snippets of pertinent information in bullets and boxed for high visibility. Glossary, index. Use for units in sports, popular culture, transportation, and for recreational reading. *Subjects*: Mud Racing; Automobile Racing.

Savage, Jeff. *Supercross Motorcycle Racing*. Parsipanny, NJ: Crestwood House, 1997. Action Events Series. Hardcover $14.95 (ISBN 0–89686–887–7); paper $4.98 (ISBN 0–382–39292–2). Fry Reading Level 4+. Interest Level Grade 5–Adult.

About the action sport of supercross racing and what is required to do it well. Shows both indoor and outdoor events and discusses championship people and events. Reads and looks as though it is a magazine article. Colorful illustrations and a clever format. Index, glossary. Use for recreational reading and for units in sports, popular culture, and transportation. For reluctant readers. *Subjects*: Motocross; Motorcycle Racing.

Savage, Jeff. *Truck and Tractor Pullers.* Parsipanny, NJ: Crestwood House, 1997. Action Events Series. Hardcover $14.95 (ISBN 0–89686–886–9); paper $4.98 (ISBN 0–382–39296–5). Fry Reading Level 4+. Interest Level Grade 5–Adult.

County fairs and racetracks across the country, particularly in small towns, are home to this sport. Shows how the tractor and truck pulls have replaced many of the horse-pulling contests of the past and shows the raw power needed. Describes the events and the people involved. Colorful illustrations and attention-getting format. Index, glossary. Easy-to-read book for the truck and car people and reluctant readers. For supplemental reading. *Subjects*: Tractor Driving—Competitions; Truck Driving—Competitions.

Sheely, Robert, and Louis Bourgeois, *Sports Lab.* New York: Silver Moon Press, 1994. Science Lab Series. Hardcover $12.95 (ISBN 1–881889–49–1). Fry Reading Level 2–4. Interest Level Grade 5–Adult.

Sports labs and sports medicine presented in a highly readable manner for use in classroom settings and in the gym. Students doing papers on sports labs and sports medicine can find current information, complete with color and black and white photographs. International implications are discussed, as science has become an essential part of sports in the training of world-class athletes. Machines, computers, and studies that go into improving athletes and athletic performance are illustrated and discussed in easy-to-read fashion, and readers learn how computers are used to simulate what athletes are doing wrong, or right, so that they can correct or improve their performances. Of interest to student athletes, sports fans, and those interested in medicine and technology. Bibliography. *Subjects*: Sports; Sports Medicine; Sports Technology.

Shoemaker, Joel. *Skateboarding Streetstyle.* Minneapolis, MN: Capstone Press, 1995. Action Sports Series. Hardcover $17.50 (ISBN 1–56065–261–6). Fry Reading Level 3+. Interest Level Grade 5–Adult.

Presents the development of skateboarding since its inception in the 1920s as well as the techniques involved. Discusses how to move, how to turn, and how to stop. Notes the protective clothing and equipment needed. Excellent color action photographs. Easy to read. Brief glossary, other reading, addresses. Use for units in fitness, sports, popular culture, and for recreational reading. *Subject*: Skateboarding.

Smith, Jay H. *Humvees and Other Military Vehicles.* Minneapolis, MN: Capstone Press, 1995. Wheels Series. Hardcover $18.40 (ISBN 1–56065–219–5). Fry Reading Level 4+. Interest Level Grade 5–Adult.

Movies and the armed forces have kept the interest in these vehicles alive. Easy-to-read source for material on land rover–type trucks, desert patrol vehicles, and the Humvee itself. Discusses the uses of these vehicles in Desert Storm and the civilian model of the Humvee (the Hummer). Glossary, brief index, addresses. Illustrations. Good background material for those interested in vehicles. For history classes and supplementary reading. *Subject*: Vehicles.

Smith, Jay H. *Powerboat Racing.* Minneapolis, MN: Capstone Press, 1995. MotorSports Series. Hardcover $17.80 (ISBN 1–056065–231–4). Fry Reading Level 3+. Interest Level Grade 5–Adult.

Easy-to-read book about the sport of motorboat racing. Covers racing from its beginning in France using boats with automobile engines to worldwide competition with specially made water craft. Explains different kinds of races and different types of boats. Half text, half color action illustrations. Addresses, glossary, index, brief bibliography. A world-popular subject. Use for units on water sports, racing, extreme sports, or popular culture as well as for recreational reading. *Subject*: Motorboat Racing.

Stewart, Gail. *Horseback Riding.* Minneapolis, MN: Capstone Press, 1995. Action Sports Series. Hardcover $17.80 (ISBN 1–56065–263–2). Fry Reading Level 4+. Interest Level Grade 5–Adult.

Discusses learning to ride, different kinds of riding, and different types of horses. Explains the relationship between the rider and the horse. Points out clothing for the rider and equipment needed for the horse. Glossary, index, brief list of other readings, addresses for further information. Appeals to younger students. Use for units on animals, sports, fitness, and competition, as well as for recreational reading. *Subject*: Horsemanship.

Townsend, Brad. *Shaquille O'Neal: Center of Attention.* Minneapolis, MN: Lerner, 1994. Sports Achievers Biographies Series. Paper $5.95 (ISBN 0–8224–9655–5); hardcover $17.50 (ISBN 0–8225–2879–7). Fry Reading Level 8+. Interest Level Grade 7–Adult.

The principle of respect is central to this biography of the personable and popular young basketball star. Life both on and off the court shows his humor and his love of family. Shaquille is shown to respect himself, what he does, and the people around him. Profiles his life as a professional basketball star as well as international and media celebrity. Uses a sports vocabulary to tell a warm and inspiring story. Black and white and color photographs. Appeals to basketball fans, sports fans, and people who like to read about celebrities. Inspirational supplementary reading. *Subjects*: O'Neal, Shaquille; Afro-American Men in Sports; Sports—Basketball.

Wadsworth, Ginger. *Susan Butcher: Sled Dog Racer*. Minneapolis, MN: Lerner, 1994. Sports Achievers Biographies Series. Hardcover $17.50 (ISBN 0–8225–2878–9). Fry Reading Level 8+. Interest Level Grade 7–Adult.

About the difficult and world-famous Iditarod and one of its champions. Dog sled racing provides a different slant for learning about customs in the far northern reaches of this country. Intrepid, courageous Susan Butcher and her champion dogs present an adventurous endurance tale. Discusses customs, events, weather, and the countryside. Dogs as well as people are shown, and the interplay between Butcher and her dogs is an example of teamwork and understanding at its best. Shows the mental and physical fortitude needed by both humans and dogs who participate in this race in the extreme conditions that can occur in Alaska. Presents a woman who excels in a nontraditional endeavor. Color and black and white photographs. Advanced vocabulary. Appeals to all who like adventure. For classes in geography or social studies. *Subjects*: Butcher, Susan; Dog Sledding; Iditarod.

Young, Jesse. *Stock Cars*. Minneapolis, MN: Capstone Press, 1995. Cruisin' Series. Hardcover $14.59 (ISBN 1–56065–223–3). Fry Reading Level 4+. Interest Level Grade 5–Adult.

Talks about and defines stock cars and stock car racing. Easy-to-read text illustrated with color action photographs from the National Association for Stock Car Racing. Tells how stock car racing owes its beginnings to the fast drivers who ran bootleg whiskey during Prohibition. Illustrates how the tracks evolved from cow pastures to the huge complexes today, such as the ones at Daytona, Charlotte, and Talledega. Explains driving rules, race rules, equipment rules, and skills. For history classes and supplemental reading. This can be used in conjunction with television to highlight local racing or local racing events. *Subjects*: Stock Car Racing; NASCAR (Association).

Young, Jesse. *Harley-Davidson Motorcycles*. Minneapolis, MN: Capstone Press, 1995. Motorcycles Series. Hardcover $14.54 (ISBN 1–56065–224–1). Fry Reading Level 4+. Interest Level Grade 5–Adult.

Examines the mystique of the Harley-Davidson motorcycle: its history and current popularity. Discusses touring, racing, and personal riding. Talks about the motorcycle gangs. Discusses parts, mechanics, and manufacture. Easy-to-read text well illustrated with vivid color photographs. Glossary, index, further reading, pertinent addresses. Use to illustrate the place the motorcycle has in the mythology of gangs and the 1930s depression era. *Subjects*: Harley-Davidson Motorcycle; Motorcycles.

# Appendix A: Distributors of Nonprint Materials

Nonprint materials provide an option for instructors in ESL settings to enhance, supplement, or replace print materials. These materials can include (but not be limited to) CD-ROMs, audiotapes, computer programs, films, videos, filmstrips, and Internet sites. These materials can all be used by the teacher, the learner, or the learner and the teacher together.

The Internet provides a plethora of web sites offering resources, support, and ideas as well as professional development opportunities. Digitization provides the student with a look on the Internet at the actual sights and words of history. Digitization projects at the Library of Congress have already made many of the archival documents of U.S. history available on the Internet, and in many cases sound is provided. Students using interactive multimedia programs can hear the correct pronunciation of words and phrases as they read the words. They can also see the meaning acted out on the screen. Some of the cultural and historical icons of the world can be seen and heard as they read or recite their work or as they are present at an historic event. The printed word cannot be replaced, but it can be enhanced and illuminated. Encyclopedias, dictionaries, atlases, and literary materials lend themselves to multimedia production.

Rely on catalogs from many of the distributors of multimedia, CD-ROM, and computer products and videos to keep current with what is available. Addresses are listed for some producers and distributors.

BFA Educational Media
2349 Chaffee Drive
St. Louis, MO 63146
0-1–800–221–1271
0-1–314–569–0211
Division of Phoenix Films, Incorporated; bargain films; all age levels and areas of
interest

Ecomium Publications
3639 Wiltshire Avenue
Cincinnati, OH 45208

1–800–234–4831
TOEFL Test; language; English language skills study

Grolier Electronic Publishing
Sherman Turnpike
Danbury, CT 06816
1–800–285–4534
General reference

INTELECOM
150 East Colorado Boulevard, Suite 300
Pasadena, CA 91105–1937
1–800–55–ENGLISH
Crossroads Cafe videos and television programs

Microsoft Corp.
One Microsoft Way
Redmond, WA 98052
1–800–426–9400
Reference, general materials

Pro Lingua Associates
15 Elm Street
Brattleboro, VT 05301
1–800–366–4775
Languages

Queue
338 Commerce Drive
Fairfield, CT 06432
1–800–232–2224
All fields of curricula, reference, general material

SVS
Society for Visual Education
6677 Northwest Highway
Chicago, IL 60631
1–800–829–1900
Churchill media, instructional material for all areas of the curriculum and all ages;
    many formats

Time Life Education
P.O. Box 85026
Richmond, VA 23285–5026
1–800–449–2010
General materials, history, social studies, reference

UPDATA
1736 Westwood Boulevard
Los Angeles, CA 90024

1–800–882–2844
Materials for all classes and all age groups and all levels; reference and general

These are some of the CD products that I have found useful for ESL use:

Microsoft's *Bookshelf*
*Grolier Multimedia Encyclopedia*
*Compton's Multimedia Encyclopedia*
*Encarta*

Following are some of the standard ESL publishers with computer programs that are excellent for instructional use (addresses are in the publishers list in the back of the book):

Pro Lingua
Contemporary Books
New Readers Press
Critical Thinking Books and Software
Educational Design
Raintree/Steck-Vaughn

These are a few web sites helpful for ESL:

*The Bilingual Education and ESL Homepage*
    http://www.educ.wau.edu/esl/esl/html
    Washington State University home page with links for students and professionals, as well as resources for ESL teachers
*ESL Links*
    http://www.uwm.edu/Dept . . . tResources/esllinks.html
    Online grammar help and links to student-centered web sites; study help online
*General ESL Resources*
    http://www.prairienet.org/community/esl/GenESL.htm
    Links to ERIC, Washington State, CUNY, EST Homepage, Lingua Center TESL Canada, and others
*Internet TESL Journal: For Teachers of English as a Second Language*
    http://www.aitech.ac.jp/-~iteslj
    Provides links to many other sites, as well as information on lessons, materials, networking, and available materials
*Links and Resources for ESL Teachers*
    http://www.educ.wsu.edu/esl/professionallink.html
    Classroom resources, ESL lesson plans, thematic units, worldwide address book, native literature, resources, and more

*National Institute for Literacy: LINCS*
    http://www.nifl.gov
    Provides instructors with background materials, links, regional information and hubs to contact, statistics, directories, legislation, grants, events, online discussion groups, instructional resources, technology lesson plans, information for student use

*Outreach and Technical Assistance Network: OTAN*
    http://www./otan.dni.us
    Over 12,000 ESL documents on this site; lesson plans are available as well as curricula resources and reference materials; grants and other information; particularly useful in California

*Region IV Hub Literacy Network Project*
    http://www.literacynet.org
    Literacy links, California resource centers, and more

*TESL-EJ: Teaching English as a Second or Foreign Language, an Electronic Journal*
    http://violet.berkley.edu/~cwp/TESL-EJ/index.html
    Journals date back to April 1994; indexed by title and author

*Virtual English Language Center*
    http://www.comenius.com
    For students, teachers, and speakers of English around the world to communicate and learn more about the language; in many languages for ESL learners

# Appendix B: Publishers of Print Materials

This is a selected list of publishers of print materials that are of use to teachers of English as a second language. Almost any publisher has one or two titles that can be useful, but these listed here consistently have useful materials. The annotation highlights some of the materials and subjects available.

Addison Wesley Longman
1 Jacob Way
Reading, MA 01867
ESL materials, classics, fiction, middle and secondary school materials, bilingual materials

August House
P.O. Box 3223
Little Rock, AK 72203–3223
Storytelling, folktales, ethnic stories, material for youth and adults, audio materials

CRC Publications
2850 Kalamazoo Avenue, S.E.
Grand Rapids, MI 49560
Christian publisher affiliated with the Christian Reformed church

Capstone Press
Box 669
Mankato, MN 55447
Material for youth and adults, action stories, history, multicultural, geography; includes Bridgestone Books Division; colorfully illustrated

Carolrhoda Books
Lerner Group
241 First Avenue
Minneapolis, MN 55401
Nature; well illustrated

Chippewa Valley Publishing
LVA-CV Literacy Programs
400 Eau Claire Street
Eau Claire, WI 54701
Literacy publications, new readers as authors, ESL, GED, school materials

Crabtree Publishing Company
Department 2QQ
350 Fifth Avenue, Suite 3308
New York NY 10118
Low-level reading with interest range through high school; nature, biography, ethnic
  materials, geography, multicultural studies

Creative Education
P.O. Box 227
Mankato, MN 56001
Classics, sports; low-level reading; interest level to mid–high school

Educational Design
345 Hudson Street
New York, NY 10014
Social studies, citizenship

Fearon Teachers Aids
4350 Equity Drive
P.O. Box 2649
Columbus, OH 43216
Literacy-type materials, easy readers, fiction

Greenhaven Press
P.O. Box 289009
San Diego, CA 92195–9009
Classics, literature, current issues, history, biography, science

Grolier Educational Corporation
Old Sherman Turnpike
Danbury, CT 06816
Encyclopedias, multimedia, video, languages, science, history, social studies

HarperCollins Children's Books
10 East 53d Street
New York, NY 10022
Books through high school; family, classics, fiction

Heinemann
Boynton/Cook Publishers
361 Hanover Street
Portsmouth, NH 03801–3912
Teacher resources through eighth grade, graded reading, classics

High Noon Books
Division of Academic Therapy Publication

20 Commercial Boulevard
Novato CA 94949
High interest, low reading level: reading levels 1–4 and interest level 4–adult; mysteries, adventure, nonfiction

Highsmith Press
W5527 Highway 106
Fort Atkinson, WI 53538
Specialized materials

Intercultural Press, Inc.
P.O. Box 700
Yarmouth, Maine 04096
Reference material for teacher use, material for non-Americans

International Reading Association
800 Barksdale Road
P.O. Box 8139
Newark, DE 19714–8139
Literary, teacher aids, pamphlets for parents

Jamestown Publishers
P.O. Box 6743
Providence, RI 02940
Educational materials, literacy materials, classics

Janesville Literacy Council
17 S River Street
Janesville, WI 53545
Literacy materials, new readers as authors

Kentucky Humanities Council
P.O. Box 4449
Lexington, KY
Regional materials, history

Lerner Books
241 First Avenue, North
Minneapolis, MN 55401
Literacy publications, youth,
series

Literacy Volunteers of America
2111 South Salina
Syracuse, NY 13205–0027
Literacy materials, ESL, easy materials

Marshall Cavendish Corporation
99 White Plains Road
P.O. Box 2001

Tarrytown, NY 10591–9001
History, atlases, mythology, nature, sets, reference

Morning Glory Press
6595 San Haroldo Way
Buena Park, CA 90620–3748
Teenage problems, youth problems, fiction

NTC Publishing Group
4255 West Touhy
Lincolnwood, IL 60646–1975
Travel, language, ESL, career, youth adults

New Readers Press
1320 Jamesville Avenue
Syracuse, NY 13210
Literacy publications, fiction, nonfiction, education for living

Orca Book Publishers
P.O. Box
Custer WA 98240–046
Fiction, nonfiction, sports, young adults, Native North Americans

Peachtree Publishers
494 Armour Circle, NE
Atlanta, GA 30324–4088
Fiction, nonfiction, picture book type, regional material; all ages

People's Publishing Group
P.O. Box 70
Rochelle Park, NJ 07662
Multicultural materials

Penguin USA
375 Hudson Street
New York, NY 10014
Fiction, nonfiction; all ages

Prentice Hall Associates
240 Fresch Court
Old Tappan, NJ 07652–5240
Nonfiction, ESL, teacher aids

Pro Lingua Associates
15 Elm Street
Brattleboro, VT 05301
Languages, multimedia

Project Learn
1701 Payne Avenue
Cleveland, OH 44114
Bibliographies

Project Read Press
1410 Ponce de Leon Avenue, NE
Atlanta, GA 30307
New Words Digest materials, religious materials, literacy, secular material

Putnam and Grosset Group
200 Madison Avenue
New York, NY 10016
Picture materials, nonfiction, literacy; all ages

Raintree/Steck-Vaughn
8701 North Mopac, #200
P.O. Box 26015
Austin, TX 78755
Literacy publishers, biographies, nature, science, series; all ages; ESL

Random House
201 East Fiftieth Street
New York, NY 10022
Fiction, nonfiction, multicultural, young adults

Rosen Publishing Group
29 East Twenty-first Street
New York, NY 10010
Multicultural materials; career, youth values, problems, life skills

Scholastic
(Includes Blue Sky)
555 Broadway
New York, NY 10012–3999
Middle and high school interest publications; fiction, nonfiction, history, reference

Seal Press
3131 Western Avenue, #410
Seattle, WA 98121
Multicultural materials for all ages for women and girls

Second Start Adult Literacy Program
125 Fourteenth Street
Oakland, CA 94612
Literacy publications, new readers as authors, multicultural materials

Silver Burdett Press
299 Jefferson Road
Parsippany, NJ 07054
Fiction, biographies, holidays, multicultural materials, religion, values education; high
    interest/low vocabulary; reference

Silver Moon Press
160 Fifth Avenue, Suite 803
New York, NY 10011
Literacy, holidays; all ages

Simon & Schuster School Group
1230 Avenue of the Americas
New York, NY 10020
Books for young readers; fiction, nonfiction

Teacher Ideas Press
Department T963
P.O. Box 6633
Englewood, CO 80155–6633
Resource books for elementary and secondary teachers, Division of Libraries Unlimited

Three Rivers Literacy Alliance
203 West Wayne Street
Fort Wayne, IN 46802
Literacy publications, new readers as authors

Time Life Education Materials
2000 Duke Street
Alexandria, VA 23285–5926
Science and nature, social studies, Spanish language series, how-to; audio material, videos, CD-ROMs; multicultural; all ages

Twenty-First Century Books
115 West Eighteenth Street
New York, NY 10011
Young adult through adult; reference, multicultural materials, drug education, health, science, social studies and history; Division of Henry Holt and Company

Turman Publishing Company
P.O. Box 19680
Seattle, WA 98109
literacy, reading, ESL

University of Missouri Press
2910 LeMone Boulevard
Columbia, MO 65201
Regional materials, history, local color

# Author Index

# Subject Index

# Title Index

# Ethnic Group Index

**About the Author**

LAURA HIBBETS MCCAFFERY is Librarian in the Readers' Services department of the Allen County Public Library, where she has worked with the Fort Wayne Literacy Council and the Three Rivers Literacy Alliance to develop a collection of materials for patrons for whom English is a second language. She supervised the collection and has developed a collection development policy for literacy and ESL materials that is in use in the library. A former Young Adult librarian, she has served on the Publishers Liaison Committee in the Adult Lifelong Learning Section of the Public Library Association, where she evaluated materials for literacy needs.